Men, Women, Passion and Power

This completely revised edition of *Men, Women, Passion and Power* offers a new critique of conventional notions of masculinity and femininity. Contemporary psychoanalytic debates about sexuality are explored, revealing how the cultural idealisation of men is replicated in theory and clinical practice.

Illustrated with detailed and vivid case material, this book demonstrates that it is only when the feminist perspective has been truly integrated into theory that the psychoanalytic project will realise its full radical potential. Subjects covered include:

- The power of female sexuality.
- Race, class and sexuality.
- The fragility of male sexual identity.
- Envy between the sexes.

Marie Maguire argues that an awareness of how our assumptions are influenced by social inequalities can enrich the psychotherapeutic process, and result in a more balanced psychological relation between the sexes.

Men, Women, Passion and Power will be of great interest to psychotherapists, psychoanalytic practitioners and anyone with an interest in the integration of a feminist perspective into psychoanalytic theory.

Marie Maguire is a psychoanalytic psychotherapist and clinical supervisor in private practice in South London.

Men, Women, Passion and Power

Gender issues in psychotherapy

Second edition

Marie Maguire

 Brunner-Routledge
Taylor & Francis Group

HOVE AND NEW YORK

First edition published 1995
by Routledge
11 New Fetter Lane, London EC4P 4EE

Second edition published 2004
by Brunner-Routledge
27 Church Road, Hove, East Sussex BN3 2FA

Simultaneously published in the USA and Canada
by Brunner-Routledge
29 West 35th Street, New York NY 10001

Brunner-Routledge is an imprint of the Taylor & Francis Group

Typeset in Times by RefineCatch Ltd, Bungay, Suffolk
Printed and bound in Great Britain by
TJ International Ltd, Padstow, Cornwall

Paperback cover design by Hybert Design

This publication has been produced with paper manufactured to
strict environmental standards and with pulp derived from
sustainable forests.

British Library Cataloguing in Publication Data
A catalogue record for this book is available from the British Library

Library of Congress Cataloging in Publication Data
Maguire, Marie.
  Men, women, passion, and power: gender issues in psychotherapy/
Marie Maguire. – 2nd ed.
    p. ; cm.
Includes bibliographical references and index.
  ISBN 1-58391-266-5 (hbk) – ISBN 1-58391-267-3 (pbk)
1. Psychotherapy. 2. Sex role. 3. Sex differences (Psychology)
4. Sex (Psychology) 5. Psychoanalysis and feminism.
  [DNLM: 1. Psychotherapy. 2. Gender Identity. 3. Power
(Psychology) 4. Psychoanalytic Interpretation. 5. Psychosexual
Development. WM 420 M213m 2004] 1. Title.
RC480.5.M3147 2004
616.89´14–dc22   2003022426

ISBN 1-58391-266-5 (hbk)
ISBN 1-58391-267-3 (pbk)

Contents

Acknowledgements

My greatest thanks must go to my patients, who made the writing of this book possible. I'd again like to thank everybody who helped me to produce the first edition. I am particularly indebted to Joanna Ryan for continual discussions and editorial help with this second edition. Richard Harris provided invaluable technical assistance and moral support.

Introduction to the second edition: Psychotherapy and sexual identity

Inequality between the sexes is one of the most intractable features of human culture. Even today, as the relative position of women in some societies improves, sex-based patterns of power and submission continue to be reproduced in our most intimate relationships. Why is this? How is it that gender inequities come to be inscribed in our very psyches, even when we believe passionately in the need for change? In this book I explore the ways in which psychoanalytic and feminist theorists have addressed these questions, as they examine the impact of early experience and unconscious fantasy on the formation of psychological gender.

Looking at theorists from Freud onwards, and utilising my own clinical material, I offer a critical perspective on psychodynamic concepts of sexual difference. In our society each sex has access to different forms of power and control which arouse intense envy in those who lack them. I consider the way in which psychoanalytic theories have shifted between an emphasis on the child's envy of paternal authority and potency and a focus on the mother as the more powerful and enviable parent. I examine the relationship between sexual orientation and identity, and between biological sex and gender characteristics. What are 'masculinity' and 'femininity'? Every society has ways of distinguishing the sexes – socially, culturally, psychologically. Historically, however, this division has varied enormously. What counts as maleness or femaleness in one period or cultural setting can look radically unlike its equivalents in other times or places. And similarly, how an individual comes to identify himself or herself as belonging to a gender also varies greatly. The unconscious meaning each of us gives to our biological sex depends on a complex interaction of personal and cultural factors; it is never simply a result of anatomical difference. And of course so-called 'anatomical' differences can also be culturally constructed.

According to traditional gender stereotypes in the west, women are expected to live vicariously through idealised others, including men and children, to whom they submit, denying the strength of their need and aggression. Men, in contrast, are usually encouraged to assume a stance of pseudo-independence where their own emotional need is transformed into domination of those on whom they depend. Femininity, in other words, is still associated with passivity, and masculinity with activity, as Freud argued (Freud 1905a). But, as my clinical examples show, there is as much variation within each sex as between the sexes, since women and men simultaneously conform to and resist gender stereotypes. Although individuals may present themselves as having a fixed and unified sense of what it means to be male or female, this is often a veneer, a masquerade. Sexual identity – the psychological meaning each of us gives to being a woman or a man – is always fluid, and never exactly what it seems.

One of the main contentions of this book is that the roots of gender expectations lie in cultural ideas about the psychological division in parenting. I offer a critique of traditional gender roles and divisions while simultaneously showing through clinical examples how these very divisions are reproduced – more or less effectively – within people. For instance, in many societies the mother is still expected to look after the baby's physical needs, and to help her or him to think about and eventually verbalise feelings and thoughts. The father's role is associated with boundary-setting, and helping the child find a pathway out of the symbiotic preoccupations of infancy into the world at large. However, I assume that the capacity for these parental functions exists in both sexes and, as my clinical examples show, some women prefer fathering, while men may have more highly developed maternal capacities.

One of my central themes is the way each sex deals with aspects of personality seen culturally as feminine or masculine. In many societies girls and boys react against the early power of the mother by idealising paternal authority. The work men do and 'masculine' qualities tend to be valued more highly than those associated with women. This devaluation of women has profound implications for each sex, since we all identify to some extent with conventionally 'masculine' and 'feminine' aspects of both parents, and with the paternal and maternal functions of each.

Theories about sexuality have always been central to psycho-analysis. Yet they have also been the focus of fundamental disagreements that have divided the analytic community. These disputes have coincided with rapid changes in the organisation of sexual and family life, in turn accompanied by shifting attitudes towards gender. Although the analytic and feminist literature in this area is vast, surprising gaps exist. Key papers are scattered and sometimes hard to find. The issues that have aroused most controversy over the years are often discussed from polarised positions with little dialogue between opposing factions.

In this book I draw together and re-evaluate psychoanalytic theories of psychosexuality, using case histories from my own psychotherapy practice to review issues which have recently become controversial within the analytic community. For the second edition I have made some radical changes, including a new final chapter, 'Differing desires'. This focuses on recent psychoanalytic theory about bisexuality, homosexuality and heterosexuality – sexual orientation being the area where prejudicial clinical attitudes have been most strongly challenged since the early 1990s. In Chapter 1 and several later chapters I include substantial new material on another controversial and long-neglected area: the impact of 'race', class and culture on the practice and professional organisation of analytic psychotherapy. Continuing the cross-cultural theme, in this edition I amplify my original discussion of the way our bodies are structured through culture, using recent feminist philosophy and research into the mind–brain relationship (e.g. Butler 1997, Grosz 1994, Solms and Turnbull 2002). In updating theories of sexual identity I have drawn on new psychoanalytic writing from a range of clinicians, including Jessica Benjamin, Muriel Dimen, Adrienne Harris, Judith Butler, Thomas Domenici and Juliet Mitchell. There is also an extended section on violent male fantasy and the eroticisation of emotional pain in Chapter 4.

Some of the theory I discuss in this book has been written by psychoanalysts working with patients whom they see in the classic fashion, five (or in Freud's case, six) times a week, lying on the couch. Psychoanalytic psychotherapy, although it is founded on the same basic premises as psychoanalysis, involves less intensive treatment. For practical and stylistic reasons I use generic terms such as 'analyst' or 'therapist' to refer to all who practise psychoanalytic psychotherapy.

Psychoanalytic psychotherapy is distinguished from other forms of therapy by an emphasis on helping the patient to understand their own unconscious processes as they are re-enacted within the transference relationship. The psychotherapist also uses her own countertransference – her emotional reactions to the patient, and especially to the transference – in a variety of different ways, to further the work of analysis. Some of the patients I discuss came to see me for intensive psychotherapy, two to four times weekly for up to eight years, often lying on the couch. Others came for once-weekly brief psychotherapy over a period of six to nine months, in publicly funded clinic settings. In order to preserve patients' confidentiality I have altered biographical details, omitting certain facts and fictionalising others, while doing my best to capture the essence of the therapeutic encounter. Whenever possible I asked for permission and used material from ex-patients to avoid disrupting an ongoing psychotherapy.

Although Freud claimed universality for psychoanalysis, it is the product of a particular culture and historical epoch, a social theory with moral and political effects, as well as an analysis of individual suffering and development. Different views on the interaction between unconscious fantasy, culture and physiology, including cross-cultural critiques, are therefore vital to my discussion. Since this book was first published new work has highlighted the importance of understanding more about how issues of class, culture, 'race' and racism might emerge within the clinical setting. Such critiques raise fundamental questions about the aims of psychotherapy and the stance clinicians should take towards social norms and political institutions.

Contemporary girls are brought up with a promise of sexual equality, which, for the most part, our society fails to deliver. Although individual women attain influential positions, men as a sex retain control over institutions of authority – political, economic, educational, juridical and medical. British women on average work longer hours than men, frequently doing the equivalent of two jobs where men do one. Not surprisingly, the emotional toll on women is statistically visible. Women are far more likely than men to seek psychological help of all kinds, to be prescribed psychotropic drugs, and to spend time in psychiatric hospitals.

I argue that inequality between the sexes continues to be reflected in the theory and practice of analytic psychotherapy, despite periods of intense debate between feminists and psychoanalytic clinicians. European struggles for women's suffrage shadowed the first period of controversy about female sexuality. A half-century later a new generation of feminists – myself included – turned to psychoanalytic psychotherapy during the 1970s to understand why we could not will ourselves into being the New Women we had hoped to become. Like many of my contemporaries I thought at first that I was struggling mainly with oppressive outer realities. But gradually I realised that I was also grappling with unconscious feelings and fantasies, which often contradicted my conscious political beliefs.

Like many British psychotherapists I am a theoretical hybrid, incorporating diverse influences within my clinical practice. My experience of working in two radical psychotherapy projects, Battersea Action and Counselling Centre and The Women's Therapy Centre, was formative. The founders of these organisations drew on certain British psychoanalytic theories, especially the work of W.R.D. Fairbairn, to analyse how real inequities of class, race and gender are structured into the personality and emerge within the therapeutic relationship. Despite this kind of pioneering work, which has often been inspired by the Women's Movement, we still do not yet know exactly how cultural and social changes impact on the psyche. I remain convinced that we are primarily a product of our personal and cultural histories. In this book I explore how we carve out identities for ourselves, giving meaning both to childhood experiences and to the expectations and desires of those around us. But I am also very interested in new ways of thinking about physiological experience, including recent developments in neuroscience.

Theoretically I am steeped in the tradition of British psychoanalysis, with its insights gleaned from child analysis about the infant's earliest experience of mothering and the maternal body. However, I also maintain a critical distance from this way of thinking. For instance, I am intensely aware of the value of the countertransference, but also concerned not to place too much significance on my own reactions at the expense of listening to what the client is actually saying about themselves and the therapeutic relationship. Freud's emphasis on language, his theory of psychosexuality and his focus on the way patriarchal power is structured into the personality are also vital to my thinking about the practice of psychotherapy.

New theories: body, mind and culture

Theories of narcissism are essential to an understanding of how gender power inequalities are woven into our most fundamental passions and desires. Unconsciously we all collude in the narcissistic denial that we – like other human beings – are ultimately helpless in the face of psychic pain, loss and death. Recognising that the two sexes are anatomically different yet equal would mean facing up to the fact that the most important aspects of existence elude human control. Those we love and on whom we depend are psychically separate from us. We maintain an illusion of ecstatic fusion with others (a defence associated with stereotypes of femininity) or imagine ourselves to be so powerful and independent that we have no emotional needs (the stance culturally linked with masculinity) because unconsciously we cannot acknowledge that our love-objects are essentially unpredictable.

Although I believe we are formed primarily through culture, I also think that the anatomical differences between women and men impact on the psyche, affecting unconscious anxieties and fantasies. Because male and female bodies are constructed differently and we have different physiological and sexual capacities, our experience of sex, reproduction and physiological life-stages such as adolescence and the menopause will inevitably vary.

Psychotherapists are often presented with evidence that psychological stress can manifest itself in physical ways, which can be mediated through gender. But we do not yet know exactly how this happens. In discussing clinical work we sometimes talk as if our minds and bodies exist side-by-side, interlocking, mutually influential. Or we assume that our bodies are a kind of subordinate counterpart of a more dominant psyche. However, psychotherapeutic interventions based on these assumptions are not always particularly helpful.

It is interesting then that in recent years neuroanalysts and philosophers have challenged these traditional ways of thinking about physiology and the psyche. In *The Brain and the Inner World*, Mark Solms and Oliver Turnbull show that environmental and genetic influences are absolutely inextricable. Contrary to popular opinion, sex and gender – and all that they imply – are not predetermined from the moment of conception by our genetic make-up. Nature and nurture are in dynamic interplay from the earliest moments of development. The genetic design according to which we are built can be altered in many different ways through environmental forces, which in turn shape our identity, our sense of self. While many societies place enormous stress on the difference between men and women, in genetic terms the distinctions are absolutely minimal and not always as clear-cut as we might imagine. Surprisingly often, although our bodies might seem to place us definitively on one side of the sexual divide, our genes can show us to have strong characteristics of the other sex. There is then a great deal more that we share than what distinguishes us (Solms and Turnbull 2002).

New research shows that maturation of the brain is dependent on experience. From the viewpoint of neurophysiology, all 'life events' are registered and translated through bodily processes. The mother (or caretaker) acts as regulator of the baby's covert physiology as well as its behaviour. The emotion-regulating part of the brain almost literally embodies the child's experiences of parenting. So if a child suffers deprivation, neglect or trauma during a critical period of development these experiences will be structured into the brain. But the brain can change throughout life. Being listened to will alter the structure of the brain and so the capacity to process emotions will increase (Schore 1994). Neuroscientific research has implications for the crucial issue of memory in psychotherapy. So-called 'false memory' – a source of great controversy amongst neuroscientists – is discussed in Chapter 7.

From a different vantage-point, philosophers have arrived at similar conclusions about the influence of the environment on physiology. It is not just that men and women's bodies are seen or represented differently in each society, argues the feminist philosopher Elizabeth Grosz. Different cultures *produce* different bodies. 'Our ideas and attitudes seep into the functioning of the body itself, making up the realm of its possibilities or impossibilities' (Grosz 1994: 190). What is crucial for women is the agency, mobility and social space accorded to them (Grosz 1994). In many societies women take on the function of being '*the body*' for men who are then left free to 'soar to the heights of theoretical reflection and cultural production', while people from culturally subordinate races or groups function as 'the working body' for society as a whole (Grosz 1994: 22). For sexual, racial and class equality, what needs to be transformed is attitudes, beliefs and values rather than the body itself. This is why the distinction between sex (biological) and gender (culturally constructed) has recently been challenged. The concept of gender is ultimately linked to some notion of biological sex, yet this biological division is never as entirely culture-free as it is made to seem (Butler 1990, 1993).

For instance, during the twentieth century in some societies women's relationship to their bodies changed dramatically. Women can now control their fertility while also remaining sexually active. It is possible to live openly in partnerships with other women or men. Women no longer spend much of their adult lives pregnant or breastfeeding, and therefore financial independence of men is more possible, although still circumscribed by educational opportunity and other cultural factors. In such societies the beliefs held about female bodies are changing. New physical possibilities are open to us and this will inevitably be reflected in our psychic lives.

It should be clear by now that I am not arguing for the existence of inborn anxieties or for certain preconceived patterns of feeling or fantasy. Nor do I think that any particular psychological characteristics can be found universally in one sex rather than the other. I do not believe that we are born with tendencies towards heterosexual 'femininity' or 'masculinity', or that there is any core of 'real' personality which transcends culture. In fact, language-patterns, cultural symbols, belief-systems and values will be fundamental determinants of how physiological sensation is interpreted in any given society. If we want to abolish inequalities between the sexes, we must understand and radically alter the way we interpret and symbolise the embodied experience of women and men.

Changing language, changing theory

In the years since this book was first published attention has begun to focus on whether the language used in the clinical setting might inhibit rather than promote change in gender power relations. Psychoanalytic theories of sexual identity have tended to revolve around two-way systems, such as masculine/feminine, active/passive, maternal/paternal, body/mind and homosexual/heterosexual. Recently the use of the terms 'masculine' and 'feminine' has been challenged, on the basis that they reinforce normative stereotypes of gender and sexuality even when the writer uses them – as I do – to describe culturally constructed qualities which can be found equally in both sexes (Harris 2000). 'Binary' ways of categorising experience remain emotionally resonant for many people, but they often rest on the implicit belief that one category is more 'healthy' or highly valued than the other. For example, although Freud recognised that all sexual identity is intrinsically fragile and never quite what it seems, many of his followers linked heterosexuality to the gender binary, relying on the belief that 'opposites attract', so that heterosexual desire is created through a 'natural' polarity between the sexes. The influential feminist philosopher Judith Butler has pointed out that this assumption bolsters the idea that heterosexual 'masculinity' and 'femininity' are the only 'healthy' identities (Butler 1990). Butler turns this belief on its head through her argument that heterosexual identity is built on particularly fragile foundations. In societies where heterosexuality is the only legitimate identity, Butler says, the most fundamental taboo is not against heterosexual incest – as psycho-analysts believe – but against homosexual love. So heterosexual identity is constructed on the loss or foreclosure of the child's first same-sex love-object, resulting in a profound melancholy at the root of gender identity. This loss cannot be spoken about or mourned in a society that sees only heterosexuality as 'true love', a love worth losing. Both 'masculinity' and 'femininity' are then formed partly through 'disavowed grief' about 'unlivable [homo-sexual] passion', composed through exactly what 'remains inarticu-late in sexuality' (Butler 1997: 138–9).

Changing our language means changing the way we think. In this book I maintain a critical attitude towards these binary categories. I offer a critique of conventional notions of masculinity and feminin-ity, but at the same time I argue that we all need to identify with a range of qualities associated culturally with both sexes. In my emphasis on cross-sex identifications I know that I might be seen as reinstating the basic gender binary. But we all live within language, and if we restrict our words too much we may inhibit clinical discus-sion of sexual identity. On the other hand, I am also well aware that the words psychotherapists use reflect our underlying personal and professional beliefs. Our vocabulary can be profoundly influential, structuring the way our clients think and feel. This is one way that mainstream psychoanalytic theories might reinforce normative ways of organising sexual and family life. For instance, the notion of a heterosexual relationship between a parental couple – whether actual or symbolic – is absolutely central to psychoanalytic thinking. The implicit assumption in Oedipal theory is that there is only one 'real' difference, that this is established on gender lines and that it also constitutes sexual object choice (Benjamin 1995). Often there is great confusion about whether we are talking of 'real' parental figures and what significance is placed on their anatomical sex. And what of other differences, most notably those of race and class? These issues have become highly controversial in recent debates about the con-tinuing centrality of Oedipal theory in contemporary psychoanalysis (see Chapters 1–3).

'Race' and class in psychotherapy

Recently attention has shifted back to an old idea, that cultures – as well as individual psyches – are blighted by guilt and losses which cannot be mourned (Mitscherlich and Mitscherlich 1967). This theory, once applied to post-war Germany, is now being used again as some clinicians make a sustained effort to break a longstanding silence about the impact of race and class on the clinical encounter. Black British and North American analysts have raised questions about the intergenerational impact of slavery, genocide and racial abuse on victims and perpetrators. 'Slaves were not supposed to have feelings, yet slavery formed the entire basis of Caribbean and American society. To my mind, then, trauma on a massive scale has been handed down through the generations, is still being handed down, and is hard to express and conceptualise', writes Barbara Fletchman Smith (2000: 7). Such unassimilated psychic states linger like ghosts, leaving individuals and sections of society prone to dissociated states of mind, intense feelings of persecution and melancholy.

The North American psychoanalyst Kimberlyn Leary describes the way racial experience which is not yet reflected upon or linguistically encoded remains a part of our everyday psychic grammar. The therapist's unassimilated experience may re-emerge in the analytic encounter as a 'racial enactment' through which the analyst might unwittingly re-traumatise the patient (Leary 2000).

These ideas might also help us think about a topic which has received extremely little theoretical attention – the way social class resonates through the therapeutic relationship. In Britain, as in many other countries, the class we belong to is still the greatest influence on our chances in life, yet its effects are hard to verbalise. Class is still inscribed on our minds and marked on our bodies in ways we recognise instantly, despite our wish to believe it no longer exists. But the signs of classification are likely to be felt and thought about more as evidence of personal failure and pathology than of inequality and oppression (Walkerdine et al. 2001). In later chapters, including 1, 4, 5 and 7, I return to look clinically and theoretically at the intersections between 'race', class and gender.

I begin the book with an account of the 1919–35 controversy about female sexuality. In Chapters 1–3 I summarise opposing analytic and feminist arguments about envy and power which had their origins in the early period of sexual controversy. Envy, described in Webster's Dictionary as 'chagrin or discontent at the excellence or

good fortune of another', originates in early disappointment in relation to the mother, the original source of life. To Freudians and
Lacanians the role of the father, female penis envy and male dread of
paternal castration remain central. Mother-centred theories, including those of Klein and Winnicott, emphasise that ambivalence
towards maternal power underlies all female envy of male privilege
and authority as well as men's repudiation of femininity. I look at
the relevance of these opposing theories of sexual identity to my own
clinical work with male and female patients. In Chapter 1 there is
also an extended new discussion of how racialised and class experience affects sexual identities, a theme which I pursue further through
clinical accounts in later chapters.

Since the psychoanalytic literature is so extensive, I have structured the book around the writings of those analysts and feminists
who see the early debate on female sexuality as a central point of
reference. This 1920s/1930s controversy focused on Sigmund Freud's
theories and Karen Horney's counter-arguments. Significant contri-
butions were also made by Helene Deutsch, as well as Joan Riviere
and others who were influenced by Melanie Klein's new theories.
Many feminists including Juliet Mitchell have been inspired by the
work of Jacques Lacan, who saw the controversy as a watershed
where psychoanalysis lost its subversive core. I also draw on the work
of many other analysts and feminists who address this book's central
themes. I am particularly interested in the work of Jessica Benjamin,
who analyses the way culture binds our erotic desire, and Luce
Irigaray, who also attempts to combine the insights of Freud or
Lacan with a more mother-centred perspective. I argue that we need
to draw on the strengths of different psychoanalytic and feminist
theories since no one perspective offers a complete understanding of
sexual identity.

Throughout the book I address a series of related topics that need
reassessing in the light of dramatic cultural changes. For instance,
the early psychoanalytic interest in the erotic life of adult women has
faded, to be replaced by a preoccupation with their maternal function. In many contemporary case studies the mother dominates her
children in indirectly sexualised ways, but is not the subject of her
own desire (Welldon 1988). Ironically, given women's increased sexual independence, there has been a long period where we have heard
little about their actual sexual relationships, with men or other
women. After the Second World War the father's role in the psyche
received little theoretical attention in Britain and the USA. Only

since the 1980s have psychoanalysts begun to acknowledge that in many post-industrial societies men's expectations of sexuality, marriage and fatherhood are very different from those of Freud's patients.

In Chapter 4 I ask, 'Are men really fragile?' Freud argued that men were not so prone to neurosis because of a less problematic sexual history. Later object relations theorists (e.g. Stoller 1968) emphasise the relative fragility and emotional impoverishment of male identity. Drawing on detailed clinical material from men who have lived through dislocations of class or culture I argue that this latter argument needs to be combined with an understanding of how prevailing power relations are structured into the male psyche. Masculinities, like femininities, are not fixed global entities, but are built through the layering of multiple identifications, memories and fantasies. Men can fully recognise their difference from their mothers only when they recognise her otherness in themselves, once aspects of themselves they see as maternal or 'feminine' are acknowledged rather than projected onto others. If women and the characteristics associated with them are devalued then there really is no possibility that men can achieve equality in heterosexual or homosexual relationships, since the partner who is seen as more psychically 'feminine' is likely to be denigrated and objectified. I look at some of the reasons why men are less likely to seek change through psychotherapy, noting that those who do are likely to display a particular combination of psychic resilience and vulnerability that enables them to open up to internal change.

Although some contemporary object relations theorists imply that women are emotionally the more powerful sex, the real lack of economic and social power experienced by the female sex as a whole is rarely acknowledged. In Chapter 5, 'The power of women's sexuality', I connect this discrepancy with the psychoanalytic emphasis on the elusiveness of female desire. Cultural imagery constantly depicts women as gaining pleasure from being attractive, rather than from exercising their own desires. Women who feel that desire pulls them towards surrender and self-sacrifice may choose to deny their need for erotic pleasure altogether. Other women describe a disturbing clash between internalised images of female submissiveness and conscious hopes of sexual and social equality. Again class and cultural factors resonate through these discrepancies. For the girl, some qualities associated culturally with men and masculinity might well be viewed not as threatening, as womanliness is for the boy, but as unattainable ideals (Benjamin 1988). The difficulty many women have in experiencing themselves as independent beings with their own needs and desires can be linked to the problems girls have in identifying with paternal qualities in the mother or father. I look at how far it is possible in psychotherapy to break into this cycle and help patients to develop the capacity for more equal relationships.

Writing about the analytic transference, Janet Malcolm uses the analogy of romantic love relationships, which are 'at best an uneasy truce between powerful solitary fantasy systems', where we 'must grope around for each other through a dense thicket of absent others' (Malcolm 1982: 6). Chapters 6 and 7 explore the interface between fantasy, reality and erotic desire in transference and countertransference. In Chapter 6 I look at how gender power inequalities emerge within the therapeutic setting through the impact of the patient and therapist's sex on the transference and countertransference. I ask whether homosexual and heterosexual erotic transferences are experienced differently by male and female analysts and explore some of the difficulties psychotherapists may have in working with cross-gender transferences.

In Chapter 7, 'False memories of sexual abuse?', my focus is on contemporary psychoanalytic debates about false memories of incest. It is often suggested that the psychotherapist's emotional influence could be used in ways that are counterproductive for the patient, perhaps reinforcing existing inequalities of gender or generation. I locate dramatic shifts in psychoanalytic theory about the 'real event' of childhood incest within a context of heightened public concern that psychotherapists might either deny the reality of these experiences or encourage patients to fabricate false memories. Through clinical material I explore some technical difficulties of working with those who are uncertain whether or not they are incest survivors, including the impact of cross-cultural differences on the transference.

Women's masochistic avoidance of erotic pleasure has been a constant psychoanalytic theme. Freud argued that women express sexuality indirectly through hysterical conversion symptoms and physical self-abuse. Perversion has until recently been seen as predominantly male. In recent decades it has often been attributed to the presence in men's lives of seductive, castrating mothers (e.g. Rosen 1979a). In Chapter 8, 'Female and male perversions?', I look again at psychoanalytic theories about male and female perversion and hysteria. Using detailed case material I discuss why the use of hardcore pornography as a substitute for sexual relationships might be more commonly found in men, while eating problems such as bulimia are more prevalent in women.

When psychoanalysts label sexual behaviours as perverse or pathological they are also, of course, giving clear signals about their own anxieties and prejudices. This has been particularly obvious in relation to homosexuality, where the profession is in the process of confronting a deep-rooted, partially hidden bias against homosexuals, both as patients and as potential colleagues. Contradictions in theory can be traced back to Freud, who argued that psychoanalysis should not encourage adaptation to prevailing norms of sexual behaviour since these were often a root cause of human misery. Yet at the same time he linked adult homosexuality with arrested development and perversion. Tentatively, in some psychoanalytic arenas, homosexuality has been designated as normal. However, anxieties have been expressed that bisexuality could be seen as the new pathology since it is often described in mainstream theory as infantile, rather than a valid sexual orientation. In the USA homosexuality is no longer a bar to entry to the most orthodox trainings, even though more covert prejudice may still exist. But in Britain some psychotherapists from the more orthodox trainings still feel that openly gay and lesbian clinicians are stigmatised and that negative clinical attitudes prevail (Ryan 2002).

The final chapter, 'Differing Desires', touches on fundamental questions about the aims of psychotherapy. The first edition contained many clinical examples of women patients who desire both sexes equally. This substantially updated chapter draws on this material in a new discussion of bisexuality as a sexual orientation. I also focus on recent theory which explores the impact of homophobia on clinical transference and countertransference.

Current debates over homosexuality within the psychotherapeutic world are in some respects reminiscent of the 1920s/1930s dispute over female sexuality, inasmuch as both test many of the central assumptions on which psychodynamic therapy is based. Both controversies also reflect the challenge which gender politics poses to psychoanalysis, as feminists and gay theorists offer new interpretations of psychosexual development which confront older orthodoxies. It is essential that psychoanalytic psychotherapists be willing to accept these challenges and to rethink our theoretical and clinical work in the light of new perspectives on sexuality, race, class and culture. I hope this book contributes to this process.

Part I

Theories of female and male sexuality

Chapter 1

Controversy – sexual and cross-cultural

It was in the wake of the mass feminist struggles for women's suffrage that the first significant controversy over female sexuality broke out within the psychoanalytic movement. The egalitarian demands of the suffragists formed a backdrop for the entire debate. Between 1919 and 1935 at least nineteen prominent analysts wrote papers on the topic, arguing vigorously with each other and with Freud. This debate, which centred on Freud's theory of female penis envy, set the agenda for discussions of sexual identity for the rest of the century.

Since the 1920s there has been an off-and-on engagement with the issue of how an originally male-dominated theory might apply to women. In contrast, questions about the universal applicability of psychoanalytic theories to all cultures have not been consistently addressed until very recently. This is significant since psychoanalysis developed through clinical work with bourgeois, early-twentieth-century Europeans.

Freud's attitude towards women's demands for equality was highly contradictory, in common with that of most other early male psychoanalysts. He revealed a deep ambivalence over the question of female inferiority, at times implying that women actually are inferior while at other moments suggesting that they are simply viewed in that way within a male-dominated society. For instance, in 1933 he suggested that a female patient's long-held wish for professional and intellectual success might turn out to be sublimated childhood penis envy (Freud 1933). But he had also insisted, against opposition from male colleagues, and at a time when many professions barred females, that women should be able to train and take up prominent positions within the psychoanalytic movement. He was a sexual liberal, supporting the radical causes of his day, including the legalisation of homosexuality, the liberalisation of divorce laws and a woman's right to abortion.

During the 1920s one of Freud's most influential opponents, Karen Horney, a young German psychoanalyst, accused Freud of 'male bias', of creating a theory which devalued women (Horney 1924, 1926). Freud's theory revolved around the child's relationship to the father and its struggle to come to terms with the authority and privilege of the patriarch, a struggle in which the mother seems to become almost a bystander. Horney's view was that each sex has something uniquely valuable which arouses fierce envy in the sex lacking it. This argument and other aspects of her critique of Freud won influential support from colleagues who later transformed the role of the mother in psychoanalytic theory. For British object relations theorists and North American ego psychologists, women – far from being deficient – have enormous emotional power based on the ability to reproduce the species and the utter dependence of the human infant at the beginning of life. From this theoretical perspective the influence women have over the psychic lives of children is seen as far more significant than the political and economic power wielded by men. At issue here are divergent notions of power and control and arguments about which parent is viewed by the child as more potent and enviable.

Feminists have always remained divided as to whose views on sexual identity were the more radical – Freud's or Horney's. A crucial area of disagreement was over whether women and men are born heterosexual or 'made' so by culture. For Freud, the girl only begins to desire men sexually and want their babies once she realises she can never be male; Horney, on the other hand, argued that women are born with tendencies towards heterosexual femininity. By emphasising innate womanliness in this way, Horney intended to defend women against the Freudian charge that we are merely men *manqué*. But present-day feminists have pointed out that in doing so she 'threw the baby out with the bath-water', abandoning one of Freud's most subversive insights, his theory that all sexual identities are formed through the influence of personal history and culture rather than being the inevitable outcome of biological sex (Mitchell 1974).

The dispute between Horney and Freud raised fundamental questions about the transformative potential of psychoanalysis. If women have inborn tendencies towards a certain kind of feminine heterosexuality, then the possibility of change in female identity, and any subsequent shift in power relations between the sexes, might be limited. Freud had argued against the idea that psychoanalysts should encourage patients to conform to prevailing social and sexual norms. But if his theory showed a bias against women, who was to judge what counted as genuine therapeutic success rather than mere conformity to current notions of authentic femaleness? Contributors to the debate probed such questions, wondering to what extent the prejudices of the psychoanalyst influenced the course of a treatment. They also speculated about whether the psychoanalyst's gender shaped the way the transference unfolded and whether opposing theories of sexual identity might in turn reflect varying experiences of the therapeutic relationship.

The debate was crucial to the future of psychoanalytic theory and the practice of psychotherapy. For the first time, Freud's authority as theoretical leader was challenged in an open and sustained way by dissenters who stayed to argue their case. The psychoanalytic movement began to split, its members taking fundamentally different paths, but still seeing themselves as part of the same community. Opposing factions in the debate coalesced into theoretical tendencies which continue to dominate contemporary psychoanalytic thinking about psychosexuality and identity.

Prior to the outbreak of hostilities between himself, Horney and others, Freud had had little to say about female sexuality as such. His *Three Essays on the Theory of Sexuality* (1905a) offered a general theory of psychosexual development which did not dwell on the differences between men and women. Freud asked a series of questions about what sexuality was and how it came to be associated with the onset of neurosis. He concluded that sexual libido was a wild, insatiable force, the 'most unruly' of all the instincts. In order to build civilisation it was necessary to repress desire and sublimate sexual libido into culturally constructive pursuits. But this resulted in psychic conflict in individuals who could not tolerate the way society restricted their sexuality. Neurosis was the inevitable result, particularly for women who were denied pleasure and knowledge through the sexual double standard.

Freud's infant is a hedonist who at first seeks 'autoerotic' pleasure from its own body, purely for pleasure's sake. In Freud's theory sexuality is not intrinsically linked with reproduction or with the need for closeness. (Here Freud differs from later object-relations theorists who argue that the infant seeks human intimacy rather than sexual pleasure from the moment of birth.) Neither, according to Freud, does infantile sexuality have any predetermined object. Instead it is diffuse and 'polymorphously perverse', experienced in relation to everyone and everything the infant encounters. Only after a primary period of narcissistic self-preoccupation is the infant seduced into intimacy through the physical ministrations of the mother.

Freud stresses the continuity between adult and infantile sexuality and between erotic desire and other forms of love. The mother derives erotic pleasure from her child, responding to it 'with feelings that are derived from her own sexual life: she strokes him, kisses him, rocks him and quite clearly treats him as a substitute for a complete sexual object' (Freud 1905a: 145).

Central to Freud's theory of sexual identity was his argument that all children are born bisexual, psychically androgynous, possessing a complex combination of 'masculine' (active) and 'feminine' (passive) mental characteristics. Heterosexuality only begins at the Oedipal, genital phase. As the infant becomes less preoccupied with the oral pleasures of feeding and the anal struggles of toilet-training it becomes more aware of genital sensations and the accompanying fantasies.

Until female sexuality became controversial among his colleagues, Freud had written mainly about the boy's experience. In his early writings on sexuality he assumed that the girl's experience would be a mirror-image of the boy's. For her too the opposite-sex parent, the father, would be most significant.

Freud confirmed some of his theories of sexuality through his analysis of three-year-old Hans, a 'positive paragon of all vices' (Freud 1909: 179). As his Oedipal desire for the opposite sex parent grew, Hans wanted his mother to touch his penis because 'it's great fun' (Freud 1909: 182). His father was at these moments a hated rival. He had fantasies about marrying his mother and having a baby with her. Hans also reported eroticised daydreams about the plumber visiting him in the bath and penetrating his stomach with a great big 'borer'. These homosexual desires are an expression of the negative Oedipus complex – Hans had also taken the same-sex parent as erotic love-object and felt rivalry towards his mother.

Freud says that ideally the son relinquishes his Oedipal desire for the mother because of a real or imagined threat of castration by the father. He then accepts that he must wait until adulthood to possess his own woman sexually. The little boy sublimates his incestuous desire through identifying with his father's potency and cultural privilege. This identification forms the basis of the male super-ego or conscience. If the Oedipus complex is not resolved in this way, the boy may grow up to feel an intense hatred and contempt for women. Freud argued that this kind of misogyny is an expression of male castration anxiety – the man is terrified that he will lose his masculinity and become like the women he hates and fears. It was not until 1924/5 that Freud published a theoretical account of female sexuality – and then in some haste, with incomplete clinical data. Apologising for the schematic character of his arguments, he cited his failing health as the reason for hurrying into print. It is also possible that he wanted to stake out territory and reassert his theoretical leadership against challengers such as Horney. The battle-lines were being drawn. Freud's own famous interjection – 'Here the feminist demand for equal rights for the sexes does not take us far' (Freud 1924a: 320) – indicates how heated and oppositional the theoretical atmosphere was becoming.

In spite of his provocative tone, Freud was preoccupied with questions which are still relevant for contemporary women. For instance, he noted that little girls seemed initially to be 'more intelligent and livelier than boys of the same age'. He asked how those assertive little girls came to lose their intellectual confidence and capacity to act directly on their desires (Freud 1933: 151). Whether through nature or nurture, it is at the point where the little girl becomes interested in the father and men that she appears to become more passive.

Freud's explanation for this is that the little girl goes through a phase where she is a 'little boy psychologically' and is active or 'masculine' in her love for her mother before she becomes heterosexual. It is penis envy, Freud argued in 1924, that sets the girl on the path towards psychic womanhood. As soon as she sees the boy's penis the girl recognises her inadequacy 'in a flash' and blames her mother for sending her into the world ill-equipped (Freud 1925: 336). Neither she nor the boy knows of the existence of the vagina until adolescence. Both imagine that the clitoris is a stunted penis. In bitter disappointment at her lack, the girl turns to her father in the hope of gaining a penis and becoming like him. When she realises that she can never be a man, she reluctantly accepts the second-best option of femininity. She begins to feel heterosexual desire and to hope for the father's baby – ideally a boy, a penis by proxy.

According to Freud, the girl has to make a series of renunciations in order to become a heterosexual woman, none of which are required of the boy. Most significantly she must give up her mother – her first love-object – and the active sexual strivings she felt in relation to her. Her aggressive urges turn inwards as she becomes more passive in relation to her father and men (Freud 1931, 1933). Not surprisingly, Freud thought that many girls never do become entirely heterosexual. They may remain attached to their mothers, identify with their fathers, or lose interest completely in sex. Freud described how a woman may marry in order to have a penis-baby, and then transfer her love completely to the infant. A marriage is only consolidated, Freud later said, when the woman has also made the man into her child (Freud 1933).

Freud argued that girls are further disadvantaged in the moral sphere since they cannot identify with patriarchal authority. 'I cannot evade the notion (though I hesitate to give it expression) that for women the level of what is ethically normal is different from what it is in men', he admitted (Freud 1925: 342). He went on to explain that women have a weaker super-ego and a stronger sense of pity, disgust and shame, due to the repression of their sexuality and their envy of men.

By the early 1930s, after a decade of pressure from his female colleagues, Freud had become more able to recognise the early mother–daughter relationship as a foundation and crucial determinant of later experiences with the father. He now argued that penis envy had its roots in the inevitable narcissistic wounds of breastfeeding. These only become organised into a sense of gender-inferiority once the girl sees the boy's penis. The 'reproach against the mother that goes back furthest is that she gave the child too little milk – which is construed against her as lack of love . . . the child's avidity for its earliest nourishment is altogether insatiable . . . it never gets over the pain of losing its mother's breast' (Freud 1933: 155–156).

Female sexuality always remained mysterious and elusive to Freud, but by 1933 he was more able to detect the maternal transference. For instance his patient H.D., the symbolist poet, assumed at first that he represented a father-figure, but Freud insisted that she had transferred her early feelings about her mother onto him. Mistakes had, he explained, been made in the early days because psychoanalysts did not realise that some girls never do transfer their affections from the mother to the father. He told H.D.: 'I do not like to be the mother in the transference, it always surprises and shocks me a little. I feel so very masculine.' She asked him if others had mother transferences to him. He said 'ironically . . . and a little wistfully "O, very many" ' (H.D. 1956: 147). It seems clear that Freud had always been able to elicit strong maternal transferences from his patients, but had not been able to recognise that this was happening because of his own unresolved conflicts about his sexual identity (Freud 1905b).

Some prominent women analysts, including Helene Deutsch, Jeanne Lampl-de-Groot and Ruth Mack Brunswick, declared their agreement with Freud's theory of female sexuality although each gave far more importance to the mother–daughter relationship than he had done. Some of them fully endorsed Freud's belief that as 'more suitable mother-substitutes' women analysts would have access within the transference to aspects of the female psyche that their male colleagues would never encounter (Freud 1931). 'The undeveloped, primitive woman with scant heterosexuality and a childish, unquestioning attachment to the mother, presents herself almost regularly to the woman analyst . . . [but] does not consult the male analyst because of a total lack of contact with the man', Brunswick wrote in a coda to the debate (1940: 62).

Women's sexuality: the theories of Freud's female contemporaries

Helene Deutsch

Helene Deutsch was typical of Freud's contemporary female supporters in that she always stressed her loyalty to his views on penis envy without acknowledging that she disagreed with him fundamentally about female sexuality in general. Most significantly, Deutsch was certain that the psychological differences between the sexes were rooted in biology. She also abandoned Freud's central emphasis on the father, focusing instead on a mother–daughter identification based on the shared child-bearing function over the course of the life-cycle. Her mother-centred perspective, like many contemporary theories, focuses on what women possess – the capacity to bear children – rather than on what they lack.

Deutsch argued that women tend to focus inwards, seeking gratification through children and family life, because their psychic life revolves around the reproductive cycle and sexual organs located inside their bodies. In contrast, men are driven to possess women and sublimate their sexuality in the external world. She attributed this partly to the penetrative urges of the penis, whose location directs men's attention outside themselves (Deutsch 1924).

Freud didn't know whether women were naturally more passive or became so through cultural repression of their sexuality. But Deutsch became notorious with later generations of feminists for insisting that three traits – narcissism, passivity and masochism – were integral to female psychology (Deutsch 1930). Deutsch asks, as many contemporary feminists have, why women have accepted throughout history the 'social ordinances' that prevent them from gaining sexual gratification while simultaneously denying them the possibility of sublimating their sexual urges through artistic or cultural achievement (Deutsch 1930). She argues that it must be the 'magnificent gratification' women gain from their reproductive capacities. Yet her writings are concerned with a painful paradox in female experience. According to Deutsch, many women gain little pleasure from the passivity and self-sacrifice required of them in vaginal intercourse and motherhood. This is because they are born with a component of active 'masculine' sexuality – the clitoris, a stunted penis, the remnants of which do not allow them to submit without conflict. Therefore many women find little gratification in heterosexual intercourse, to which they feel they must resign themselves. They may also be highly ambivalent about pregnancy, childbirth and mothering, especially if their identifications with their mothers are ambivalent (Deutsch 1924, 1930).

This biological reinterpretation of Freud became profoundly influential and was widely perceived as the Freudian orthodoxy, particularly in the United States after the Second World War. It was hardly surprising, then, that feminists coming to psychoanalytic theory in this period perceived it as deeply conservative, particularly when influential analysts actually used the theory as a stick with which to beat the feminist movement. Freud, as we have seen, did this. So too did Karl Abraham, who in 1920, in the first shot fired in the debate, argued that feminist demands for equality were not just a response to social inequities but also a sign of penis envy, the desire to be a man (Abraham 1920).

Karen Horney

Like all the other contributors to the debate, Karen Horney agreed that penis envy existed but saw it as transient and relatively unimportant (Horney 1924). In her view girls are born 'feminine' with heterosexual tendencies and an early awareness of their vaginas (Horney 1924, 1926). Penis envy that is strong and persistent is usually a result of the little girl's guilt about powerful inborn Oedipal desires and her anxiety that her father will actually penetrate and damage her small vagina. So, rather than being impelled towards hetero-sexuality by penis envy, as in Freud's theory, Horney's little girl regresses into the wish to be a man because she cannot tolerate the intensity of her own sexual longings for her father (Horney 1924).

One of the many ironies of this debate is that Horney was replacing Freud's penis envy theory with another father-focused argument, at the time when Freud himself was exploring the influ-ence of early mothering. Furthermore, if a contemporary girl was terrified of paternal rape we might wonder about the nature of her father's desire, but Horney's focus on the girl's 'natural' Oedipal desire prevented her from considering such questions.

Freud often responded to followers who deviated from his theories with scathing attacks. His 1924 paper certainly could be read as a direct rebuttal of Horney's earlier paper – a fact she may have found wounding (Odes Fliegel 1986). At any rate, from that point on Horney's own writings became increasingly polemical, concentrating on a 'male bias' within psychoanalysis which seemed to reflect the sexual fantasies of the little boy (1926). 'Men are evidently under greater necessity to depreciate women than vice-versa', Horney remarked tartly (1926: 12). It is womb envy that causes men to dominate women and exclude them from culture.

> At this point, I . . . ask in amazement . . . what about mother-hood? And the blissful consciousness of bearing a new life within oneself? . . . And the deep pleasurable feeling of satisfac-tion in suckling it and the happiness of the whole period when the infant needs her care?
>
> (Horney 1926: 10)

According to Horney, a 'dread of the vagina' – originating in early envy and fear of sexual rejection by the mother – emerged rapidly in the transference between male patients and female analysts.

> When one begins, as I did, to analyse men only after a long experience of analysing women, one receives a most surprising impression of the intensity of this envy of pregnancy, childbirth and motherhood, as well as of the breasts and the art of suckling.
>
> (Horney 1926: 10)

Horney's theories won influential support, notably from Melanie Klein, who settled in London in 1926.

Melanie Klein

Klein did not directly join in the debate, but issued a strong indirect challenge to Freud (Klein 1928). Disagreeing with his account of Oedipal feelings arising at three or four in relation to the father, she argued that the first signs appear in early infancy in relation to the mother's body. According to Klein, the father can be significant to the infant from early on, but he is at first experienced only as part of the mother.

Through the influence of Klein, Horney's theories – particularly her emphasis on womb envy and her argument that each sex had its own separate line of sexual development – became subsumed into the mainstream of British mother-dominated psychoanalysis. Klein saw penis envy as a defence against a deeper dread – that in retaliation for the daughter's own envious fantasies her mother will destroy her child-bearing capacities. The girl does not go through a 'masculine' phallic phase before she becomes heterosexual. Instead, children of both sexes go through a primary 'femininity phase' where they identify with their mothers, want babies and try to steal the imagined contents of her womb. The girl dreads retaliatory attacks to the inside of her body, whereas the boy fears that the mother will retaliate by attacking his genitals.

From 1935 the debate on female sexuality petered out, ending in deadlock rather than resolution. Present-day psychotherapists and feminists continue to discuss issues left unresolved about the nature and origins of sexual identity. I prefer to believe, as Freud sometimes seemed to, that our bodies and minds might be structured through patterns of cultural power. The radicalism of Freud's theory is flawed, though, by his phallocentrism. Horney's spirited womb-envy analysis has earned her a place in feminist and psychoanalytic history. Nevertheless, Horney's theory of inborn femininity remains highly problematic. For instance, how are we to view the many female contributors to this debate who either did not become wives and mothers, or did so only with great ambivalence? Theories which revolve around a 'natural' femininity – including heterosexual desire and the wish for children – pathologise women who choose other paths to happiness. Freud, in contrast, argued that there was no point in encouraging people to conform to what society demanded of them, particularly in the sphere of sexuality and gender, since they could never fully do so and repressed desire might well lead to neurosis. He also raised crucial questions about the origins of the passivity and self-abnegation so often associated with female sexuality and mothering. He argued that it is when the girl becomes heterosexual that she relinquishes her active 'masculine' strivings. This line of thinking is still of interest to those who question whether, for instance, heterosexual women who enjoy mothering might also be forceful and competitive enough to survive in the world of work outside the home.

Ultimately the theories that we feel are right will probably be those that resonate with our own personal experience of family and cultural life. For example, Horney may well have been able to stress the positive, enviable aspects of motherhood, and challenge Freud so forcefully, because of her identification with an idealised dominating mother and her intense hostility towards a denigrated father. Deutsch's more negative identification with a harsh mother who seems to have wanted her to be a son might have predisposed her towards Freud's theory of female penis envy. Because of her early experiences Deutsch could not celebrate womanhood, childbirth or mothering as Horney did. Deutsch idealised her father and this may also have prevented her from being able to state her quite considerable theoretical differences with Freud (Sayers 1991).

Why did Freud win so much support from his other female colleagues for his views on the centrality of penis envy? Perhaps in his day women actually were more preoccupied with envy of men, copying them in their dreams because they had no female role models. In 1972 Helene Deutsch said, 'Yes there is penis envy, but in a society open to women, with accepting parents, the impact will be very different than it used to be' (Strouse 1985: 165–166).

Freud and Horney's opposing views on penis and womb envy still resonate through contemporary theories which privilege the power of one parent or the other in the mind of the child. But some clinicians are now fundamentally challenging Oedipal theory. Increasingly doubts are raised as to whether basic analytic concepts can be applied across cultures and about their continuing relevance to societies where gender power relations are undergoing dramatic change.

Women's sexuality: feminist debates in the new millennium

Horney believed that men's cultural dominance is built on fragile and defensive foundations – an argument that has huge relevance for societies where traditional male power is being eroded. She probably would have agreed with those psychoanalytic feminists who argue that while cultural inequality still exists women are indeed the stronger sex, on whom men rely for emotional support, while enviously depreciating 'feminine' emotional intelligence and caring skills (Chodorow 1978, Orbach 1999).

In contrast, some modern-day feminists support Freud. They draw on Lacan to argue that when Freud focused on women's penis envy he was not devaluing women but simply describing their unenviable position in a society where they were seen as second-class. 'No phallus, no power, except those winning ways of gaining one', Juliet Mitchell wrote in 1974 (Mitchell 1974: 96). But is this really what Freud meant? As so often, it is very difficult to tell.

Freud's equivocal position towards women lives on. It resonates through some recent studies of Freud's concept of hysteria (neurosis), including Juliet Mitchell's *Madmen and Medusas* (Mitchell 2000). Mitchell's emphasis on the psychic importance of siblings is illuminating. She sees the hysteric's dramatic symptoms and envious longings as a protest against traumatic displacement, often by a real or imagined sibling. Mitchell describes how male and female hysterics deny the Oedipal 'reality' of sexual difference and develop an illusion of being able to give birth to their own self-generated (sibling) babies.

Provocatively, Mitchell throws down the gauntlet to those feminists who argue that we should focus on what links the sexes together as well as on the (biological) differences that distinguish us. They 'see only gender uncertainty', she argues, and therefore 'forget the problem of engendering' (Mitchell 2000: 324). Like Freud, she argues that girls' and boys' major task is to define themselves as different sexually and reproductively. Her book has become controversial because she often seems to offer women only a choice between conforming to prevailing gender norms and succumbing to hysteria. It is, she says, 'probably correct' that 'there are psychical consequences to anatomical differences'. Inevitably, then, the physiological difference between girls and boys 'confirms their different social fate: girls must be like mothers and boys must aspire to possess their replacements . . .' (Mitchell 2000: 324–325).

The child obviously does need to recognize a sense of difference or 'otherness' if it is to separate psychologically from its earliest love-objects, especially the mother, but does the 'third term' or agent of separation have to be a male father-figure? Pointing out that nowadays women may well have many options other than reproductive heterosexuality, social psychologist Lynne Segal declares that Mitchell's increasingly biological version of psychoanalysis does nothing to help us combat the pervasive denigration of women, whether as 'hags, whores or hysterics' (Segal 2000: 15).

Mitchell also dismisses the idea that we can all gain psychological strength from identifying with qualities associated culturally with the opposite sex and that ultimately this will contribute to sexual equality. She does not acknowledge that those who do not conform to conventional patterns of identification may be making a creative and enriching choice. According to New York psychoanalyst Adrienne Harris, the tomboy may be playing with and imaginatively transcending restrictive gender categories. Or she might be using a boyish persona defensively to protect against unresolved traumas in her own life or 'ghosts, demons or losses' resonating through generations of family life (Harris 2000: 224).

Harris and her colleague Jessica Benjamin are precisely the kind of feminists Mitchell argues against. Benjamin believes that mainstream psychoanalysis overemphasises the difficulty of recognising difference and 'otherness' and places too much significance on biological sex-differences. We do need to acknowledge difference, Benjamin says, but it is just as great a challenge to acknowledge our similarities to those who appear different. Identification with difference is crucial, Benjamin says, stressing that the girl – like the boy – needs to identify with a 'masculine' sense of agency and potency within a loving father–daughter relationship if she is to avoid experiencing herself as a submissive victim or an object of desire for others (Benjamin 1988, 1995). If this need for identificatory love with a father-figure is not met, Benjamin argues, children of both sexes may succumb to the cultural pattern of devaluing women and enviously submitting to idealised men.

Benjamin's fascination with bringing together insights from opposing theories remains for me one of the most valuable aspects of her work. She has made a radical attempt to integrate the strengths of father- and mother-centred theories into new understandings of sexual identity. This is particularly refreshing in the British context, where for decades mainstream psychoanalytic writing has focused on the psychotherapist as mother-figure, with the consequent danger of neglecting Oedipal sexuality, fathers, and siblings.

Benjamin continues to explore the question of who or what the 'third' might be if it is not simply the father or patriarchal law. 'I do not see the third as someone (a child, a former lover) who interrupts or even as some otherness that unravels, but as a mental function or capacity' she says, drawing on post-Kleinian theory (Benjamin 2000: 304). As she points out, we need to be able to think symbolically about ourselves and our interactions with others if we are to go beyond rigid 'binary' gender relationships.

But can the capacity for triangular relationships develop through the relationship between two people, as Benjamin suggests? In a critique of Benjamin's work, Judith Butler suggests that Benjamin displays an 'untenable hopefulness' about this (Butler 2000). Twosomes exist only fleetingly: there are triangular echoes in all sexual relationships, she argues. Neither heterosexual nor homosexual desire exists alone: one is always the arena for the other. This renders the relationship between sexuality and gender intensely complicated. Butler wants to envisage a society where homosexuality and heterosexuality are equally valued and continuing desire for both sexes can be thought about freely. So she wants to think about triangles including both sexes without returning to Freud or Lacan – 'the prison-house of Oedipus'. She wishes to move on from mother–infant dyads but she is also 'no great fan of the phallus' (Butler 2000). Benjamin agrees with Butler, acknowledging how far she has been influenced by the object-relations tradition which privileges the mother–infant relationship as the basis on which more sophisticated relationships are built. Insofar as we forget that the 'other', the third force is present in any couple we may reinforce a 'binary' either/or way of thinking about gender and sexuality (Benjamin 2000).

This discussion brings us back to a question which is central to this book: How can we integrate theoretically the power associated with both parents without devaluing women or pathologising homosexuality? A triangular theory of identity and desire which does not involve making an absolute and irrevocable choice for one sex or the other would indeed be more appropriate for societies where sexuality and gender are seen as more fluid and open to change and development than traditional Oedipal theories. Are these ways of thinking helpful to a consideration of other kinds of difference – such as those of 'race', culture and class?

Sexual identity – is it universal?

Freud frequently suggests that he is describing fundamental human conflicts and symbolic systems that prevail in the unconscious regardless of cultural variation. In contrast, anthropologists and archaeologists argue that no universal symbolism can be attributed to the penis (or phallus). For instance, Lucy Goodison points out that women's different, more highly valued status in prehistoric Crete is reflected in religious symbolism that revolves around powerful images of the female body and womb, rather than the male penis (Goodison 1990).

Does the pattern of our anxieties vary from culture to culture? Some of Freud's contemporaries argued that this was so. In 1929 Girindrasekar Bose, founder of the Indian Psychoanalytic Association, wrote to Freud that Oedipal anxieties in boys from the Indian subcontinent were different from those of their European counterparts. It is obviously very difficult to generalise about such a vast geographical area containing so very many cultural groups, languages and religions. But Bose did nevertheless feel able to argue that Indian men's cross-sexual and generational identifications were more fluid and that they more able to accept conscious fantasies of being female (Bose 1929, quoted in Kakar 1989). In his reply to Bose, Freud was polite and equivocal. But he told the poet H.D. during her analysis in 1933, 'On the whole, I think my Indian students have reacted in the least satisfactory way to my teaching' (H.D. 1956: 68).

The anthropologist Bronislaw Malinowski was given similarly short shrift when he challenged the universality of the Oedipus complex during the same period. Malinowski argued that Oedipal theory 'corresponds essentially to our patrilineal Aryan family ... buttressed by Roman law and Christian morals'. Malinowski went on to ask whether infantile conflicts, accentuated as they were by 'modern economic conditions of the well-to-do bourgeoisie', would be the same in the cabin of the peasant or the one-room tenement of the poor working man (Malinowski, quoted in Jones 1928). The early psychoanalyst Ernest Jones dismissed Malinowski's criticisms of psychoanalytic ethnocentrism as 'unconscious resistance' to a painful psychological truth (Jones 1928, Walton 1995).

Decades later Franz Fanon again challenged the universality of the Oedipus complex, arguing that the father who existed under colonial rule – or was a slave – had a completely different relationship to the state and cultural power than that of the white colonialist or slave-owner (Fanon 1967). Similarly, the working-class man who becomes middle-class might feel that he had betrayed rather than triumphed over his father if that father was proud rather than ashamed of his working-class identity (Blackwell 1998).

Klein's theories are often used to describe the way racism draws on infantile mechanisms of splitting and projection. We project aspects of ourselves we cannot face onto people of different races and classes, denying what is admirable and enviable in them. For instance, the racist white man might project his own powerful repressed desires – homosexual and heterosexual – onto the body of the black man, seeing him as a constant threat to his sexual monopoly of white women. Racism, according to this view, is a kind of sexual revenge (Fanon 1967).

However, racism, like class prejudice, arises also from power relations and requires evidence of people or groups of subordinate social and economic status (Frosh 1991). This becomes clear in clinical practice when we see patients who have previously benefited through cultural exploitation – through racist regimes, class privilege or sexual inequality. When their circumstances change they can appear quite bereft psychically, economically and socially. Previously they lived a parasitic existence and now they feel unequal to those they used to see as inferior. This helps us to understand how the exploited group is a product of the oppressor's need.

Kleinian theory helps us to understand the individual psychology of racism, which draws on infantile mechanisms of splitting and projection. But how do prejudicial attitudes perpetuate unequal power relations? And how are we to understand the sexual dynamics that seem so intrinsic to racism? Recently it has been argued that human relations 'internal and external, are colour-coded' (Dalal 2002: 227). Racist value judgements about blackness and whiteness are implicit in language and enter our psyches before we can think, according to Farhad Dalal. During slavery the black body was appropriated and controlled in fantasy as well as reality as the slave-owner re-enacted unresolved Oedipal wishes, using blackness and especially black skin as a container for the urge to triumph over and possess the once unattainable parents (Mohamed 2000). If we are to understand how these intensely complex issues emerge in the consulting-room, we need then to draw together mother-centred insights into splitting and projection with contemporary writings about triangular sexuality.

Joan Riviere: racism and the clinical relationship

Bearing in mind that most of the patients seen by psychoanalysts during Freud's lifetime were white, how would 'race' and racism have impinged on their dreams and fantasies? The feminist academic Jean Walton draws on one of the most interesting papers written during the 1920s debate, Joan Riviere's 'Womanliness as a masquerade', to explore the racialised sexual fantasies of these early psychoanalytic patients (Riviere 1929, Walton 1995). Riviere's paper focuses on a North American intellectual who spent part of her childhood in the Southern states and frequently dreams and fantasises about a sexually threatening black man.

Riviere's concern is with the growing number of women like herself who divide their time between traditionally 'feminine' and 'masculine' spheres of activity. She is puzzled about how to classify these new women who want the best of both worlds: women who, she says would until recently have made no secret of their wish to be like – or even to be – a man.

Her patient, who combines marriage and family life with a successful lecturing career, dreads retaliation from men and wards it off through ostentatious flirting with 'father-figures' after every successful public-speaking engagement. In this way she assumes womanliness like a mask to hide her professional competence as some men hide their homosexual desire through exaggerated displays of heterosexuality. Riviere describes how many women conceal their 'masculine' skills, taking up an attitude of extreme passivity with men, as if to say, 'I must not take. I must not even ask. It must be given me' (Riviere 1929: 101). The patient dreads retaliation from her mother even more than from her father. She constantly tries to put her 'masculine' skills at her mother's disposal, seeking to restore the father's penis, which she feels she has stolen from her mother. Riviere asks a question which has intrigued readers of her paper through the decades: Is there some core of 'genuine' femininity which can be clearly delineated from the pseudo-womanly masquerade? She answers that, whether 'radical or superficial', womanliness and the masquerade 'are the same thing' (Riviere 1929: 94).

Although the patient has a fulfilling heterosexual life, Riviere says that psychically she is a lesbian because she has frequent homosexual dreams with intense orgasms. Apart from that, her other dreams and fantasies revolve around the sexualised experiences with black men described earlier. Walton argues that throughout the decades psycho-analysts have consistently used white European subjectivity to represent all female identity. She points out that Riviere does not comment in any detail on her patient's racialised fantasies, focusing instead on aspects of sexuality that appear universal. This neglect also resonates through the writings of the myriad famous psychoanalysts and feminists who have written about this now iconic text – including Luce Irigaray, Judith Butler and Jacques Lacan (Walton 1995).

Riviere's patient uses this fantasy of racial difference to negotiate forbidden 'masculine' aggression and proscribed sexual desires. She imagines that she will protect herself from attack by seducing the black man, with the thought that she might eventually hand him over to the authorities. Riviere sees him as another powerful father-figure who must be reassured that she hasn't stolen his masculinity. But Walton points out that the black man in the 1920s American South occupies a similar position to the woman. He might also have needed to adopt a masquerade to ward off retaliation from white men who feared he would usurp their sexual and political power. The woman can 'turn her pockets out and prove she has no penis after all', but the black man cannot do so and in the American South at that time his horrific punishment would have been 'literal castration and death' (Walton 1995: 231).

Riviere's paper revolves around masquerades of sexuality and race. However, I have always assumed that, as in so many clinical accounts, there might also be another masquerade connected with identity. The patient may well not have come from the American South. The few biographical details that are given might be an attempt to disguise her true identity. It has even been suggested that Riviere herself had autobiographical links with the patient (see O'Connor and Ryan 1993). Nevertheless, Walton has still provided us with an outstandingly illuminating insight into the fundamentals of psychoanalytic and feminist racism.

Race and class in the countertransference

Racism, homophobia and misogyny are vectors of power which require and deploy each other. They do not run in parallel or function as separate entities (Butler 1993). How are these interlinked sources of control reflected in the therapeutic relationship?

First of all, psychoanalytic clinicians may have assumed in the past – and perhaps even assume in the present – that people with different cultural values and ways of thinking about emotional unhappiness are less able to think symbolically and are therefore less suited to analytic treatment. Barbara Fletchman Smith describes how in her experience some Afro-Caribbean people have been thought to lack 'psychological-mindedness' because they present a body rather than a mind that is 'going mad' (Fletchman Smith 2000). Once psychotherapy begins, the white therapist may well bring a negative cultural agenda constituted through sources such as fairy tales, jokes and media images – a kind of 'pre-transference' – into the clinical relationship with a black patient (Thomas 1992). The therapist may become overwhelmed, 'blinded by colour' or 'colour-blind', unable to think at all about the significance of racial difference, so that the black patient once again feels marginalised, misunderstood (Dalal 2002).

When racism, colonial or class oppression plays a significant role, the therapist might need to prepare herself to create a space for the patient to explore the interaction between the psyche and socio-economic or historical factors. Profound self-hatred or deference is often generated by racism or class prejudice, and some parental failings may be understood differently if they are placed in their original political and economic context. So the analyst needs to help the client think about the relationship between their psychological problems and their cultural history. At the same time the psychotherapist must try to understand the anxieties generated by his unintended racial thoughts and feelings, so that he can think about his own 'racial enactments' in a productive way (Leary 2000).

Class, a particularly un-theorised area, is fertile ground for unconscious countertransference enactments. Alienation – the psychology of class – takes the form of 'demoralisation, shame and inflamed psychesomas' (Dimen 2003: 93). If patients have moved out of the class they were born into they may have a particular need to explore the invisible wounds inflicted during that transition, but many psychotherapists lack the cultural awareness to respond to such needs. Since classification operates in and through all of us it may be structured into the therapeutic relationship in ways that neither participant can see or understand. For instance, a supervisee described how a patient from a working-class white immigrant background had at fourteen been put in a remedial class for a subject in which she had come top in her entire year. At first the therapist, who came from a rather privileged background, had been incredulous that the school could have done this. The patient went on to explain that although she excelled in some subjects she had stopped trying in others, since she felt that the teachers in her 'good' state school did not seem to expect her to succeed. She also mentioned that her middle-class 'English' best friend was generally treated more respectfully. The patient had urged her mother to complain while sensing that her mother would not be able to do so effectively – which turned out to be the case. When the therapist said how difficult it must have been for the patient to have a mother who was not able to 'fight' for her daughter, the patient suddenly became enraged. She shouted that she had already said how grateful she was to her parents for all they had gone without to help her get a good education. She was fed up with the therapist not listening. How could the therapist, with her big house, smart car and posh accent, know what it was like to be treated as she had been?

The usually very competent therapist felt shocked and helpless and became uncharacteristically quiet for the rest of the session. In supervision we tried to unpick this complex 'class enactment' wherein the therapist had become paralysed through anxiety and guilt about her own upper-class background. Clearly she had also felt as helpless and incompetent as the patient's mother had when her own intervention had been so unsuccessful. We speculated that the patient might have felt all over again that she and her family were being publicly humiliated as the therapist was experienced as behaving like the uninterested 'snobbish' teachers and the more privileged best friend.

Interestingly, in a recent study of class and gender in London the tendency of teachers to expect working-class girls to fail, and the ability of middle-class parents to 'fight', even to the extent of getting incompetent teachers removed, is seen as crucial to the success of middle-class girls educationally. The authors argue that when a middle class girl underperforms she is seen as lacking motivation, while the working-class girl is expected by teachers to fail, and so is judged to be lacking in ability if she does not do as well as she might (Walkerdine et al. 2001).

Each clinical encounter is laced through with myriad unacknowledged, perhaps unthinkable culture-based feelings and fantasies. Based as it is on a combination of psychic, economic and political factors, racism would seem to be an ideal topic for exploration by psychoanalysis – the 'science of the irrational'. After all, the role of psychoanalysis is to confront aspects of ourselves we would rather avoid rather than to 'resolve' or prescribe (Frosh 1991). Hopefully when we are able to take back our projections, accepting parts of ourselves that we previously discarded, psychotherapists may be able to work with and even enjoy differences rather than defending against them.

Joan Riviere's question about how women can draw on their psychic 'masculinity' while also preserving more traditionally feminine strengths and activities is central to this book. I ask how women can take possession of their lives and see themselves as agents of their own destinies, without renouncing their own emotional needs or giving up on the possibility of sexual passion. The question is just as fundamental when reversed: how can men integrate qualities associated culturally with femininity? Can they be strong without depending on women as a receptacle for disowned aspects of psychic life? The difficulty both sexes have in this area is compounded (or perhaps created) by the fact that women and 'femininity' are still valued so much less than men and 'masculinity', and by the power differentials between the sexes. Men and women are very differently located in the cultural hierarchy, and this difference also affects the analytic encounter, a topic raised by Horney. She described how rapidly envy, fear and contempt arise in the maternal transference with male patients. Likewise, Freud acknowledged the discomfort he felt when his female patients perceived him as feminine or maternal.

This brings me to the second major theme of this book – the clinical and political implications of power and envy. Freud and Horney's opposing theories have found expression in different analytic traditions revolving around 'maternal' and 'paternal' power. What do these terms mean exactly? We need to understand much more about the interaction between 'real' experiences of parenting, parental functions, cultural symbolism and fantasy.

Only now that more black and working-class clinicians are entering the psychoanalytic world are the issues of 'race', racism and – to a much lesser extent – class receiving serious attention. Racism, class oppression, sexism and homophobia are inextricably linked, operating in and through each other. Rooted in envy and hatred of our own early vulnerability, irrational feelings interact with economic and political mechanisms. As a profession we are only just beginning to think about the way complex cultural inequalities are played out within the transference and countertransference. Can the theory and practice of psychotherapy help us understand and change cultural power-differentials rather than merely replicate them?

Some themes of the debate remain central to recent discussion of sexual identity although they are addressed in different ways. Nowadays we would not ask whether women are more masochistic than men. But contemporary analysts and feminists still question why women tolerate cultural restrictions and painful or frustrating personal relationships. Some symptoms prevail in one sex rather than the other, such as serious eating problems and certain male sexual perversions.

Examining such phenomena invariably raises all the questions so central to the earlier debate. What are 'masculinity' and 'femininity'? How do they arise, and are they more the property of one sex than the other? Given the way inequitable divisions of power and prestige have permeated the erotic life of women and men, is it ever possible to eliminate such deeply entrenched inequalities or have they become necessary to our sexuality? Uncomfortable questions, with still no easy answers.

Chapter 2

From the penis to the womb: male sexuality

During my training as a psychoanalytic psychotherapist in early 1980s London I barely heard mention of Freud's concept of penis envy. Most of my colleagues and teachers seemed to regard this aspect of Freud's theory as too anachronistic and irrelevant to merit serious discussion. In those years only Lacanians criticised the prevailing view of the mother as the most powerful and enviable parent. Juliet Mitchell, who drew on Lacan in her early writing, said: 'The debates of the 1930s bequeathed, instead of an interest in the psychology of femininity, a heritage of a mother–child obsession' (Mitchell 1974: 229). In North America and France the psychoanalytic climate was different. Freud's theory was reformulated and his writings on female sexuality have continued to be taken far more seriously as a subject of debate.

Debate over female sexuality had abated after the 1920s/1930s controversy, and did not revive until the 1960s, when feminism generated a new wave of interest in the psychology of gender. In the intervening years there had been some significant theoretical shifts in British psychoanalysis and North American ego psychology. This chapter focuses on how changing theories about envy, the Oedipus complex, and the father in the male psyche might affect clinical practice.

Freud had prophesied that his theory of a subversive sexuality which could never be fully tamed by culture would alienate many of his psychoanalytic followers. This was indeed the case with British object-relations theorists, who argued that Freud focused too much on the relief of physical tension, rather than always linking erotic desire with loving intimacy or defences against it (Meltzer 1978, Symington 1986). Most British psychoanalysts moved away from Freud's emphasis on incestuous desire, concentrating rather on the need to renounce the illusion of fusion with the mother. Until recently relations with the father were virtually ignored.

This view of the father as an increasingly peripheral figure both reflected and reinforced social trends during the era when object-relations theories were developing. Freud's perspective was formed through the experience of Victorian upper-class European families, where mothers were often squeezed out by authoritarian fathers and a parade of nannies. The theories of Winnicott and Bowlby, by contrast, were forged in post-Second World War Britain. There, panic during 1945–7 about the falling birth-rate ensured that the target of post-war social policy was the mother, who was spoken about as if she constituted all there was of the family. Increasingly the mother was seen by policy-makers as a synonym for all women, the needs of other female groups being ignored (Riley 1983). Today theories which stress male fragility and womb envy may reflect men's current anxieties about the erosion of patriarchal power as traditional family structures disappear and women's lives appear more enviable.

As the 1980s went on, however, there was also a noticeable revival of analytic interest in the role of the father. Men expected to be far more actively engaged with their children than their own fathers had been. Yet the increasing economic dispensability of the father (given the growth in female employment) has induced anxiety in some male analysts. In 1991, for example, the British psychoanalyst Adam Limentani lambasted a feminist clinician who had suggested that children often benefit from being brought up solely by the mother (Limentani 1991). At the same time, feminists have also become concerned that in psychoanalytic theory mothers are being held solely responsible for the problems of their children. Clearly this is a critical moment in the changing patterns of male–female relations: can psychoanalysis take on board these shifts in family life, and the way they reverberate in the individual unconscious? If the actual power of men is under threat, what meaning does this have for psychological gender?

The British School of psychoanalysis: womb envy

Writing as a turn-of-the-century patriarch, Freud was well aware of the benefits men gained from identification with the father's authority and cultural privilege. He also idealised the mother–son relationship, saying: 'A mother is only brought unlimited satisfaction by her relation to a son; this is altogether the most free from ambivalence of all human relationships' (Freud 1933: 168). According to Freud, men's greatest rivalry is with other men. The woman-hater dreads submission to another man and therefore abhors the female sex and qualities he sees as 'feminine' in himself and other males. If men avoid psychotherapy or become resistant to the process, this is because they see accepting help as synonymous with humiliating submission to (or castration by) the analyst within the paternal transference.

In contrast, Klein and Winnicott argue that it is envy of the mother rather than rivalry with the father that impedes psychic change. Klein, who believed that the boy's early rivalry with his mother was particularly intense and asocial, created a new psychoanalytic reading of envy. She described how all infants are born with varying tendencies towards envious hatred which is experienced most strongly towards the mother in infancy rather than the Oedipal father in toddlerhood (Klein 1957). Klein radically redefined the Oedipus complex, focusing as much on emotional and intellectual development as on erotic desire. For her the child's most crucial task is to tolerate the guilt and depression that follow the recognition of destructive feelings towards love-objects. Psychic health, including the capacity for self-reflection and symbolic thought, is dependent on tolerating the mother as a separate being with a life of her own, including a sexual relationship with the father.

Klein's views on envy touch on psychoanalytic controversies about how far aggression is inborn and the extent to which the very young baby feels itself to be separate from other people. Winnicott's completely different argument that envy can only arise as a reaction to severe pain or frustration is more in line with my thinking.

Winnicott barely mentioned fathers. When he did it was to assign them the auxiliary role of providing a 'protective covering' for the mother–infant couple against external impingement (Winnicott 1957). Later the father might also balance the mother, providing a more objective attention that would help the child to cope with emotional ambivalence.

Despite his emphasis on environmental factors, Winnicott, like most British object-relations psychoanalysts, believes that there is a congenital disposition to be psychologically, as well as anatomically, masculine or feminine, maternal or paternal. Winnicott believed that upbringing is crucial, and this is why some men are more maternal than their female partners. But he also wrote that ideally the environment reinforces innate tendencies. Therefore, most 'males become men and most females become women' (Winnicott 1964: 184).

Winnicott agreed with Horney that male womb envy and fear of domination by the female is far deeper than women's envy of men. He argued that human beings would not need to wreak revenge on 'Woman' through cruel and discriminatory customs if they could face up to the absoluteness of their early dependence on the mother. Winnicott also traced men's tendency to seek out danger, in fighting wars for instance, to envy of the risks women take in childbirth. These insights are, in my view, absolutely crucial to a feminist understanding of gender power differentials. Yet Winnicott, who remained profoundly ambivalent about women's struggles for equality, argued in the same essay that feminism is an identity disorder – the result of the girl's inability to accept that she could not be male (Winnicott 1964).

This emphasis on overwhelmingly maternal power led to the widespread view that mothers were almost entirely responsible for the psychological problems of their offspring. For 'most men the problem is women', we are told in a contemporary American anthology on male psychology (Fogel 1986: 9). The father is no longer seen by his sons as a threatening patriarchal presence but as absent or ineffectual, leaving his son at the mercy of the parent who really is imagined to be powerful – the mother. This results in a 'martial masculinity', a brittle, artificial and aggressive version of manhood formed as protection against identification with the powerful mother, argues Munder Ross in the same volume. In a classic British object-relations anthology on sexual perversion, almost all the patients described are male, and maternal castration, seductiveness or neglect is given as the main reason for the son's difficulties in almost every case (Rosen 1979a).

There is a tendency for psychoanalysts who emphasise women's power in psychic life to ignore men's financial and social power. They disregard the way motherhood is circumscribed by medicine and the state, often in ways that increase women's sense of helplessness and isolation. This can lead to the assumption that women, as the stronger sex, simply give away the emotional power they gain from their procreative role. The reality is that in our culture qualities seen as 'masculine' are more socially valued and linked with mental health.

Men who want to be female

Maleness, in our society, is a sign of power and privilege. Yet, given this, why do some men wish to abandon it? Indeed, far more men than women seek actually to change their gender, penis envy notwithstanding. Why is this?

The North American psychoanalyst Robert Stoller argued that because men have to 'dis-identify' with the mother after an initial period of female identification, their gender identities are more rigid and fragile than women's (Stoller 1975). He traced male hatred of women and the wish to be female to a three-way conflict – between the desire to regress to an illusion of symbiosis with the mother, a dread of the ensuing loss of male identity, and a longing for revenge on her.

Stoller argues that an immutable sense of being male or female – a 'core gender identity' – is fixed mainly through cultural rather than biological forces by the age of three. The boy who is not encouraged to 'dis-identify' and continues a 'timeless, excessively close physical and emotional intimacy' with his mother may in extreme cases become transsexual, convinced that he is a psychological female trapped in a male body (Stoller 1979).

It is striking that Stoller barely mentions the role of the father except to say briefly that in these cases he is either absent or oppressive and threatening. The British psychoanalyst Adam Limentani has slightly more to say about the father's role. He argues that male transsexualism develops from early disturbance in symbol formation exacerbated by intrusive or absent fathering. Similarly, female transsexuals are, in his view, unable to think symbolically and so can conceive only of the most extreme and concrete way of differentiating themselves from a feeling of fusion with their mothers – through gaining a male body surgically (Limentani 1979, 1991).

Juliet Mitchell offers a different perspective, arguing that many male patients described as 'feminine' by psychoanalysts – including Limentani's famous 'Vagina-Man' – might actually be suffering from hysteria (Mitchell 2000, Limentani 1984). Hysteria in men, which ranges from a temporary Oedipal response to a delusionary psychosis, is always rooted in powerful fantasies of possessing the mother's body and her procreative powers, according to Mitchell. She describes how British psychoanalysts turned away from the concept after its wide-scale occurrence in soldiers during the First World War because they were unable to face the prevalence of male hysteria.

One of the most radical challenges to mainstream psychoanalytic theories has emerged from US feminist clinicians such as Jessica Benjamin, Virginia Goldner and Adrienne Harris. They all reject the idea that there is a single clearly definable entity called male 'identity', consolidated through becoming like the father and unlike the mother. Describing gender as both 'tenacious and fragile, reified substance and dissolving insubstantial', Benjamin describes how all identities are structured gradually, through 'multiple differences and unstable identifications' with real and imagined love-objects rather than through the dramatic – even traumatic – process of differentiation or 'dis-identification' (Benjamin 1995: 70). Disagreeing with Stoller, Benjamin argues that the boy does not need to 'dis-identify' with or separate more from his mother than the girl. At the point where the boy develops a 'core' sense of belonging to one sex he may still imagine that he possesses the physical capacities of both sexes and his parents may be only partially differentiated in his mind. In reaction to this early 'over-inclusive' phase, the Oedipal child develops an extremely rigid view of what each sex is like, enviously repudiating anything that differs from this stereotype. Later, if castration anxiety and repudiation are toned down, a range of identifications can be reintegrated (Benjamin 1995).

In some cultures nowadays it is possible for both sexes to 'play' creatively – even ironically – with gender convention, points out Virginia Goldner. But while some people are able to experiment with gender, investing it with personal and symbolic meaning, others experience their gender as rigid and restrictive, imposed on them from outside (Goldner 2003). The boy who obsessively rejects identification with his own sex or is unable to move between a range of identifications may be reacting to personal or familial trauma. His 'girlish' persona may represent a desperate attempt to keep an abandoning or rejecting mother inside his psyche (Coates 1990). According to Susan Coates, who studies boyhood identity confusion, the mother's withdrawal can lead to a profound melancholic identification which shows itself as an excessive 'femininity' in boys as well as girls. Alternatively, the boy who feels himself to be more female than male may be serving as a container for a parent's dissociated self-states. He may be struggling unconsciously to maintain his father's very fragile sense of masculinity, perhaps acting out an unacknowledged 'girl' part of the paternal psyche (Harris 2000).

It is also increasingly accepted that quite distinct 'masculinities' are built around a range of real and imagined experiences of 'race', ethnicity, social class and sexuality. So, growing up Muslim is different from growing up white in Britain. Both these kinds of masculinity are 'also experienced in the context of fantasies of African Caribbean black masculinity with its associations of attractive style and physical "hardness" ', according to a recent study of London boys (Frosh *et al.* 2002: 258). Assumptions about physical prowess and heterosexuality indicate that class and sexual orientation are also crucially entwined with fantasies about race and culture. The struggle to establish oneself as 'normatively heterosexual' in contrast to a repudiated 'gay' identity is fundamental to the construction of these young masculinities.

Sexual identity is then always complex and potentially unstable, however male the boy believes himself to be. 'Masculinities' are structured differentially within each localised cultural and familial context and may be experienced as restrictive and inhibiting or as personally meaningful. A boy may draw on his mother's 'masculine' potency or on his father's maternal qualities, absorbing these real or imagined attributes through loving identificatory relationships or through dissociated trauma which has reverberated through the family for generations.

I go on now to describe how a male patient's maternal transference triggered a nightmare early in therapy. In discussing the dream he revealed how social class, including an extremely impoverished childhood in a rough and violent inner-city area, had a crucial impact on his sexuality and identity. The dream also raised questions about the interaction between so-called 'real' events and fantasies, since the patient, whom I call Mr C, had very sparse memories of his early years.

The spider dream

Mr C had been coming to see me for two months before the Christmas break. Returning from the break, he told me of a disturbing dream in which he woke up and noticed a small multi-coloured spider on his bedroom door. He went to pick it up gently but saw that it was growing larger and moving nearer to him. It was made of shiny foil with a lot of red in it, like Christmas decorations. Bits of it kept sticking in him 'like fibreglass, which gets under your skin and becomes infected if you don't protect yourself'. It then changed, becoming a matchstick animal, standing on the table near him. It was mainly female but also a bit male.

Eventually as the spider/animal continued growing he told it, 'I'm bigger than you and can walk away'. Mr C woke up immediately the dream was over, feeling overwhelmed by powerful, confused feelings. Although it was still the middle of the night he started to write about his feelings about psychotherapy. He associated the shiny red spider with me, since I often wore red. He went on to say: 'These sessions have become very important to me, but I realised that I did feel very angry about you being away. I started to write down things you'd said to me before the break. At the time, they made sense, but later I felt criticised by you.' When he finished writing his mood changed. He had acknowledged his own ambivalence towards me, so his depression lifted.

The primal spider creature might have combined elements of fantasy and real experience. Mr C's insecure relationship to his mother was exacerbated by an intolerable feeling of exclusion from parental sex. The entire family, who had been very poor, had slept in the same room until he was four. Mr C had witnessed drunken, chaotic scenes, including his father's violence towards his mother. Their living conditions were a source of great humiliation to the family since they did not come from a culture where children and adults routinely shared sleeping quarters. He also told me that several times in his teens in the swimming-pool, adult men had rubbed themselves against his genitals. He had found this both exciting and profoundly disturbing, and wondered whether he had suffered any sexual abuse earlier in his childhood. When he was fourteen he had also made several attempts to force himself on his elder sister sexually, and she had only managed to fight him off with great difficulty.

Contemporary Kleinians argue that if parental intercourse is felt to intrude into the child's mind before she or he has internalised a secure maternal object, the full recognition of parental sexuality is then dreaded as a mental catastrophe, or even experienced as a threat to life. The predominantly female multi-legged spider who is also a bit male would, from this perspective, be a very primitive early infantile image of combined parental intercourse. The break from me just as he was beginning to form an attachment had been experienced as a disaster by Mr C.

Discussing the dream, he told me that there was something sexual about the spider/animal. Just before Christmas he had become aware of feeling attracted to me. During the break he felt so abandoned that I, like the little spider, altered in his mind, becoming an increasingly overwhelming, predatory and threatening figure. Whereas he had previously found my interpretations helpful, now he experienced my words as having pierced his skin. Left to fester they had become as painful and hard to remove as bits of fibreglass.

Mr C went on to tell me that there had been a 'lack of empathy' in his 'baby-relationship' with his mother, for which his rather distant, uninvolved father could not compensate. Mr C had therefore not had anyone who could help him to tolerate and understand his own raw pain, wild passion and rage. He could only project these states of mind outside himself so that other people, including myself, were liable to turn into nightmare creatures, looming dangerously over him like the spider in the dream. It was also easier for him to see me as a wicked retaliatory maternal figure than to face his fear that I, like his sister, might become the object of the violent sexual and possessive impulses he had exhibited in his teens.

Mr C longed for the kind of intense intimacy with a mother-figure of which he had always felt deprived, but he simultaneously dreaded being swallowed up in an incestuous symbiosis where he would lose any sense of being male. Mr C admitted in the session that he would like to tell me, as he told the spider, that he is bigger than me and can walk away. The boy may repudiate the mother and his own identification with her through an assertion of his more privileged position within patriarchy. Many boys unconsciously decide then that the mother is not worth the pain of so much desire and that they will never again allow a woman to have so much power over them (Jukes 1993).

From a Freudian perspective Mr C's dream might represent an attempt to incorporate a paternal element into a potentially suffocating therapeutic dyad. Lacanian clinicians would argue that Mr C needs to confront the existence of the Other, a paternal force who can help him to face Oedipal issues, rather than to internalise a more secure maternal presence, as recommended by object-relations theorists.

Mr C was grappling with a range of disturbing questions. He wondered: Was his abusive attack on his sister a re-enactment of his own experiences of abuse – or an identification with his father's violence? Did he have a strong component of homosexuality, or was he lacking paternal love and attention – or both? His dream raised issues about the interaction between male desire and father–son identification. Where mother-centred theory prevails, such issues are often neglected in favour of maternal nurturing and its vicissitudes. In the following section I discuss a variety of contemporary views on the role of the father in the male psyche.

The return to the father

Since the 1980s there has been renewed interest in the father and in male psychology among British and North American psychoanalysts. In an interesting reappraisal, Adam Limentani admits that in his own past work he sometimes colluded with the family's desire to exclude the father from psychotherapy consultations. He himself overlooked the way in which he became a positive paternal figure in the analysis of patients, including transsexuals. If the psychotherapist focuses only on the mother this may fulfil the patient's unconscious desire to preserve the illusion of being central to the mother's life. The theoretical neglect of the father may mean that little is expected of him or that important facts about his position in the family are ignored in clinical work. Especially in the latter part of the analysis, the 'acquisition of the second object is our fundamental therapeutic task, a fact that is so obvious that it gets overlooked' (Limentani 1991: 577). From a similar perspective it is argued that initially the boy internalises the father as an ally, the 'wall of a fortress' against fears of merger or annihilation by the mother. The father will then gain significance as an alternative object of love and identification (Glasser 1984).

Some psychoanalysts, including some contemporary Kleinians, have adopted a more radical stance on the mobility of parenting functions, arguing that fathers may provide 'maternal' containment, and that mothers too help children gain a sense of psychic autonomy and assist their move into the wider world. Kleinians in general have always placed some emphasis on the father's importance both as a real figure and as an object of early fantasy. Since the 1980s Kleinian theorists have demonstrated the crucial role played by a child's feelings and fantasies about the father in the formation of its early relationship with the mother. They stress that a child's capacity to tolerate the emotional and sexual links between its parents is crucial to the capacity for distinguishing internal and external reality, self-reflection and objective thinking about others (Britton 1989).

Despite these efforts at rehabilitation, the father remains a shadowy figure in much contemporary theory. He is still secondary to the mother and does not intervene as a powerful sexual presence, a representative of authority and culture, as in Freud's theory. British psychoanalyst Gregorio Kohon draws on Lacan to argue that object-relations analysts 'have managed to castrate the father, and desexualise the theory; the penis of the father has become another breast, an

organ of warmth and reparation, the giver of babies but not of
sexual pleasure'. He quotes a senior British woman analyst: 'What is
the function of the father,' she exclaimed, 'but, of course, to fuck the
mother?' (Kohon 1987: 225).

The recourse to Lacan in Kohon's essay is significant, since it
points to one of the most fully elaborated – and controversial –
attempts to reinstate the father at the heart of psychoanalytic theory.
Lacan was deeply critical of the contemporary psychoanalytic preoccupation with the mother–infant relationship. In particular he
identified the Oedipal moment – rather than the pre-Oedipal relationship with the mother – as the crucial point of psychic structura-
tion. The preverbal child, dwelling in its dyadic union with the
mother, is living inside an imaginary world which must be ruptured
by the entry of a 'third term', the symbolic father, if the child is not
to become psychotic.

Lacan argues that the boy suffers in a particular way from being
'idol-ised' by his mother, who does not envy or idealise the girl in
the same way. The boy needs his father to break into the intense
'luring' mother–son relationship, structured around the mother's
lack of a penis and the son's wish to become the 'phallus', the sole
object of maternal desire (Lacan 1964). Lacan is describing the
role of the symbolic, rather than the actual, father. His focus is on
the way patriarchal laws are reproduced in the unconscious. It is the
father who helps the child to face reality, originally of the differences between the sexes and the generations, while the mother is
associated with helpless dependence and the dangerous lure of
psychotic illusion. Inevitably, then, his theory reflects the devaluation of the mother and idealisation of the father which prevails in
our society. There is a paradox inherent in it too, since the 'liber-
ation' offered by the father places the girl and boy in different
positions in male-dominated culture. Through identification with
paternal power the boy can triumph over the mother and deny the
strength of his early physical and emotional dependence on her. It is
also worth noting that in most actual families the mother does
much of the work of preparing the child for independence, while
the father may well provide some maternal containment for the
infant.

How useful are theories which assume that the father becomes
significant only as an Oedipal patriarchal rival when the boy is three
or four? Benjamin argues that the process of identification is successful only when it is reciprocal – when the father recognises the boy's

need to be like him within the context of a loving relationship. This kind of homosexual identificatory love serves as the boy's vehicle for establishing masculinity both defensively and creatively, according to Benjamin. It confirms his sense of self as subject of desire, master of his own destiny. Thwarted identificatory love, on the other hand, often turns into a submissive or hostile tie to a powerful admired father who emasculates rather than confirms the boy's identity (Benjamin 1995).

Another North American clinician, Thomas Domenici, emphasises the boy's need for a loving relationship with his father from infancy. When the boy experiences his father only as a prohibitive figure who dismisses the boy's need for reciprocatory love and tenderness the boy – whether gay or heterosexual – will internalise a contemptuous hostile attitude towards love-relationships between men. As a result all male identity is built on the fragile basis of a denied love for the father (Domenici 1995, Butler 1997). This does of course cast light on the way so many adolescent boys band together around a shared repudiation of homosexuality.

Changing clinical practice: integrating the father

Different theoretical views about the importance of the father will obviously influence the way psychotherapists work. For instance, some object-relations psychotherapists expect to be seen mainly as a maternal transference figure during the early stages of treatment (Limentani 1991). This reflects a belief that the patient must internalise a secure enough maternal object before he or she can face the existence of the father. Intersubjectivists, including Jessica Benjamin, argue that the child – or patient – must feel fully recognised by another person before he is able to begin the process of psychic separation. The patient may then begin to acknowledge that the therapist is separate, outside himself, not merely the sum of his projections or the object of his need.

In contrast, Lacanians believe that the patient needs to experience the intervention of a third force. The analyst must speak from the position of the symbolic father, locating the child's desire to move out of the narcissistic position associated with the early mother. Too great an emphasis on 'internalising' a maternal good object could strengthen the patient's illusion that he exists in an exclusive therapeutic dyad. The patient has to come to terms with a sense of lack:

the object of our desire is always outside us, and we can never fully possess the presence or qualities of another.

Is it possible to integrate the insights of Freud and Lacan with more mother-centred theories? Or are these approaches too difficult to combine? Certainly the psychotherapist must be aware of Oedipal issues from the beginning of therapy, but some patients will be able to face these issues more rapidly than others. Mr C showed through his spider dream that he had very little capacity to recognise triangular relationships, because they represented such a threat to his psychic equilibrium. The next patient I describe had as a child begun to recognise his parents' sexual closeness, but his pain at exclusion was so intense that he avoided the full significance of this knowledge. In psychotherapy he was so determined to avoid facing his Oedipal rivalry and humiliation that he barely mentioned his father for the first two years of twice-weekly psychotherapy.

The father eclipsed

Mr E told me in his first session that his problems had begun in his fourth year. A first child, he was greatly cosseted and indulged by both parents, but was expected to grow up suddenly when a sister was born that year. He felt that he'd been ejected with traumatic abruptness from a womb-like atmosphere. In that fourth year his family had also moved house and he had been sent to a nursery school some distance from home. At fourteen he had hit his sister on the chest and his father had responded by hitting his son – something he had never done before.

Psychically Mr E had wiped his father out because he had not wanted to acknowledge that he himself was not the sexual and emotional centre of his mother's life. The arrival of a third – the new baby – had destroyed his fantasy of existing in an exclusive couple with his mother. He defended himself against feelings of humiliation and inferiority in relation to his father by illusions of triumph. In one dream he climbed out of bed with his mother while his father glowered impotently from the other side of the room.

As he began to work through some of his overwhelming grief about abandonment, Mr E began to acknowledge that in fact his father had given him considerable attention during that traumatic period after his sister's birth. The relatively strong relationship he had had with his father had been covered up and buried by his pain at the loss of his mother.

During psychotherapy he gradually became less preoccupied with losing or being rejected by mother figures, including myself. Then, for the first time, Mr E began to recall through dream images the hours his father had spent with him playing patiently with maps, trains and models. The uncovering of these memories coincided with a period of dramatic progress in his career. Mr E connected his increasing intellectual confidence and organisational skills with those early experiences of father–son intimacy.

If the psychotherapist focuses entirely on early conflicts about the mother, a sense of stagnation may begin to prevail within the thera-peutic relationship. The therapeutic discourse may suddenly come to life again once a sense of otherness within the transference is acknowledged. The first time I became aware that I represented Mr E's father in the transference was during a session when he com-plained bitterly that he couldn't listen to me, although he agreed rationally with what I was saying. The problem, he kept reiterating, was that although my consulting-room usually felt warm and soft, today it did not provide the womb-like, softly-upholstered environ-ment he needed. Eventually I began to feel useless, impotent, invis-ible. I mentioned this and linked the feeling with the way his father had been wiped out, never mentioned in the sessions. I suggested that he was unable to make use of what I was saying to him today just as he had been unable to assimilate the hours of patient attention his father had given him after the birth of the new baby sister. The atmosphere changed when I said this and he began to listen intently. He then replied that perhaps he had felt too upset about losing his sense of me as a comforting motherly figure to think about me in a different way. He felt that I was speaking to him in a paternal way whereas he wanted everyone to be the same and to treat him in an identical way, he explained.

As his fantasies of being female became evident, Mr E described himself as having been '24 when his mother was born'. He'd always had fantasies about heterosexual intercourse with me. Now he described bisexual fantasies about having my body inside his, keep-ing him warm. 'It feels as if I've got a baby inside me, and that the baby is you', he told me. This reminded him of how he had told his teacher 'I'm having a baby' before the birth of 'my baby', as he had called the second sister, born when he was eight. Later in psycho-therapy he came to understand that the reason he had always wanted many children was so that he could outdo his mother. For him the minimum number was one more than she had.

As Mr E's identification with his father grew stronger, he began tentatively to confront the intimacy between his parents. He dreamt about them as a united couple, but when I mentioned this he said, 'I don't like you putting both of my parents together and talking about them in one sentence'. After this, though, he gradually became able to notice and even enjoy the fact that his parents really did seem even now to gain great pleasure from physical and emotional closeness with each other. He also began to express the hope that I had a sexual partner, because he did not want me to be lonely. Once he had mourned the illusion of a lost exclusive relationship and recognised the link between his parents, he became increasingly able to reflect on his own experience and to observe relationships between others. As psychotherapy progressed it became clear that his father had been exceptionally involved in his son's early childcare, even though his mother had remained the primary parent. He became convinced that his father had contributed to the early feeling of womb-like security he had experienced in infancy.

If I had been more Lacanian I might have confronted this man much earlier with the fact that he was obliterating his father from the therapeutic discourse. Would earlier, more forceful interpretations about the absence of a third have had a positive effect? Mr E's father had a far stronger presence in his mind than in that of Mr C, whose dream I described earlier. But in childhood he had been expected to grow up too suddenly. If I had confronted him earlier with his pain about having to share his mother with a sexual rival he might have experienced me as repeating his parents' mistake. I think that one of his reasons for choosing a female psychotherapist was an unconscious wish to avoid facing the existence of his father too soon. However, as I show in Chapter 6, it is questionable how far the therapist's sex does impede the emergence of such transferences.

Mr E thought of himself as a 'New Man', but his apparent gentleness and sensitivity belied hatred and envy towards women. He could be described as a male hysteric, since he had defended against displacement by a sibling through fantasies of creating his own babies. Driven by powerful fantasies of being female and having a woman's body, the archetypal male hysteric is a Don Juan figure who appears heterosexual, although his wish to identify with his female lovers is stronger than his desire for them (Mitchell 2000). Abandoning and betraying his partners, the serial seducer evokes in them his own intolerable pain and jealousy.

Towards the end of psychotherapy Mr E felt able for the first time to choose a woman he desired and wanted to be with, rather than someone he wished to be. He was able to make this choice because he was now less envious of his mother, having accepted that he could be like her psychologically even though he could not possess her sexual or reproductive capacities. Although he felt more able to draw on identifications with his father's professional acumen, he still thought of himself as 'feminine' and nurturing. He was able to use these 'maternal' qualities – which he felt had been there in both parents – to make innovations in his traditionally male workplace. I learned when he returned to psychotherapy briefly in a crisis that he had become a very motherly father, having married a woman who was well able to lay down the law and set 'paternal' boundaries.

Male-dominated social structures provide opportunities for men to deny their own envy and dependency needs while forcing women into confrontation with infantile aspects of their own experience. Indeed, in our society it is still socially acceptable for a man to put his female partner into the position of childlike helplessness he once occupied with his mother, although women's increasing economic independence is giving them more possibility of resisting emotional subservience, and even reversing those roles. Another way in which men can deny their emotional need for others is by treating objects as a substitute for people, and relating to them with a fervour once reserved for the mother. Some men form their richest relationships with systems of ideas or pieces of machinery, relating to people as if they were things.

The boy who does not have experiences of loving paternal intimacy may become aware of his father for the first time only as a forbidding Oedipal figure who rejects his desire for closeness as 'feminine'. In identifying with this rejecting patriarchal figure a renunciation of homosexual desire, originally for the father, would be structured into his identity. For the adult man, internalised homophobia would then underlie all desire, rendering heterosexuality tenuous and homosexuality fraught with shame (Domenici 1995, Butler 1997). I return to this topic in Chapter 9.

Conclusion

Since the 1980s there has been a new attempt to bring both parents together in the theoretical mind and to re-examine different aspects of the boy's relationship with his father. Contemporary theories focus on the much-neglected early father–son relationship as well as on Oedipal fathering. There is now more recognition of how hard it is to differentiate the process of identification from the developing capacity for intimacy. Throughout life there will be an element of identification in our love relationships and vice versa.

New theory continues to explore the fluid complexity of identities formed through a range of shifting likenesses and love relationships. In psychotherapy we need to be aware of the different ways 'masculinities' can be formed, bearing in mind that aspects of gender which are defensive against pain and trauma may well be experienced as restrictive and inhibiting, rather than enriching and personally meaningful. Despite this new emphasis on multiple identifications, 'binary' theories focusing around likeness and difference to a parental couple are still so influential that until recently the impact of other family members on the psyche has been ignored. So, although we all know from personal experience that siblings – or their lack – have an enormous impact on our identities, only now is this being recognised theoretically.

It is often unclear in theoretical and clinical accounts whether it is the actual behaviour of the parents or their symbolic function that is under discussion. Many unanswered questions emerge. For instance, is it desirable to have two parents who fulfil different functions? Or is it possible for the biological mother to fulfil the paternal role of facilitating psychic separation? Can a grandmother, aunt or lesbian lover play the part of father, or should we then assume that the child has two mothers? Such queries are fundamental to my exploration of the interaction between male social and female psychological power within the psyche and the therapeutic relationship.

Similarly, we are only beginning to explore how race, culture, class and caste impact on male psyches. Men are expected to negotiate same-sex desire and character-traits deemed 'feminine' in different ways in each culture. A repudiation of same-sex desire is structured into the identities of all men in societies where heterosexuality is seen as the only 'true' way of loving. In Chapter 4 I return to explore how men cope with changing images of class and racialised identity in societies where gender power-differentials are shifting rapidly.

In Chapter 3 I discuss sex-based discrimination and women's own psychic prohibitions against the realisation of their own needs and desires. In particular, women's eroticism, like men's, often seems bound up with prevailing patterns of power and submission.

Femininity, like masculinity, is a psychosexual product of the most intimate inequalities, although how the psychically female person is created continues, as we shall see, to be a source of intense controversy.

Chapter 3

What do women want?

Women 'frequently do not feel whole, we feel undeserving and fraudulent in significant ways', the feminist psychotherapists Susie Orbach and Luise Eichenbaum claimed in 1987; 50 years earlier Freud had described how all women develop a sense of inferiority 'like a scar' (Eichenbaum and Orbach 1987: 56, Freud 1925: 337). That women somehow become bruised and scarred by the process of becoming female has been an ongoing theme within psychoanalytic theorising, although the ways the process has been understood have often been very different.

What Does Woman Want?, Freud demanded in 1933, and four decades later a new generation of British and American feminists returned to this question. Initially the answers they gave were, for the most part, fiercely anti-psychoanalytic. In North America a strongly biological version of Freudianism had become assimilated into the medical establishment, where it was often used to bolster conservative ideals of 'women's place'. British psychoanalysis likewise aroused feminist suspicions, since the mother-centred theories of Bowlby and Winnicott had been used after the Second World War to justify the withdrawal of nurseries for working women who were encouraged to return to the home, vacating their jobs for returning soldiers (Riley 1983, Ernst 1987).

But gradually during the 1970s some feminists began to look towards psychoanalysis for a better understanding of why it was so difficult to alter feelings or fantasies through willpower or collective action alone. As this turn 'back to Freud' (or versions of Freudianism) occurred, so the issues raised in the 1920s/1930s controversy reappeared, with theories polarising around problems left unresolved by that earlier debate. In this chapter I outline recent attempts to integrate mother-centred perspectives with new views on the father–daughter relationship – including feminist critiques of French Lacanian theory and the work of North American intersubjectivists. Finally I discuss clinical examples of what my patients themselves described as 'penis envy' in the light of these different theories. Through exploring the intricate interplay between what these women wish to possess and what they want to be, I raise questions about the interaction between envy and desire.

Women's lack: a feminist perspective on mothers and daughters

Freud described how the mother could not adore her daughter as she did her son since the girl could not provide her with masculinity by proxy (1933). This failure to arouse idealised desire in the mother later becomes organised into penis envy, a narcissistic wound which leads women to become highly dependent on the love and esteem of others. Women love in order to be loved, to compensate for their own feelings of inferiority, according to Freud, in contrast to men, who love in order to satisfy their instinctual needs (Freud 1914a).

A half-century later, pioneering feminist psychotherapists strongly refuted this theory. This maternal ambivalence would disappear, they argued, if both sexes were seen as equals. They argued that mothers transmit to their daughters a sense of emotional inadequacy and a deep ambivalence about the right to sexual pleasure, derived from the experience of cultural subservience. In an effort to gain attention and loving care vicariously the daughter begins to nurture her own mother, so embarking on a lifelong habit of putting others' needs before her own. Although men and children are nurtured emotionally by women, the skills of 'feminine' caring are devalued in a society which prizes 'male' characteristics, such as emotional detachment and rationality, more highly (Eichenbaum and Orbach 1982, Chodorow 1978, Orbach 1999).

In Britain the writings of Eichenbaum and Orbach have had considerable popular, as well as professional, success, probably because they articulate the very deep feelings of vulnerability and inadequacy many women have, without pathologising individual mothers. The writers transmit their own passionate conviction that women can transform themselves through psychotherapy while simultaneously fighting to improve the social status of their sex. The validation of culturally denigrated characteristics and the presentation of positive role-models seems to be a vital part of the process by which oppressed groups gain confidence in their capacity for personal and political change.

Despite an initial feminist tendency to emphasise the similarities between women, without acknowledging how very diverse their experience actually is, Eichenbaum and Orbach in particular did address a significant and often neglected difference between women. Unlike many psychoanalytic feminists in the 1980s, they wrote about the experience of lesbians. As the 1980s progressed, psychoanalytic feminist writing placed far more stress on how stereotypes of femininity vary within as well as between cultures and historical epochs. The sexuality of black women, for example, is usually represented in western society as primitive, powerful and 'free' from cultural constraints, as opposed to the delicate, repressed hysteria associated with white middle-class women for much of the twentieth century.

Originating in a period of optimism after the cultural flux of the 1960s, some feminist psychoanalytic theories assumed a quite fluid interchange between the psyche and the external world; a certainty that as culture changed, so would internal reality (see Chodorow 1978, Dinnerstein 1978). It is now clear that many psychic and social obstacles stand in the way of sexual equality. For instance, statistics show that mothers are still primarily responsible for childcare. Where fathers have tried to take a leading role, the impact on gender stereotypes has not been as dramatic as was originally predicted.

Female identity is not seamless and stable, but complex, chaotic and shifting, built around multiple identifications rather than just one or two. A daughter may simultaneously resist and absorb the awareness that she is female, knowing she is a woman yet feeling that she is disturbingly male or masculine psychologically. Mothers may identify strongly with a son rather than a daughter and fathers are sometimes more conventionally 'maternal' than their wives. Some families unconsciously value daughters more than sons. In certain classically patriarchal societies girls are still taught that they should submit to and serve their fathers, brothers and husbands, while other cultural groups inculcate daughters with the belief that women are far stronger and more dependable than men.

These variations will affect a girl's sense of identity and self-worth. But in a society where women are second class, an unconscious knowledge of her inferior social status will inevitably be imprinted on her psyche. Nevertheless, there is plentiful evidence that girls do not slip easily into the restricted roles that society continues to offer them. The infant does not remain passive while outside forces stamp themselves on its personality. Identification – through which the subject assimilates aspects or attributes of another and is transformed partially or entirely after the model the other provides – is a process in which the child engages actively and creatively, although unconsciously. She (or he) takes inside herself – introjects – bits and pieces of experience which have been infused with fantasy and makes of them something new. The child's view of the world around her is also structured through what she projects onto it from inside herself. Identifications are formed through a subtle and intricate process of layering and fusion of memory, fantasy and desire. Fragments of language and image are constantly worked over, influenced always by fantasy.

We all know that the world around us is altering, but psychoanalysts have always had very different views about whether cultural change impinges on the depths of the psyche immediately, after a time-lag, or not at all. Parents may consciously believe in equality between the sexes while transmitting unconsciously a belief that women would be happier in their traditional roles. In periods of rapid cultural alteration new prohibitions develop and others lose their old authority, but something in the psyche may resist easy change. Reserves of primitive moral feeling may remain beneath a façade of liberal personal change leading to the periodic resurgence of self-proclaimed 'traditional' mores. The internalised value system seems to be constructed not through what children are actually permitted to do or prohibited from doing, but through what they absorb unconsciously of their parents' own super-egos, the conscience or values of a generation before.

Women, so the feminist arguments I've been discussing generally run, are trammelled socially and psychically by cultures in which femininity is a subordinate state. Women themselves do not bear responsibility for this situation, it is implied: they are its unhappy victims. But some psychoanalytic feminists disagree, believing that women have a more active part to play in our life destinies. They look towards Klein and Freud, both of whom emphasised the ways that individuals participate in the intrapsychic processes which shape their lives.

Female 'masculinity': a stolen desire?

'Basically penis envy is the symbolic expression of another desire. Women do not wish to become men but to detach themselves psychically from the mother and become complete autonomous women' (Chasseguet-Smirgel 1964b: 118). Many girls, when faced with early difficulties in separating psychically from the mother, resort to the culturally favoured solution of denigrating their own sex and enviously idealising the father. But this idealisation of the father often masks envious hostility towards him as well as difficulties in relation to the mother. Fearing her own destructive wishes, a woman may relinquish her own needs and beliefs and see herself as the object of male desire. Whatever her sexual orientation, conflicts about damaging others or being damaged through certain kinds of physical contact – including vaginal penetration – can lead to sexual inhibitions. Guilt about her envy may also cause a woman to feel that she has no right to venture into traditionally male spheres of activity. Many women are also intensely preoccupied with a fear of being envied and ultimately rejected by their own sex if they appear too contented or successful.

We all unconsciously collude with outdated gender power arrangements because we cannot face the loss of an imagined blissful mother–infant unity or the inevitability of human frailty, psychic pain and death. Women who retreat into motherhood and family life attempt to recapture their imagined fusion with the maternal body, so avoiding responsibility for the challenges of history-making. Men – and to some extent women, nowadays – can deny the strength of their early link with the mother through a preoccupation with mastery over the universe and with that which can be predicted, possessed, piled up and counted. Arguably men still benefit more from gender inequities and therefore are less inclined to expose them (Dinnerstein 1978).

How can the girl identify with the father and psychic 'masculinity' – however that is defined in her culture – without feeling that she is stealing something that does not belong to her or that she is an inadequate woman? That is the question addressed by a number of female analysts, most recently Jessica Benjamin. To both sexes the father may well represent exuberance, excitement and agency. Culturally he comes to represent a subject, someone who knows who he is and what he wants, rather than an object to be possessed and desired by others. Above all he is autonomous from the mother and his authority may appear more limited. The girl's need to be like her father is often mistaken for Oedipal desire. Whether someone is like us or different is not necessarily to do with their sex (Harris 2000). Also, we may love others who are different with the hope that eventually we can become like them (Benjamin 1988).

The girl whose omnipotence is deflated too early, who does not get her need for recognition met by a father-figure, may later become self-abnegating, forming relationships tinged with subservience. This might cause her to idealise grandiosity in men, including her own sons (Benjamin 1995). Unable to put herself centre-stage in her own life, she may submit herself to others, living out her own need for success, excitement or adventure through 'heroic' male or female partners who tantalise her emotionally.

Might contemporary mothers also represent the 'subject' of desire, appearing excitingly self-directed and different? Certainly a mother nowadays may have more power in the outside world than her male partner. This is an interesting question, raising funda-mental issues about the interaction between 'real' experiences – including parental personality and child-rearing patterns – and fantasy and cultural symbolism.

Some daughters dread arousing maternal envy and retaliation if they are happier or more successful than their mothers. Envy and guilt towards the father may combine with real external discrimin-ation to create serious inhibitions about professional competition and self-assertion in personal relationships. And, in a society where each generation of women has more opportunities than the last, the mother – and indeed the father – may in reality envy the daughter.

In order to break into this cycle of cultural subordination, the girl needs to identify with psychic masculinity without devaluing womanhood. But how can she separate psychically from the mother without entering into another relationship where she relinquishes her will and desire? First of all we need to recognise that the girl gains positive strength from her early identification with the mother, who can encourage her to move out into the world. The girl's desire for autonomy need not simply represent a contemptuous rejection of the mother or hatred of dependency. The daughter needs to have an identificatory relationship with the father without idealising his sex. But how is this to be achieved within a social system where both she and her mother are valued less than the father? Some feminists have turned to Lacan's theories, arguing that the Women's Movement needs to look again at Freud's father-centred theory in order to understand the resilience of patriarchy – the way it continues to reproduce itself in the unconscious mind however family life is structured (Mitchell 1974).

Lacan – the return to Freud

> If feminism is to change a phallocentric world, phallocentrism
> needs to be dealt with and not denied.
>
> (Gallop 1982: 18)

Lacan believed that the 1919–35 debate on female sexuality marked
the beginning of the deterioration of psychoanalysis, where the subversive and radical core of Freud's theory – his stress on sexuality
and the unconscious – was abandoned. In his theory Lacan focused
on these two basic Freudian concepts, adding a new concern with
linguistics. Lacan argued against Klein's theory that the baby arrives
in the world with tendencies towards a male or female sexual identity, which is confirmed (or not) through real interactions and
fantasies. Lacan saw biology as having no place at all in psychoanalytic theory and stressed instead that the unconscious is constructed through the words of others – the language of the family,
culture and epoch into which we are born. Lacan kept a sceptical
distance from all prevailing notions about self, truth, knowledge and
power. In some object-relations feminist writings there is an implica-
tion that we should and can feel 'whole' psychically, entirely sure and
confident in our sense of sexual identity. This is impossible, Lacanians argue, since human beings are fundamentally alienated from
both themselves and each other. What appears to be an identity is in
fact a mirage arising through identification with others' perceptions
of, desires and expectations for the subject. Although a woman may
consciously believe that she is certain of her identity, her
unconscious will reveal a fragmented subjectivity, which is shifting
and precarious (Mitchell 1984).

Lacan criticised those object-relations theorists and ego psychologists who chart an ideal line of development from infantile satisfaction at the breast through to adult heterosexual fulfilment, describing
some relationships or states of mind as 'mature', 'healthy' or 'ful-
filled'. Such notions, he argued, romanticise conventional ways of
structuring sexual and family life (Lacan on Dora, 1985). Instead
Lacan stressed that adult sexual relations are inevitably unsatisfying
because the loved one is always a displacement of, and a substitute
for, the primal maternal lost object. Desire comes into existence
through experiences of absence or lack (of the breast or the mother
initially), not as the result of satisfaction. There is then something
intrinsically painful and insatiable about desire itself. Any later

experience of satisfaction always contains that first loss within it. Lacan drew on Freud, who argued that something in the nature of the sexual instinct itself might be unfavourable to the realisation of complete satisfaction.

Lacan returned to Freud's theory that it is the possession or absence of the penis (phallus) that distinguishes one sex from the other, rather than the existence of different sexual and reproductive capacities. But Lacan rewrote Freud's theory in linguistic and symbolic rather than biological terms, differentiating the penis from the phallus more than Freud had done. In Lacan's theory the paternal figure separates the child from the dangerous engulfing mother, as representative of the Law and an embodiment of the power of the phallus. The child must accept the Father's authority and phallic status in order to have a place in the socio-symbolic order, a name and a position from which to speak. There can be no symbolisation without the phallus, the 'signifier of signifiers', the mark which positions the subject as male or female, and locates him or her in terms of power, authority and speaking position. The phallus signifies what men think they have and what women are believed to lack. Under patriarchy, women represent for men a lack which men have disavowed (Lacan 1977).

However, Lacan's theory is, like Freud's, deeply ambiguous. Lacan argues that neither sex possesses the phallus, but each sex longs either to possess it (in the case of the boy) or to be it (if a girl). Yet at the same time the male enjoys a special relationship to this privileged, albeit symbolic, term. Although Lacan rejects the idea of the 'natural' or pre-given, he says that the name of the father has been identified with the impersonal law which structures the personality at the Oedipal phase since 'the dawn of history' (Lacan 1977: 67). At times Lacan seems to echo Freud's uncertainty about whether women really are in some way inferior. For instance, he states that:

> the fact that the penis is dominant in the shaping of body-image is evidence of [an autonomous, non-biological imaginary anatomy]. Though this may shock the champions of the autonomy of female sexuality, such dominance is a fact and one moreover which cannot be put down to cultural influence alone
>
> (Lacan 1953: 13)

Certain feminists argue that Lacan and Freud were simply describing what they saw around them: a world where women were second-class and entirely unenviable (Mitchell 1984). But to arrive at this conclusion Freud and Lacan must be read in a very selective way. I agree with Grosz, who says, 'Unless the symbolic order is conceived of as a system where the father and the penis are not the only signifiers of social power and linguistic norms, feminism is no better off with Lacan than without him' (Grosz 1990: 145). It is quite clear that Lacan's theory has the same weaknesses as Freud's. Both are fundamentally profoundly phallocentric, and focus primarily on male subjectivity. Lacan's lack of attention to female subjectivity resulted in a French feminist backlash. Under pressure he acknowledged the strength of female sexual pleasure and tried to sidestep the controversy aroused by his theory that women were the complementary sex. He now described women as having a 'supplementary jouissance' that men know nothing of. Like Freud, Lacan stressed the mysterious inaccessibility of women's desire, and sought enlightenment from female colleagues which he was unable to gain in the usual analytic way – from his patients. At the same time Lacan made a sardonic dig at the feminist predilection for theories of female sexuality which revolve around mothering: 'We have implored our women psychoanalysts, on our bended knees, to tell us about it (the enjoyment of the women) but mum's the word' (Lacan 1972–3, cited in Benvenuto and Kennedy 1986: 69).

Post-Lacanian feminism: back to the mother

Lacan is so ignorant of women's 'incalculable pleasure, which grows indefinitely from its passage in/through the other' because he does not know how, or where, to listen (Irigaray 1977: 350). Luce Irigaray, a French feminist psychoanalyst, claims that Freudians and Lacanians recognise only masculine desire and see all desire as masculine. Psychoanalysis reproduces one of the 'sexual theories of children', Irigaray argues, the fantasy that there is only one – male – sex, and that women are castrated, defective versions of men. Her project is to seek other ways in which women can speak of and for themselves.

Irigaray argues that the only way forward for women is to assert their difference through the creation of a powerful female symbolic to represent them against the omnipresent effects of the male imaginary, which negates their existence as subjects. Many psychoanalysts and feminists argue that the only way to break into the cycle of suffocating merger between mother and daughter is for the father to intervene or become involved in early childcare. In contrast, Irigaray believes that it is women themselves who must alter their position in society by creating new ways of speaking about and for their sex. This may mean existing separately from men for a period of time.

According to Irigaray, the problem for women is that the relationship to the mother and the mother's body is not symbolised often or adequately in our culture. At the moment women exist in a state of 'dereliction', outside society and the symbolic order, as if abandoned by God. Deprived of their own symbols, gestures, imaginary, denied access to their own autoerotism, the mother–daughter relationship is the 'dark continent of the dark continent, the most obscure area of our social order'. And, without that 'interval of exchange, or of words, or gestures, passions between women manifest themselves in a rather cruel way' (Irigaray 1984: 103, quoted in Whitford 1989). Both mothers and daughters must create a new language in which their identities as women can be articulated. At the moment the daughter has no woman with whom to identify.

Since, in her view, psychoanalytic theory is not sexually neutral, but specific to men, Irigaray argues that the model could be inadequate for women, and imposing it on them could reinforce their inferior position within patriarchy. For instance, classical psychoanalytic interpretations might block rather than free the expression of women's desire. Through research into senile dementia and with analysands diagnosed as hysterical or obsessional, Irigaray claims to have discovered that there are significant differences in the impairments of women and men's speech. She has also explored the parameters of the psychoanalytic session, looking at factors such as the gender of the analyst and analysand, and the effect of gesture and other non-verbal factors on patients of both sexes. For instance, she discusses the different meaning for the woman and the man of lying down in the presence of another, who sits behind them. She also implies that women should create forms of psychoanalysis appropriate for them, as various groups of women have tried to do (Whitford 1989).

Irigaray points out that Freud and Lacan constructed their theories around the boy's experience of his body while denouncing as biologist anyone who attempts to do the same for the girl. She explores the female body as it is made meaningful in language, articulating the ways in which it is used as a site both for patriarchal power relations and for symbolic representational resistance. When she describes some typical female erotic pleasures, such as 'Caressing the breasts, touching the vulva, opening the lips, gently stroking the posterior wall of the vagina, lightly massaging the cervix', it is immediately obvious that such experiences are rarely if ever referred to in psychoanalytic literature (Irigaray 1977: 348). Instead we hear much about the power of the penetrating penis, and the smothering potential of the womb. Women do not need, Irigaray argues, to find something external to touch themselves with – a hand, women's genitals, language – as men do: 'A woman "touches herself" constantly without anyone being able to forbid her to do so, for her sex is composed of two lips which embrace continually' (Irigaray 1977: 345). Woman 'has sex organs just about everywhere. She experiences pleasure almost everywhere . . . one can say that the geography of her pleasure is much more diversified, more multiple in its differences, more complex, more subtle than is imagined – in an imaginary centered a bit too much on one and the same' (Irigaray 1977: 348).

Irigaray is right in arguing that our culture represents all agency and power in phallic terms and that there is no equivalent symbol to suggest female desire or potency. Does the hidden nature of women's sexual and reproductive organs reinforce this cultural inequality? Freud and Klein both contend that men may find it easier to mobilise aggression and desire because they can symbolise these powerful emotions through the more visible penis which they can imbue in fantasy with magical powers (Freud 1924a, Klein 1928). Is it easier to control anxiety through a symbolic and physical focus of sensation? Jessica Benjamin notes that women often experience intense sexual excitement as dangerous, perhaps because they cannot so easily link it to any external organ that would localise it in space and allow them to visualise control of its duration. This lack of anatomical anchoring could have a correlative effect at the symbolic level. The difficulty for women, Benjamin argues, is in recognising our desire as truly inner. Spatial images can be used to convey images of female desire, as opposed to phallic activity. We need metaphors for describing inner space, she argues, metaphors which emphasise holding and self-exploration as the active side of receptivity (Benjamin 1988).

Ideas of women's sexuality as an 'internal' experience are integral to mother-centred psychoanalytic theories but it is not clear that all – or indeed most – women experience their erotic life in this way. Our reproductive organs may be inside our bodies but does this actually mean that sex is for us more of an interiorised, inside the body experience than it is for men? After all the clitoris – which many women feel to be the most powerful sexual organ – is located outside our bodies. Some women are more aware of the sensual capacities of their whole bodies, including the outside surfaces, rather than experiencing their sexual life as 'internal'.

Psychoanalytic theories of female sexuality arise within particular cultural contexts – which they also help to define. Paula Bennett (1993) links the inferior status of the clitoris in contemporary western thinking to Freud and Lacan's assumption that the dominant sexual organs are the vagina and penis. Bennett argues very persuasively that the idea that the clitoris is – like the penis – a powerful sexual organ has been lost since Freud: artistic, literary and linguistic representations of the clitoris which were popular before the twentieth century have been eradicated in favour of symbolism of the vagina and womb. Freud's assumption that the clitoris was 'accidental' enabled women to be defined as the opposite or complement of men rather than as sexual beings in their own right (Potts 2002). Psychoanalytic imagery of women's bodies as containers for the penis or the unborn child – as houses, vases or enclosed spaces – reinforces the link between female eroticism and maternity. Can we find new ways of theorising sexuality which allow women – whether or not they are mothers – to have their own autonomous identities, their own sexual lives?

Each of the theories I have described has strengths, but some of them neglect important aspects of female psychic life. Lacanian feminism provides a powerful challenge to conventional ideas about identity, power and language, and a counterbalance to the idealism and romanticism of object-relations theory. Study of the role of the (symbolic) father is also vital for understanding how patriarchal structures reproduce themselves even when parents make a conscious effort to avoid reinforcing them. But Lacan also ignores female experience and denigrates motherhood, associating it with boundless narcissism and regression. The possibility of early paternal receptivity, or the father 'holding' the infant emotionally, is ignored in these theories. Neither is it considered that the mother – or the child itself – may have urges towards moving out into the world, although many mothers are heavily committed to employment outside the home as well as to childcare.

In contrast, object-relations and post-Lacanian feminists struggle to articulate women's previously hidden experience as mothers, daughters and autonomous sexual subjects. Girls may well have particular difficulty in separating themselves psychically from the much-envied early mother because they, unlike the son, possess no mark of difference or privilege. Many girls also have problems in identifying with the father and qualities seen culturally as 'masculine' in both sexes.

The girl needs to be recognised as being like both parents psychologically. She also needs to have access to images of women as active sexual beings and agents of their own destinies. But how is this to happen? And how far must women rely on a change in male attitudes towards emotional life and family responsibilities? It is vital that men become more involved with early childcare, and fulfil conventionally maternal functions, as well as helping the daughter find a pathway to the outer world. However, women can also perform this traditional paternal function.

And it is women themselves who must continue to think about the symbolism we use and create new forms of imagery to represent all aspects of female experience. The expectations and wishes which are transmitted from generation to generation cohere around bodily experience. We need to understand more about how physiological sensation is mediated through culture and inscribed on the psyche, so we can read and interpret it in new ways. Only then will girls and boys come to see women as full subjects with their own needs and desires.

It is necessary, then, to combine the object-relations emphasis on the way second-class status is structured into the personality through early maternal identifications, with a feminist Freudian analysis of how, during the struggle for psychic autonomy, her perception of sexual difference becomes distorted. Female difficulties in articulating aggression and desire are heightened by the fact that agency and potency tend to be associated with men and masculinity.

Penis envy in psychotherapy

Although many women express dissatisfaction with their cultural position, they often feel ambivalent about fighting for change. In this section I use clinical examples of female penis envy to explore how women's fighting spirit can become twisted into envy, self-devaluation and contempt for their own sex. Freud's present-day critics imply that it may have been Freud himself who created the chronic envy, guilt and despair he detected in his female patients, by interpreting their penis envy in a dangerously literal way as the desire for something unattainable – to be a man, or to possess a penis (Grossman and Stewart 1976).

In Britain, clinical discussion of penis envy is rare. In the papers that do exist, object-relations theorists can be extreme in their refusal to recognise that penis envy might represent a desire for the privileges of men. For instance, Enid Balint argues in 'What does a woman want?' that a female patient who dreams of going to the chemist to buy a penis unconsciously wishes to use the penis to 'warm up' a depressed internal mother with whom she is overwhelmingly preoccupied. The woman is not seeking masculinity and is not lesbian, Balint says. What she lacks is an internal sense of 'mutual concern', something she did not experience with her mother (Balint 1973). I find Balint's argument unconvincing. Why, for instance, should her patient want to warm up her mother with a penis, unless she feels some erotic desire, or believes that she would be more attractive and lovable if she were male?

No doubt psychotherapists find ways of confirming their own beliefs. Freud and his colleagues assumed the centrality of female penis envy and therefore found it where many contemporary clinicians would find unresolved early conflicts about the mother. Freud's father-centred theory and his own gender may have elicited envy of men in his female patients. Or perhaps women then did feel more envious of men?

It is also true, though, that patients sometimes seek out psychotherapists whose theories make sense of their own experience. For instance, I found that women who came to see me during the 1980s at The Women's Therapy Centre, which was well known for its focus on early mothering, were likely to be preoccupied with mother–daughter envy, while those referred to my private practice from more orthodox psychotherapy organisations were as likely to have psychic conflicts about the father.

A significant number of women describe their fear of losing the love of significant female figures (including the therapist in the maternal transference) if they succeed at work or in personal life. This may be both a defence against their own envy of their mothers and a reflection of the reality that many women do envy their daughters. Perhaps women are more conscious of their envy of their own sex now that, theoretically at least, they have access to many traditionally male as well as female spheres of activity. Yet fear of success due to a dread of other women's envy is still a significant factor in holding women back.

Where extreme penis envy does exist it often seems to be associated with an early life where the general cultural devaluation of women has been reinforced through intense sexual denigration, or discrimination in favour of boys within the family. Through two clinical examples I show how, in order to understand the complex and multifaceted nature of penis envy, we need to draw on theories which locate it in early envy of the privileges and functions of both parents.

The gender of my soul is male

A woman patient, Ms M, told me: 'The gender of my soul is male. I can hear Freud saying, "I told you so." He'd say I suffer from penis envy . . . Deep down I am a man.' This woman had four elder brothers and two older sisters. She described how in her working-class family 'men were always right'. 'Women in my family had no status . . . the girls in my school talked only about marriage. The boys expected jobs, and I wanted that too', she said. Remarkably in the light of this history, she was the only member of the family who was academically successful. However, when she first came to therapy she moved from one utterly different job to another, sabotaging her chances quickly. She had no image of how a woman might find fulfilment through work outside the home, she said.

For Ms M, conflicts about identity were heightened by her move away from her working-class origins. She felt considerable guilt that she had been given greater opportunities than her parents and siblings, and she was desperately frightened of their envy and retaliation. Transforming herself into a middle-class professional engendered a deep sense of shame about rejecting her background, a shame that could not easily be acknowledged. Just as she felt that she was not a 'real' woman, in the world of work she felt that she was 'passing' as middle-class, and that she would inevitably fail or be exposed.

She described her mother as emotionally distant, yet also rigidly controlling of her bodily functions. She had consoled herself by being close to and feeling similar to her father and brothers. Going fishing with them rather than shopping with her mother and sisters, she told herself that she was glad to avoid female talk of 'diets and hairdos'. However, in her teens she felt that no amount of make-up and feminine clothes could make her feel attractive and womanly. In her adult life she described how, when she was with a lover and his male friends, her greatest pleasure was in imagining that she was 'one of the lads'.

She told me that the men in her family made denigratory jokes about women's bodies and she came across 'girlie' magazines lying

around the house. This had a profound effect on her erotic imagination, leaving her with the sense that sex for her would always involve
objectification of the female body.

Paradoxically her fantasies of belonging to the more highly valued
sex further increased her envy of women, including myself, whom
she perceived as more comfortable with their femininity. She told me
how profoundly out of place she had felt when with a group of
women who all seemed to dress in a stereotypically feminine way. In
the session she asked, 'What makes me a woman – is it my body? Is it
because I dress in female clothes? Or do I have a woman's mind?'

Ms M disparaged my appearance and that of the other women in
her family, saying that everyone preferred the looks of a younger
woman. But as time went on, it became clear that she had felt great
sexual rivalry towards her mother, which was emerging towards me
in the maternal transference. Her dreams and fantasies also revealed
attraction towards other women. She told me that she had never
acted upon these desires because she felt that lesbian sex would be a
'pornographic act, driven by a desire to humiliate and gain power'.
She was afraid of objectifying another woman as she had felt
objectified. And also, she imagined that lesbian sex would make her
feel very envious of men since she felt her body was not designed for
intercourse with women.

She told me:

> It was my father who decided whether or not I looked attractive
> and what should be done about it . . . It's all about needing to
> have my sexuality controlled and directed by men because it's so
> rampant. My father thought there were women who did – dirty
> bitches – and women who didn't. My mother's attitude was that
> it is dangerous to give in to appetite.

Ms M could only imagine herself in control of her own sexuality by
putting herself in the position of the male. 'What I need is something
to express my aggression with sexually, and what else could that be
but a penis?' she asked. However, her image of a voyeuristic, dominating male figure may have gained some of its strength from her early
experience of her mother as rigidly controlling and physically intrusive. As Benjamin points out, the phallus can represent (paternal)
power of desire or (maternal) power of control, either excitement or
obedience. She goes on to say that, since the father of identificatory
love stems from a phase when the child does not see gender as fixed,

the early paternal transference is particularly volatile, and the analyst must be prepared to see it in numerous different guises (Benjamin 1995).

Ms M described her companionship with her father as alarmingly sexualised even though there were no sexually abusive acts. 'You notice little girls having heterosexual love-affairs with their fathers,' she said, 'but at a certain point he says, "Enough!" My father didn't set any boundaries so I had to, by dressing like a boy.' Though her father made inappropriately sexualised comments to his daughters, he was actually far more preoccupied with his wife than with his children. As a result Ms M felt simultaneously overexposed to and painfully excluded from the parental sexual relationship.

Ms M's devaluation of women was also a defence against feeling rejected by and envious of her mother. After a few months of psychotherapy, she discovered on her bookshelves a book I had co-edited with a chapter by me on mother–daughter envy. She told me, 'I never look at names on covers . . . I enjoyed it but can't remember what your chapter was about.' She went on to tell me that non-fiction was much less creative than novels, poetry or drama. When she eventually did remember my chapter we were able to begin looking at how she devalued what she admired in me, as a defence against feelings of inferiority and envy.

Having rejected the idea of being like her mother, Ms M then had no protection against internalising her father's contempt for female sexuality. But penis envy can originate in other ways. Daughters do not necessarily idealise their fathers more than their mothers. Some women maintain an envious idealisation of their mothers and depreciate their fathers. But, whatever the family constellation, the girl still has the same dilemma: how to value herself as her own woman, while identifying with a range of emotional attributes associated in her culture with both sexes.

The next patient I discuss did not suffer from any strong wish to be a man. Instead she felt all too feminine, too like her mother and myself.

The experimental penis

Ms L was in her fifth year of three times weekly psychotherapy and was beginning to think about the possibility of leaving. She told me:

I dreamed a wonderful dream. You'll love it. I was fascinated by an ENORMOUS erect penis. I was in a kitchen. Actually, the penis was on a man. The man was the brother of my teenage friend. She was someone I really loved. I started to play with the penis, and then I took it right off (effectively castrating him, but painlessly). I carried on playing with it. Later, I was putting it in my mouth, trying it on for size, when I heard someone coming into the kitchen. I think it was a man but he was too shadowy to see. I quickly hid the penis in the drawer. Later, when it was all clear, I pulled it out, only to find it had shrunk. Now this was a letdown in some ways, but a blessing in others – I could slip it into my pocket to play with it later. When the time came I did my best to make it 'come alive' again and cause an erection, but it didn't work, so I tried to eat it. It tasted foul, perhaps dead, like chloroform and very rubbery.

Ms L associated her attempt to devour the penis with the lack of her father's influence in her childhood. He had died when she was two. Now she wanted to strengthen her identification with him, partly in order to differentiate herself from her mother psychically. When she thought of leaving psychotherapy she realised that she lacked a paternal figure who would intervene between us, within the maternal transference. It was traditional in her culture for male relatives to step into the role of a dead father, yet her mother had resisted family pressure to share her parental duties.

If my father had lived there might have been a balance in the family. My mother was very rigid, but she didn't help me develop any boundaries or limits of my own. I can't get away from her. I have her body.

Psychotherapy had enabled her to become more professionally successful but she still described herself as a 'people-pleaser', who dared not fight aggressively for what she wanted. She wanted to see what men had that enabled them to assert their desires with more apparent ease. She also responded to the male penis whenever she saw it with a complex combination of fascination and repulsion. This combination of feelings – 'penis awe' – results, Phyllis Greenacre has argued, from abusive or frightening exposure to the male penis in childhood. My patient did in fact remember at least one man 'flashing' his penis at her in an alarming way (Greenacre 1979).

Discussing the dream, I referred to her 'wanting a penis'. She responded indignantly, making it clear that her desire for a penis was not predominantly to do with any wish to be a man.

> What gave you that idea? Do you think ALL women want a penis? . . . I wanted it to try on, to experiment and play with, to see what it's like. I didn't actually want to have a penis permanently attached to me. Though I suppose there is what having a penis represents . . . In my experience, men are always more confident sexually, more assertive and able to get what they want.

What she coveted was the ruthless determination to put her needs first in professional and sexual life, a quality she associated more with men than with women. But some women had it too, she pointed out. She thought her father might have been more 'soft' and conventionally maternal than her tough dominating mother, whom she saw as quite psychically 'masculine'. She also saw this ruthlessness in my adherence to my own holiday times, and the endings of sessions. 'You do what suits you and don't alter your plans because of my needs', she complained enviously. When she had first come for psychotherapy she had felt obsessed with looking at herself and with being watched. No longer content to be the object of others' desire, she wanted to experiment with having the potency and privilege she associated with the penis.

Ms L had not made up her mind whether she wanted a male or female sexual partner more. Her image of a combined nipple–penis provided a temporary solution. She told me that in the dream she had put the penis into her mouth as a baby does when it explores the world around it, sucking on it as she once sucked on the nipple. 'The penis was like a tough, springy plastic toy,' she said, 'a kind of eroticised nipple.'

The dream reflected her current 'part-object' relationships with men. In the past she had had sexual relationships with both sexes. Now she was going through a phase where she loved women and desired them a bit, while having heterosexual affairs where she often made it clear that she was only interested in having a bit of the man – temporary use of the penis during sex. She was curious, she told me, about what men had that made her women-friends attracted to them, rather than to the 'other half of the human race, nice people like me'.

Hélène Cixous, a French feminist, wrote:

> I do not want a penis to decorate my body with. But I do desire the other for the other, whole and entire, male or female; because living means wanting everything that is, everything that lives, and wanting it alive. Castration? Let others toy with it. What's desire originating from a lack? A pretty meagre desire.
>
> (Cixous 1976: 262)

Ms L, who identified with this quote, wished to experiment with the attributes and privileges of both sexes. She wanted to see whether a penis would make her more desirable to women. And she wanted to be the agent of her own destiny, to be in command of her own needs and passions. Identification with the paternal penis also represented the possibility of greater autonomy from her mother. But once she felt more separate from her mother, then she might also be able to draw on her identification with maternal 'masculinity'.

To understand female sexuality more fully we need to move beyond theories which privilege the power of one parent rather than the other in the mind of the child. As a result of this polarisation certain features of female experience are neglected, or discussed in a limited way. It is interesting that both of the patients I describe were either actively bisexual or desired both sexes. Little has been written about bisexuality clinically or theoretically, although it is widely recognised as a key element of female psychology. Freud said, 'Some part of what we call "the enigma of women" may perhaps stem from this experience of bisexuality in women's lives' (Freud 1931: 385).

Women's continuing attachment to both sexes is crucial to the central question of this chapter: What does a woman want? The woman who seeks to answer this question will need to explore the complex interaction between her identifications and her desire. It is clear from the clinical material I have discussed that sexual identity is convoluted, tenuous and fragmented. An image of feminine certainty may be a response to real or imagined cultural demands. But it may also be a masquerade, unconsciously designed to hide conflicts about identity or sexuality.

Penis envy – which is intense in some women and almost non-existent in others – has a different meaning for each individual, depending on numerous factors including class, culture and family attitudes. Envy and the dread of retaliation from both parents can combine with real external discrimination to create difficulties for women in personal relationships and in the workplace. Recent theories address the question of how women can experience themselves as acting in their own interests and controlling their own destinies without feeling that they have cheated or taken something that does not belong to them. If we could re-own characteristics projected into men, such as anger and forcefulness, these qualities could then be used constructively to improve our lives. Furthermore, women's sexual lives would be enriched if they could tolerate their aggression enough to acknowledge the strength and power of their sexual desire.

Mainstream psychoanalytic theories – and some feminist reinterpretations – might reinforce conventional ways of thinking about female experience. There is an urgent task for women to articulate our previously unvoiced experience as mothers, daughters, sexual subjects and agents of our own destiny through new symbols and imagery. We can only hope that eventually children will be able to see both sexes as autonomous beings with their own wishes and needs.

The great difficulty many women have in fighting for what they want sexually and professionally has led some to argue that women unconsciously collude in their own oppression. In Chapter 5 I look at how the gender power imbalance has become eroticised, so that women's powerful desire sometimes emerges through images of powerlessness and subjugation. Chapter 8 focuses on the tendency some women have to express psychic pain through physically located, indirectly eroticised symptoms, such as eating problems, in contrast to men whose unconscious conflicts are often more floridly sexualised. In Chapter 9 I say more about female bisexuality, as well as looking more closely at lesbian issues. In the next chapter I return to the theme of male sexuality, exploring the rigid fragility of identities built on a repudiation of early helplessness and vulnerability.

Part II

Contemporary debates in clinical practice

Chapter 4

Are men really fragile?

Cultural conceptions of masculinity and femininity vary between cultures and alter over historical time. But since the beginning of the twentieth century the speed of technological and political change in the western world has been dazzling. 'We are part of a reversal of history, an absolute shift in the quality of reality', wrote Elizabeth Janeway, the American novelist and critic, describing in 1982 the revolutionary changes she had seen in the organisation of sexuality and gender since her birth in 1913 (Janeway 1982: 17). Men's position in the family has been irreversibly transformed since the 1950s. Today they are expected to have a much closer relationship with their children and it is no longer automatically assumed that women will service men in the home.

Alongside these changes there exists a widespread sense that men are in a crisis over their social role and identity. These uncertainties manifest themselves in violence, increased levels of suicide and abusive behaviour towards themselves and others. Growth of feminist awareness is generally cited as a reason for this, but also crucial are changing patterns of work. Traditional male occupations are disappearing, a continually evolving technological culture cannot be passed on from generation to generation, and girls' socialisation equips them better for the growing sector of office-work. But the situation is complex. For instance, there is increasing concern about boys falling behind as girls surpass them academically. Janet Sayers attributes the 'current laddish anti-learning culture' to teenage boys' illusion that they are 'already the grand figures their sex is often depicted as being' – a belief that leads many not to do the work necessary to achieve the glory they feel they deserve (Sayers 1998: 139). In spite of this, middle-class men still retain control over institutions of authority – political, educational, juridical and medical.

In reality it is, as always, working-class boys – and girls – who are 'failing' and later becoming trapped in low-paid unskilled work, or unemployment. If working-class children do succeed they do this against the odds, since British schools tend not to notice or foster their academic abilities as they do with middle-class pupils. Yet for all our concern about contemporary boys, the fate of 'failing' working-class girls is rarely if ever mentioned publicly (Walkerdine *et al.* 2001). And work outside the home is still mainly organised according to traditional gender roles, with the work women do being less well-paid and socially valued.

Bearing these factors in mind, it can be argued that contemporary fathers have the best of both worlds. They retain power in the public sphere while having greater access to the satisfactions, often without the frustrations, of family life. Yet contemporary men are struggling with their ambivalence and confusion about what fathering actually is. They may well not have the emotional resilience to nurture small children, having lacked a close physically affectionate bond with their own fathers, and yet they cannot retreat into the role of the prohibitive value-enforcing patriarch because authority has become diffuse and is no longer embodied by individuals. We do not have an 'Oedipal father [available to any of us] for as we approach him, or try to become him, we find he is being worked by some unseen hands' (Frosh 2002: 31).

Indeed, according to a recent study of London boys, those very adolescent males who might have benefited from greater paternal intimacy in recent decades report a profound feeling of lack as a result of the impoverished emotional contact they have with their fathers and other boys (Frosh *et al.* 2002). The authors of the study argue that this deeply disturbing taboo on close contact with other males leads to a stereotyped idealisation of girls and women which alternates with overt misogyny. The danger of wandering from the path of 'true' masculinity – associated with toughness, authority and the subordination of gay men – has to be continually monitored. So the boys ranked each other on a hierarchy involving both racialised and class consciousness. However, they produced 'softer' versions of masculinity in the more intimate one-to-one research interviews than in the group interviews, showing more 'girlish' emotional vulnerability. The interviewers draw on Judith Butler (1993), who stresses 'the complex and active ways in which gender is produced and performed through repetitive acts, giving it the appearance of something solid which individuals possess' to argue that the boys were not being more truthful or authentic in some situations than others. They were simply showing different aspects of masculine identity construction – different ways of performing or 'doing boy' (Frosh *et al.* 2002: 32).

It is widely acknowledged in psychoanalytic literature that men's repudiation of aspects of themselves which they see as 'feminine' results in male fear, contempt and cruelty towards women and also towards men who do not appear stereotypically 'masculine'. Freud's male case histories focus on unresolved conflicts about passive and active homosexual attachments, originally to the father. He observed that treatment often foundered on men's inability to understand that a passive attitude does 'not always signify castration and that it is indispensable in many relationships in life' (Freud 1937).

Mainstream psychoanalytic theories still tend to assume that, although boys may initially experience themselves in a state of blissful unity with the mother, ideally they should then go on to become psychologically akin to the father, who is assumed to be stereotypically 'masculine'. However, our identities are not dominated by just one or two identifications with parental figures, and the sex of childhood love-objects does not necessarily determine how a child sees them. The boy's father could be more conventionally maternal in personality while his mother might be more oriented towards the external world, working longer hours or investing more of herself in life outside the home.

In this chapter I suggest that psychoanalysis may – along with other influential ideologies – promote and sustain conventionally predictable ways of understanding and enacting our sexual and emotional lives even though the world around us is changing rapidly. I explore the complex interplay between the psychological patterns of male social dominance and female emotional power as they are acted out between myself and male patients. Bearing in mind the way very specific cultural beliefs are often presented as unchangeable physiological realities, I emphasise the blurred demarcation between mind and body. For instance, it is often assumed that male sexuality is intrinsically more powerful and that men are driven by wild and urgent desires that can easily overrule rational thought.

Major shifts in class or culture can exacerbate contemporary men's confusion about rapidly altering images of masculinity. Focusing on such issues as violent fantasy and the sexualisation of psychic pain, I discuss in some detail the psychotherapy of a man who made a major shift from one class to another. I show how, in order to cope with the rigours of more equal emotional relationships between the sexes, he needed to integrate a range of gendered identifications within the therapeutic transference relationship. I then explore how cultural dislocation impacted on a high-caste Hindu man as he struggled with entirely different conceptions of masculinity. To understand this clinical material I supplement mainstream psychoanalytic theory with radical critiques that focus on how power-differentials between the sexes are structured into the psyche.

Changing views of masculinity: theory and clinical practice

Mr A sought psychotherapy because of serious panic attacks and phobias. At work he found it difficult to use his personal authority and initiative. Despite a brilliant academic record, professional promotion eluded him. Mr A described a disturbing gap between his competent, sophisticated man-about-town exterior and the distraught toddler he felt himself to be. This disjunction was reflected in the clothes he wore to sessions, which ranged from pinstripe city suits through jeans and leather jackets to a torn and grubby blue running suit that became known as his 'baby-gro'.

When he moved to London from a small town in Scotland, Mr A lost the traditional structures of lower-middle-class life. In contrast, his father had not needed to make many individual decisions. He'd relied on the bureaucracy of work and solace from the Church when in personal difficulties, whereas his son had needed to pay for my professional help. His father could also rely on clear, even rigid, expectations of male and female behaviour.

Mr A's father had been, my patient told me, 'propped up' by the networks of Scottish small-town life: 'another dependant, nesting under my mother, the Queen Bee. My father had three maternal figures, wife, mother and mother-in-law, within the space of half a mile to support him as a father and authority figure.' In contrast, Mr A was not able to hide unresolved infantile conflicts beneath a veneer of patriarchal authority.

At four, after his sister's birth, Mr A had felt 'pushed out of a love-nest' with his mother. Up to that point he had been 'swaddled . . . emotionally protected in a close and attentive way'. Then he was suddenly sent off to school dressed up in a formal uniform. He blamed himself for the way life had suddenly changed so dramatically for the worse. His parents had very high expectations for him, the only son, and he envied his sisters who seemed to be loved just for who they were.

After graduating from university Mr A married. The couple had a child and resolved to operate as personal and financial equals – a difficult task, even with the support of his men's group. Mr A found himself taking over the household completely, as if he were, like his mother, a conventional 1950s housewife. Or he would go to the other extreme and collapse into the role of the helpless, cosseted son who must be totally cared for by an all-protective maternal figure. When his wife left him after three years, Mr A's mother-in-law told him that he 'hadn't let his wife be a woman'. This increased his confusion, since his wife had been adamant that she didn't want to play a traditional housewife role.

After the separation Mr A, absolutely bereft, became a part-time single parent. Isolated and without practical support, he nevertheless expected himself to play a far more active role in mothering his daughter than his own father had done. He also lacked the internal resources to mother, since he could not process and think about his own emotional life. However, she was a companion and a consolation to him. Eventually the phobias and panic attacks which had begun during a prior separation from his wife intensified, until he felt forced to seek professional help.

Mr A's psychotherapy was to last seven years, twice-weekly. At first he could not bear to have the consulting-room door shut. He felt trapped in psychotherapy as in the nursery classroom and wanted to curl up like a foetus in a corner of the room or crawl under the table as if into a womb. He felt himself to be an utterly uncontained 'skinless' creature, bursting with anguished and violent feelings.

Mr A defended against these experiences of infantile helplessness through fantasies of absolutely controlling or annihilating me, as the much-needed maternal object. Halfway through his last session before my first long summer break Mr A mentioned an old lady he'd read about who'd been murdered. I suddenly sensed an alarmingly strong murderous feeling in the room. 'I noticed that, as usual, the flat is empty apart from us. I never hear any neighbours around', he said. Feeling utterly chilled by this, I then said that I thought he was having murderous feelings about me. Through letting me know about these feelings he was trying to make me feel as frightened and vulnerable as he did about my impending holiday. 'I don't know. Perhaps I am trying to frighten you', he replied, before going on to talk more lucidly than he had before about his fears of loneliness during the break. He agreed surprisingly compliantly with my interpretations. But, whereas I had felt quite shaken by the strength of his violence, I was not sure he had fully recognised the intensity of his own emotions. These persistent murderous fantasies had started after his sister's birth: 'It's not a man attacking a woman. It's a child attacking a mother and a child', he said later.

Whenever I said something that put Mr A in touch with early vulnerability and humiliation, he would retreat into grandiose fantasies of winning my admiration with heroic feats, or overpowering me passionately. He fantasised that he was Albert Einstein, and I was an adoring student or a secretary, hanging on his every word. He imagined himself piloting Concorde outside my window rather than having to listen to me.

At other times, feeling trapped and humiliated, he withdrew into florid sexual fantasies. Sexuality had become powerfully implicated in his unconscious attempts to maintain an illusion of fusion with maternal figures. His fantasies ranged in atmosphere from childhood innocence to adult conquest to a cold and – to me – quite terrifying violence which seriously frightened me. He began with talk of 'tearing my body to bits' – criticising me – and went on to his thoughts of raping me. In his dreams he'd seduce me powerfully, and I'd submit passionately, or we'd sit on the floor and play with toys.

Mr A's fantasy of existing in a symbiotic 'love-nest' with me was shattered by another separation – my unexpected absence after a sudden bereavement. Initially he retreated into murderous fantasies and threats of rape as a defence against anxieties about abandonment. I worried that I might be in real physical danger. I explored my own fears of male violence while thinking about the precautions I might take in case he really did act on his violent or murderous feelings. Gradually both my own anxiety and the intolerable fear of his own aggression projected into me by Mr A subsided as he became able to articulate the feelings of loss beneath his murderous rage.

> I used to exist in a bubble here. My mother didn't make me feel secure . . . she needed me to grow up suddenly when she had my sister . . . I'm not so important in your life, just any old therapy client. I used to feel special. You could stop therapy with me.

The catastrophic shock of my absence was ultimately a growing-point. Mr A dreamed of a baby wearing his blue baby-gro who played with himself and his daughter. 'I realised the baby could look after itself ... change nappies, put itself on the pot. ... I'm less helpless.' Through the experience of having me listen and reflect on what he was telling me, Mr A was becoming more able to process and understand his own anxieties. He still felt like an infant who could change its own nappies – a pseudo-grown-up baby.

Another dream illustrated the interchangeability of the female figures in his life, all experienced alternately as mothers, sisters and erotic love-objects. In the dream he was dipped in a swimming pool filled with chemical water that had magical properties, by two young girls wearing print dresses identical to each other and also to one he was wearing. He stayed in the pool long enough to be changed, but not to burn his skin off. 'Probably,' he said, 'your caustic comments.' The two young girls represented myself and a new girlfriend. He associated the printed dress he was wearing with his 'pretty looks' and likeable manner. Psychotherapy, like the caustic pool, was dangerously powerful in its transformative potential. He was responding passively 'with his dress on' because it was difficult for him to listen to what I was saying and then examine it for himself.

Narcissism is present in all of us to the extent that we yearn for the illusion of fusion with an idealised other – originally the mother – as happens, for instance, when we fall in love. Narcissistic relationships are superficial, with friends and lovers being seen as interchangeable, as part of the self rather than as separate beings. In fantasy Mr A glued himself onto me, like a piece of sticking plaster, rather than interacting with me. So strong was his illusion of being identical to a part of me, that he had convinced himself that we were exactly the same age. In a similar way he often felt like his daughter's peer, one of her playmates.

Mr A needed to be able to face his own feelings of loss and guilt before he could become able to love someone while recognising their imperfections. In his third year of psychotherapy he began for the first time to express remorse about his sadistic feelings towards me and his attempts to sabotage the psychotherapy process. He was worried that he might actually damage or destroy me. This became noticeable after a session two weeks before my summer break when he withdrew into a fantasy about me as a 'disembodied cunt', perhaps the lower half of a Greek statue which he would keep for himself in a lonely moorland grotto, making visits whenever he felt like it. I connected his desire to mutilate and control me with his feelings of rage and loss about my break. He agreed rationally with this, but went on elaborating the fantasy. Apparently he was trying to avoid the emotional impact of what I was saying. He also told me that work commitments would prevent him attending his last two sessions before I left, so that he could only come twice more before my holiday.

In the following session he described how he was making his current girlfriend feel insecure because he was afraid she would finish their stormy relationship. I linked his treatment of her with the fantasy he had had about mutilating and controlling me, saying that he wanted her and myself to be the ones to feel humiliated and abandoned. 'I feel really worried', Mr A said. 'There isn't much time left in the session . . . and you're going on holiday soon . . . I feel remorse towards P . . . and towards you . . . I feel I've destroyed the relationship.' He returned the next week telling me that he had managed to rearrange his office timetable so that he could come to his two last sessions 'because I realised you were concerned about my welfare'. He had also tried to repair the damage he had done to his relationship with his girlfriend.

Mr A now became more able to use me as a figure who possessed the characteristics of both sexes and less frightened of fusion with me within the maternal transference. He then began to explore his passive homosexual desires for his father, as well as his Oedipal rivalry and humiliation.

Gradually, as Mr A began to work through some of his overwhelming grief about abandonment by his mother, he began to acknowledge that his father had given him considerable care and attention around the time of his sister's birth. They had played 'atlas games . . . train-sets on Friday evenings . . . he made me feel important'. After winning strong praise for standing in for his boss at an academic conference, he dreamt that he was starting off on a new and exciting journey with his father. During this voyage towards manhood, Mr A and his father were travelling 'in a small wooden boat that I'd built, that had been covered up or neglected for years'.

After acknowledging that he saw me as a paternal as well as a maternal figure, Mr A became more able to delve into 'the very dangerous territory . . . the fundamentals of who I am'. He embarked on an exploration of his own repudiated identification with his mother and his passive homosexual desires towards his father. He remembered giving his father 'lingering kisses' and speculated that his parents had noticed his sexual interest in adult males. Maybe this was why they had forbidden him to go on a trainspotting expedition with older boys and men?

Mr A now began to face his intense envy of my reproductive capacities. He complained of a persistent hollowness in his stomach, associated with an inability to conceive ideas. He mourned the fact that he couldn't validate his existence in a fundamental way by bearing children. My capacity to link together a series of ideas about him was, he felt, tantamount to conception – a creativity of thought – and he hoped he could identify with that. He was in rivalry, then, with my capacity to make both a real baby and a thought baby.

Feeling bolstered by a stronger internal relationship with his father, Mr A began to discuss his feelings about me as an object with the attributes of both sexes. He dreamed of me as a woman doctor, a TV presenter who possessed a professional authority he saw as male. He envied her prominent position and the style in which she conducted the 'Seven O'Clock Therapeutic Show'. At work he felt dominated by what he saw as a feminine desire to be needed. He could not set the kinds of limits he associated with a benign internal father. He compared his masculinity to a Meccano construction, rigid yet fragile. But he hoped within the boundaried structure of the sessions to build something more solid and resilient.

In one of his last sessions Mr A said, 'I don't feel I'm waiting to grow up any more. I've become a man.' He now felt equal with the heads of the organisations in which he worked, he said. Recently he'd been 'head-hunted' for a prestigious and lucrative new job, having during his years of therapy developed his own area of professional expertise.

In describing his new workplace, Mr A let me know about the structural changes in his internal world. This new building had wide, very light corridors, filled with paintings and sculptures by young artists. There was even a very innovative sculpture of a water-mill in perpetual motion. He was now more accessible to himself. There were fewer dark secrets and hidden passages inside him now that his aggressive urges had become more integrated. He could accept that his parents were still sexually happy with each other and now felt more able to welcome and look after any younger siblings (young artists) they might produce. Through psychotherapy, Mr A had developed a far greater capacity to think symbolically about his own emotional experience and to be innovative in his working life. The symbolising functions of the artist can be compared with those of the psychotherapist and the parent, each of whom nourishes and develops the internal creativity of those who engage with them (Waddell and Williams 1991).

This new organisation had (like himself now) less of a liberal image, but was if anything more genuinely humanitarian. For instance, there were people with severe physical disabilities in the top jobs. The firm was also putting considerable resources into training women for leadership roles. Mr A told me that, despite a progressive veneer, his previous firm would not have placed people with physical disabilities in prominent positions because of a fear that they'd have put off important clients. Mr A compared this to his own tendency to project his own vulnerability outside himself onto less privileged social groups:

> I might go out of my way not to be prejudiced. But underneath, I might not want to look at people with physical disabilities. But really, it's the frail part of me, the disabled part ... 16 years ago, a weakness came to light – an emotional stroke. You have therapy for strokes. Therapy is still going on inside me, healing me.

It is significant that Mr A's psychological frailty emerged when he became a part-time single parent and was forced to confront the infantile states of mind which men have traditionally disowned and projected onto women. Within the maternal transference Mr A unconsciously dehumanised me, making me in fantasy into an object he could control and abuse. This lessened only once he faced the fear that he might absolutely destroy me and the therapeutic relationship on which he depended. Then he began to confront the fact that I was essential to his process of psychic transformation.

Through a prolonged period in psychotherapy of experimenting with cross-gender identifications and expressing desire for both parents, Mr A became more sure that he was heterosexual. Since he no longer had to work so hard at excluding his own vulnerability, which he saw as womanly, he experienced me as less dangerous and alien. He could recognise some of his own qualities in me while also acknowledging the differences between us. This contributed to his realisation that he could find a partner who would love him: he was relinquishing his quest for the unattainable incestuous object – myself within the maternal transference – and was willing to accept a woman who was emotionally available. 'I realised that people are not interchangeable', he said. 'Only a few people are really valuable.' This enabled him to grow passionately attached to a woman he had known a long time, whom he later married.

Men (or women) who project all their need and emotional fragility onto others do not usually commit themselves to long-term psychotherapy. They are often able to use stereotyped modes of behaviour to protect them from their own pain and so it is more likely to be their sexual partners who seek psychological help. Or they may seek help in a crisis and stay in psychotherapy only until their most pressing problems are resolved.

In the following section I look at psychoanalytic and feminist theories about the male propensity towards acts of violence and the sexualisation of psychic pain, which was so obvious in the therapeutic transference with Mr A.

Male violence and sexualisation of pain: psychoanalytic explanations

Of all the patients I describe in this book, the only one who had a history of violence in adult life was a woman, Ms V (Chapter 6). At one point she also threatened me with physical and sexual assault. Nevertheless, I have found powerful, highly developed violent and murderous fantasies towards me as a mother-figure far more common among male patients. Mr A is also typical of his sex in his tendency to sexualise his aggression – for instance through fantasies of raping me – as well as defending against his feelings of infantile vulnerability through thoughts of his own sexual prowess.

Men's greater difficulty in processing their emotions may leave them feeling in real danger of acting on extremely violent, even murderous fantasies. Violent impulses are often associated with an intense longing for indissoluble union (originally with the mother) combined with a terror of being merged and annihilated. For the man who cannot think about or symbolise his feelings, the 'other' becomes the container of unwanted, terrifying aspects of himself. In violence or suicide the body (of the self or other) become concretely identified with the lost and hated person (Hyatt-Williams 1998, Campbell 1999). Mental and physical processes become confused. Then real or imagined violence seems the only feasible way of getting rid of unbearable states of mind. As psychotherapy progresses it is crucial for the therapist to be experienced as an intervening presence – as different, other than the mother: a presence usually described as 'paternal' in psychoanalytic theory.

Contemporary psychoanalytic discussions of male violence tend to focus either on the suddenness with which the boy is expected to relinquish mother–infant intimacy or on his particular difficulties in identifying with the father and men. Physiological factors are sometimes seen as central to the way each sex mobilises powerful emotion. For instance, Melanie Klein argues that the boy has a different, potentially advantageous, means of externalising aggression because of his belief that he possesses a penis with magically destructive and reparative powers, unlike the girl, whose psychic life continues to revolve around the inside of her body. But the boy's fantasy that he has a deadly weapon at his disposal will also increase the likelihood of direct aggression if he cannot resolve internal conflicts in any other way (Klein 1928). Men cannot identify directly with their mother's procreative power. Might women have more respect for the continuity of human life because they can symbolically enter again into the maternal womb through identification with the mother? Men, in contrast, can only fantasise about forcible re-entry to their place of origin through violently destroying all obstacles in their path, according to Chasseguet-Smirgel (1986a).

Other theories about male violence emphasise the role of the father. Some Freudian psychoanalysts attribute many of the contemporary social ills of this age, including increased male violence, to the loss of traditional patriarchal authority within the family. The French analyst Grunberger argues that the unstable contemporary family does not foster the Oedipus complex as Freud described it (Grunberger 1989). While Freud saw human beings as suffering from too much guilt, Grunberger says that people today have too little guilt. The absence of the father who can provide a model of self-restraint results in a super-ego or conscience which remains fixated at a pre-Oedipal stage of narcissistic self-absorption, argues Grunberger. Cruelty and destructiveness towards the self and others may result from a super-ego which is harsh and punitive but without moral values.

Narcissism is sometimes seen as an individual pathology which reveals a social malaise. Christopher Lasch, a cultural theorist, argues that narcissistic ways of functioning, where people are interchangeable and relationships superficial, are used as a widespread defence against the terrifying fluidity and fragmentation of the modern world, where violence always threatens to break through the brittle glamour. In contemporary western societies some people do not build their own destinies through work and responsibility towards others, but instead seek immediate experiences of power, glamour and excitement, or at least identification with those who appear to have access to these qualities (Lasch 1979).

Undoubtedly psychological difficulties can arise if the boy becomes fixated, unable to think symbolically about what it means to be a boy, as happened with Mr A who felt traumatically abandoned by both parents after his sister's birth. This may lead to the idealisation of a caricature of manhood, 'false emblems of masculinity, faceless bureaucracy, violence, torture, the jackboot and the whip' (Chasseguet-Smirgel 1986a: 73). Such a boy may develop a sado-masochistic admiration of powerful men, while treating women and 'feminine' men with abusive contempt. If they are to avoid this, boys need a positive experience of loving identification with a responsive paternal figure – a homoerotic love affair with their ideal (Benjamin 1988).

While mourning the demise of the traditional patriarchal family, Grunberger and Lasch idealise traditional Oedipal ideals associated with the father: values which grow increasingly elusive. Simultaneously they devalue the early infantile mother–infant dyad, which they see as regressive, the locus of illusion. But this early relationship is also a potential source of emotional strength. It is also unclear in their theories whether the subject of discussion is the actual parents or what they symbolise in our culture. For instance, aspects of the traditional fathering role may be played by a number of figures nowadays, not all of them men. It is also important to remember how male identities are structured differently through a variety of cultural, class and 'racial' experiences and fantasies.

From a more general point of view, theories which stress the barren fragmentation of modern relationships also disregard the tendencies that enrich contemporary family life, such as fewer children, the possibility of increased paternal involvement in early stages of childrearing, family leisure and the tendency to understand rather than to discipline children (Benjamin 1988). Although contemporary men are losing some of their traditional privileges, there is much in today's society that benefits women. Now that women's workload in the home has been dramatically reduced, they have greater access to equality in the workplace and can choose to live outside nuclear family units if they wish.

Are men and women fully equal? The hidden power-differential

'Men's loss of absolute power over women and children has exposed the vulnerable core of male individuality, the failure of recognition which previously wore the cloak of power, responsibility and family honour', writes Jessica Benjamin (Benjamin 1988: 191). Her argument is that the breakdown of paternal authority has revealed men's failure to recognise women as separate and equal beings with their own will and desire. The more fragile their sense of masculinity becomes, the more desperately many contemporary men cling to its vestiges. They struggle to become what mothering and 'femininity' are not, but this leaves them even less equipped for the demands of modern emotional life. Defending against anxieties about the loss of their identities, men can become trapped in a terrifying spiral of inconsistency, obsessional behaviour, narcissistic rage or violence.

From his experience in working with violent men, British psychotherapist Adam Jukes argues that male abusiveness, aggression and contempt for women is not just a psychological phenomenon but is powerfully implicated in the attempt to sustain male dominance. Consciously or unconsciously, the violent man seeks to re-establish patriarchal control over women and their bodies. Jukes points out that mother–son incest is much rarer and less acceptable than father–daughter incest in most societies because of the powerful cultural assumption that the woman/mother is male property (Jukes 1993). In male-dominated cultures 'the body' tends to be associated with femininity, and the female form is seen as an entity to be viewed and owned. The subject status of males (sons) and the object status of women (mothers) remains deeply engrained in all of us. This is why we become so protective of 'failing' boys, and why so many modern men themselves find it hard to adjust to a relative erosion of power.

As with Mr A, the lost and hated mother returns in fantasies revolving around a denigrated female body that can be controlled and humiliated as the boy once felt himself to be. Through fantasies and real external relationships of domination over women on whom they depend, men can disown their own psychic 'femininity' – their infantile helplessness and wish to return to an early illusion of infantile symbiosis. Unresolved infantile conflicts can also re-emerge as exaggerated sexual needs and narcissistic overvaluation of the male penis. An example of this is the common male fantasy of a powerful woman who is always present and sexually available. In order to satisfy such a woman, many men imagine that they possess a penis 'two feet long, hard as steel' which 'can go all night'. Through this fantasy the man assuages oral needs, as well as Oedipal anxieties about male potency and sexual rejection by the mother (Spector Person 1986: 84).

But men pay a price for this denial of emotional equality. Their relationship to their own bodies can often seem limited and functional, as they disavow their origins and their primal link with the mother's body. Imagining themselves self-made creatures of intellect (rationality) and culture, they lose access to sensuality and to the early infantile pleasures of the body (Irigaray 1977). The messiness and uncontrollable muddle associated with 'the body' is then associated with women and motherliness.

Stephen Frosh describes how western men see their sexuality as bestial, animalistic – rather like madness, producing a similar fascination and fear. As a repudiated obsession, their erotic wishes then become controlling. They are not seen as part of 'man', that 'advanced creature of rational mastery' (Frosh 1994: 104). The New Zealand academic Annie Potts describes how in her research interviews the men often talked as if their penises had a mind of their own. A 'man with two brains' (Potts 2002: 113) emerged in her interviews: both sexes assumed that the man had a passionate amoral 'penis' brain that might easily conquer his rational, conscious brain. Potts explores the assumption that a man may be so driven by lust that a violent streak accompanies it: he wishes to damage or destroy what cannot be entirely possessed and controlled. She points out that, although the penis-brain can be disciplined and men are expected to learn to mentally control their sexual responses to become 'good lovers', nevertheless the penis is seen as something that must always be supervised, like a wild creature that can never fully be let off the leash (Potts 2002).

It is very difficult to know quite what – if any – effect the body has in shaping psychological differences between the sexes. But sexual difference could have an impact on our mental representations – the way in which we symbolise and conceptualise sexual experience. However, what is significant is the way in which we read or interpret such symbolism and how it is represented within culture. For instance, psychoanalysis may well have played a powerful role in shaping western thinking about sexual difference and erotic experience.

How can men regain a relationship to their own bodies and their sexual experience? We need to question the relationship between phallus and penis – so crucial to Freudian and Lacanian psychoanalysis. The dominant idea of male bodies and psychology as closed and impenetrable fits in with the belief that men's genital needs are so overwhelming that they cannot be denied: the penis must have what it wants. This way of thinking often prevents men from feeling that they can explore the erotic potential of their entire bodies and see themselves as receptive and yielding as well as 'hard' and forceful. It also means that when they feel overpowering sexual passion they may lose the capacity to think about and engage emotionally with their bodily responses.

Psychoanalysis may well have played a powerful role in shaping western thinking about sexual difference and erotic experience. It is obvious that men gain positive advantages in societies where they are dominant politically and economically and where phallic imagery has a favoured position. I can only imagine that there must be potential for change in representations of female and male sexuality when societies are altering rapidly. Indeed, such changes are reflected in my clinical examples, which show how far individual men's lives have altered in the course of a generation.

Cultural dislocation

Men who control and dehumanise their female (or male) partner deprive themselves of the possibility of intimacy, since the other cannot be recognised as equal but different. In this way sexism is similar to racism. When these states of mind are dominant a vicious circle is set up, whereby the person who is attacked or abused in reality or fantasy becomes threatening and dangerous, so that more violence is deployed against them, or a greater amount of emotional distance arranged. Gaining a sense of personal power through destroying the unsettling difference represented by the feminine other impoverishes the male personality, creating a structure that is rigid yet precarious.

Cultural critiques of narcissism have been used to explain the impact of the 'great structuring dominations' of race, class and gender on the psyche (Frosh 1989). It is argued that contemporary cultural fragmentation militates against the creation of an atmosphere of reverie or containment in early life. The confirmed existence of the self can then be buttressed only through denigration of the other. So each racial, class and gender group projects its own sense of weakness onto those who have less power and destroys the conscious knowledge of this projection. This destructiveness may be wrought for instance in sexist or racist fantasy or acted out in real acts of violence (White 1989).

However, these projections are not necessarily received passively by different ethnic and cultural groups, who may absolutely reject the values of the dominant culture and bring their children up with different ideals of male and female identity and family relations. So far I have described a man who moved from one class to another, but men who move between different cultures are often presented with even more drastically different conceptions of manhood. While recognising the profound implications religion and caste have on identity in general, I focus only on their implications for gender and sexuality.

Mr D

A 23-year-old man, Mr D, whose family were high-caste Hindus, expressed his conflicts about sexual identity through intense confusion about the different versions of masculinity to which he had been exposed. When he had arrived in Britain with his mother and siblings at the age of six, to join the father he had last seen five years before, he was moving to his third different continent and culture.

Mr D came to psychotherapy because of a painful, conflict-ridden love-affair. He urgently needed to resolve questions about the way of life he wanted to follow. In his first session he described himself as passionately involved with the only woman he had ever loved. But revealing the ambivalence he could not tolerate in himself and habitually projected onto her, he made a slip of the tongue, telling me that he had come to psychotherapy to break up with her. It gradually became clear that he had unconsciously made a series of decisions, and had come into psychotherapy because he feared he would be unable to tolerate the ensuing pain.

His lover was regarded by his family (and perhaps by a part of himself) as an unsuitable marriage partner because her cultural and religious background was different from his. Mr D remained obsessed with the idea that she would return to one of her previous lovers, who had been Afro-Caribbean or white. His unresolved Oedipal rivalry was projected onto these men, whom he imagined to be bigger, more 'macho' and more potent than himself. He felt painfully inferior to all the ideals of manhood to which he had been exposed. The greatest pressure seemed to be coming from his family, who disapproved of his lifestyle and advised him to build a future through hard work, responsibility towards others, and immersion in the family's religious and cultural heritage, instead of seeking to aggrandise himself through superficial glamour and rapid ways of making money.

Mr D knew that he was much sought after as a husband in his own community. He described how he was mobbed by young girls and their mothers at religious festivals because of his family background and his personal qualities, including his gentle demeanour and his delicate, almost pretty looks. His family were extremely concerned that their offspring should do well, and had therefore set up a business to be shared by Mr D and his siblings. But at the moment the wages were low for long hours' work, and Mr D said that he did not trust the family. He feared that his older relatives would always retain control of the organisation, since nothing was written down.

Psychotherapy represented an individual solution to problems, and in this way it too represented a part of the conflict Mr D had come to solve. In fact, psychoanalytic notions of autonomy or individualism are a Eurocentric or at least a 'modern' phenomenon, and have little relevance to some cultures (Littlewood 1992). Mr D did not know whether to throw in his lot with European individualism or to identify himself as part of his family unit, which would include helping to develop the family business.

Mr D felt ambivalent about what he saw as a strong component of 'femininity' in his personality. One of his strongest identifications was with a depressed, self-sacrificial maternal figure. For several years during puberty he remembered having dreams in which he was a girl. He associated these with a terrible humiliation of which he had hardly spoken before – the experience of having been sexually abused by a previously idealised slightly older relative, when he was nine. He had been in search of fatherly affection, he told me, and bitterly resented the fact that his parents had not protected him, or realised what was happening. Mr D felt it was much easier for his brothers to feel proud and sure of their masculinity and their place in the world. He attributed this to their having had more stable parental relationships in early life and being old enough to find alternative paternal figures among the extended family during the separation from their biological father. When his father was reunited with the family Mr D had felt unable to identify with what he perceived as cruel, dictatorial paternal authority.

But there may also have been strong cultural reasons for Mr D's frequent fantasies about being a woman. Since the 1920s, Indian psychoanalysts have argued that men from the Indian subcontinent are more able to integrate and remain conscious of their own feminine identifications, and their womb envy, than their European counterparts (Kakar 1989). Kakar, a contemporary Indian psycho-analyst, argues that psychoanalysis operates from within the heart of European mythology, from the myths of Ancient Greece to the 'illusions' of the Enlightenment, and there has been little attempt to observe from within the way in which other mythological systems influence personality development. He points out that the dominant narrative of Hindu culture is neither that of Freud's Oedipus nor that of Christianity's Adam. In fact one of the dominant mytho-logical figures is Devi, a personification of the Great Goddess. The powerful mother Goddess, as depicted in folk beliefs, proverbs, symbols and religious ritual, is always omnipotently fierce and ter-rible, and possesses an inexhaustible sexual energy, which inspires intense awe and dread in the Hindu male.

Her significance is reinforced by certain aspects of Indian family life, including the fact that within the extended family the boy will have not one but many maternal figures, who will all assume responsi-bility for his physical care. In contrast, the father in Indian mythology is often presented as unassuming and remote, yet powerful. Kakar argues that in the face of such an overpoweringly sexual, omnipresent maternal figure, the boy deals with his anxieties about differentiation in certain culturally favoured ways. The fantasies of being a woman which are often close to conscious awareness in the male psyche, and the image of the goddess as a man–woman are, according to Kakar, expressions of the Indian male's wish to become a man without having to separate psychically from the mother (Kakar 1989).

There were indeed many maternal figures in Mr D's family. For instance, at one point he wondered whether to go to a religious cere-mony, where he would receive maternal attention from his many sisters, or to come to his session, where there might be only one mother-substitute. But in spite of this Mr D felt that he had lacked consistent mothering as well as fathering. His mother's depression, the birth of a new sibling when Mr D was one, just before his father left the family, and the many moves and separations had all been factors in this. As a result of these experiences he had developed a cruel super-ego with which he attacked himself and those he was close to, including myself. Unlike Mr A, described earlier in this chapter, Mr D disowned his own destructiveness and ruthlessness, seeing himself as his lover's rejected victim. Whenever I referred to his once stated desire to break up with her, he would smile wryly, acknowledging that he had said it, but never fully accepting the wish as part of himself.

During six months' psychotherapy, focused around his conflicts about his love-relationship, Mr D bombarded me with intensely emotional barrages of words, leaving me little space to speak. He generated intense anxiety in me about his destructiveness towards himself and all his enterprises, including psychotherapy, his attendance at which was constantly in doubt. Despite the fact that he rapidly became dependent on me, he found breaks and gaps between the sessions extremely difficult and frequently missed sessions. He continually attacked all the ties that bound him to other people, whether relatives, lovers, business associates, or myself. After attempting to repair the broken links between himself and others, he would then make further attacks, always conveying a sense of anguish and helplessness about his own destructiveness.

Although Mr D saw himself as genuine and caring, this was not the experience of those on whom he depended, including myself. His states of inner persecution were another form of self-absorption. It was this lack of concern for others that he kept reproving himself for. Without realising it he was subjecting other people to ruthless emotional control, projecting onto them the same sadistic states of mind he experienced in childhood. In psychotherapy these cruel aspects of the self may become integrated with more loving feelings, eventually becoming the source of a fantasy life that generates emotional contact between people. Mr D did make the first tentative steps towards this process in his psychotherapy, beginning to acknowledge and make up for his attacks on himself and others, including me. Eventually he decided that his future lay in integrating his own western upbringing with the advantages of immersion in a very resourceful, traditional family structure where he had considerable status by virtue of caste and sex. His relationship with his lover also ended, ostensibly through her volition.

Mr D's tendency to disown aggression and to experience the self as a caring, loving victim of others' destructiveness is often described as stereotypical female rather than male behaviour. Nevertheless, everyone has the capacity to bully as well as to be victimised. Gender and culture will influence but not absolutely determine which aspect of personality any individual can more easily act out. Mr D may have drawn more on identifications with long-suffering mother-figures because he dreaded facing a strong likeness to his cruel authoritarian father.

Conclusion

Ideals of manliness vary both within and between cultures, but if the society around us dehumanises and denigrates women and the qualities associated with them our psyches will continue to reflect this. Men who for cultural or personal reasons are more 'feminine' than the dominant ideal may find themselves being treated with a fear and contempt usually reserved for women. Racism, gender rigidity and violence are each in their different ways defences against anxiety about the dissolution of identity, ways of protecting the self against the fear of losing all psychic boundaries.

In profound ways patriarchy impoverishes the male personality, creating identities that are rigid, yet frail. For instance, in cultures where men's erotic life is seen as being beyond their conscious control, governed by a more 'primitive' form of intelligence, male sexuality may take a limited range of predictable forms.

Men have little possibility of equal intimacy with women who are deprived of the possibility of autonomous selfhood. The cultural repudiation of femininity may well have a profound impact on gay relationships. It certainly fuels homophobia. Only when men begin to mourn the early loss of intimacy with parental figures of both sexes and acknowledge their womb-envy will they be able to feel more equal to women and other men.

Mainstream psychoanalytic theories focused around the boy's need to renounce early likenesses to the mother in favour of a sturdy autonomous identification with the father belie the complex fluidity of our inner worlds, which are formed through a variety of identificatory relationships. Conventional differentiations between maternal and paternal roles seem increasingly difficult to delineate theoretically. Undoubtedly engagement with involved and caring men is extremely helpful for both sexes in early life. The boy who has sustained experiences of physical care and intimacy with father-figures who are unafraid of rivalry or confrontation might be able to move beyond traditional limited ideas of what a man should be. However, he also needs to build on nurturing experiences with a range of 'maternal' figures of both sexes.

As cultural notions of 'masculinity' shift, contemporary men struggle to find new ways of expressing aspects of themselves previously seen as 'feminine' or 'irrational' – including their passion and embodied emotionality – without losing access to reason. It is crucial for us to understand more about how our experience of physicality is mediated through language and cultural imagery. As men re-own the gentleness and receptivity previously seen as womanly, they may also discover a more immediate link with their bodily experience and a greater capacity for sensual pleasure.

Although patriarchal relations profoundly cripple the male psyche, men still benefit from them. Inevitably, then, it was the female sex that struggled for equality throughout the twentieth century. In many cultures women also express unhappiness with their lot through seeking psychological help far more often than men do. In the next chapter I explore how far women can break the cycle of personal domination, claim their own autonomous subjectivity, and operate more as equals in their sexual relationships.

Chapter 5

The power of women's sexuality

Women in psychotherapy often talk about their struggles to break free from self-imposed suffering, including relationships where they feel trapped with sexual partners who are cruel, tantalising or unsatisfying. Despite psychoanalytic theories that describe women as the more masochistic sex, it is widely acknowledged that men are more likely to be sexual masochists, who can obtain gratification only through physical pain or humiliation. Yet female desire often emerges in fantasies of being punished or overpowered. And some women have a highly ambivalent relationship towards all life's pleasures, including sexuality.

In this chapter I explore the difficulties many women have in recognising their own desire and asserting their needs directly. I begin by discussing female patients who describe a disturbing clash between their conscious hopes for equality with men and an erotic life structured around images of female submission. These women seek the desire they cannot recognise in themselves through a powerful other who releases them into abandon but remains in control. This often reflects a more general difficulty in seeing themselves as the driving force in their own lives. They may invest their personal potency in others, or their desire for self-fulfilment might emerge only in alienated forms, for instance through envy or self-abasement.

There has been much focus in contemporary psychoanalytic literature on mothers who become erotically preoccupied with their children (Welldon 1988). In the second part of the chapter I look at the relatively neglected question of how motherhood affects women's adult sexual relationships. Drawing on clinical material, I suggest that withdrawal from sex may be an unconscious way for some mothers to gain a sense of power when they feel helpless, socially isolated or devalued.

Early in the chapter I illustrate how difficult it is for some women to break the cycle of psychic domination and submission and move towards greater equality in sexual and emotional life. In the final section I describe how it is possible for women in psychotherapy to re-own the powerful aggression and desire which they so often experience through fantasies or fears about male dominance or sexual violence. Although the case-examples in this chapter describe bisexual or heterosexual experience, the questions I raise are equally relevant to lesbian sexuality.

The female patients I discuss had great difficulty in conceptualising their own sexual pleasure, tending to imagine themselves as the object of desire for others. Psychoanalytic theories have not usually questioned the assumption that male sexuality is organised around a unifying phallic principle, with readily definable pleasure-locations, assumptions that reflect conventional western thinking. Male sexuality is often talked about as if it is easily understandable and measurable, and there is a vast and complex terminology to describe it. In contrast, controversy still surrounds the fundamentals of female sexual experience. Basic questions are routinely asked in psychotherapy and elsewhere. These include 'How do the clitoris and vagina interact?' and 'How do I know when I'm having an orgasm?'

Why do so many women feel unentitled to assert, even to recognise, their own needs and desires? From my case-examples, several reasons emerge. First, female sexuality is structured through early mothering as well as through relationships with paternal figures. To tolerate the essential unpredictability of erotic intimacy the girl must be able to negotiate a range of passionate and ambivalent feelings including physical excitement, tenderness and aggression. If she is not helped to deal with intense ambivalence, desire may become associated in her mind with fear of annihilation or enthralment to a tyrannical parental imago.

A second fundamental problem is the girl's fear that in fighting for autonomy or expressing Oedipal rivalry she will destroy her mother. Fantasies of domination and submission can express a craving for 'masculine' ruthlessness which the woman imagines might help her separate psychically from overwhelming internal parents. If she attempts to escape from a disappointing early maternal relationship into closeness with the father, the daughter may internalise a debased image of womanhood.

In the preceding paragraph I drew together mother- and father-centred theories – the Freudian and object-relations traditions. It is worth asking whether we need to continue thinking in this kind of 'binary' way, where opposing polarities are contrasted or drawn together. The feminist philosopher Elizabeth Grosz questions all such assumptions and attempts an entirely new and more open-ended way of looking at female sexuality. She wants to entirely discard such categories as 'masculinity' and 'femininity', passive and active, external versus internal. And she does not want to privilege genital sex over other forms of sexuality. Grosz does not think of something missing or absent – as in the Freudian/Lacanian view. Indeed, drawing on Lyotard, she questions whether desire – and 'woman' – have to be seen in terms of loss or lack. Might desire be seen as something positive and productive, she asks? She also rejects the object-relations view, which equates female sexuality with mothering and therefore describes a depth or 'inside' from which desire emanates (Grosz 1995).

Grosz suggests that psychoanalytic feminists have been too cerebral and analytical in their discussion of sexuality. We should not, she argues, be talking so exclusively about fantasies, wishes or aspirations. Instead we should be thinking more about the interaction between bodily and emotional experience. Energies, impulses, and pulses of feeling might be crucial to such exploration. Desire could be thought about in terms of lived experience – the pleasures gained from the eroticisation of bodily textures, surfaces and intensities. Grosz's challenge is thought-provoking. It is interesting that there are so few really lively and rich clinical discussions about women's actual erotic experience, and that feminist clinicians often take on quite conventional ways of thinking about women's erotic life. This is understandable, since it is difficult to discard 'binary' terminology entirely while continuing to think about gender power-differentials. However, our language does fundamentally affect the way we think about our clinical work, so it is crucial that we continue to question our underlying assumptions. Otherwise we might find ourselves replacing one inadequate way of theorising female sexuality with another unchallengeable feminist orthodoxy.

It is often argued nowadays that since there are few cultural images of a powerful, active sexual desire, it is very difficult for a girl to develop a sense of herself as an active and desiring female (e.g. Irigaray 1977). According to this view women need to develop ways of representing their own desire, to generate their own meanings and weave their experience into language. We could for instance draw on (possibly clitoral) symbolism, such as that of a bud, jewel, pearl, seed or berry (Potts 2002). Since the clitoris is not connected with reproduction, but purely with sexual pleasure, this would give us a way of thinking about women's desire as their own, and not mediated through thoughts or fantasies about maternity.

But will it necessarily benefit women if we develop new and accessible forms of imagery? Perhaps they will simply function as modes of control, rendering female sexuality predictable and expectable? Grosz asks whether we should be seeking to retain the inarticulacy, the labile indeterminacy of lesbian and female sexuality, or representing it as clearly as possible. These are fascinating questions which need much more discussion.

In the meantime many women, like those I describe in the following section, can only think about their passion and excitement in relation to a forceful lover who would compel them to experience their own pleasure. They imagine themselves being overtaken by a woman, a man, or both – and only occasionally think of themselves in the dominant position. This has historically made it difficult to articulate lesbian as well as heterosexual desire.

The eroticisation of power

Ms S, 35, came to see me in a crisis after her husband had walked out suddenly, leaving her with their five-year-old son. She wanted to understand why she chose men who at first seemed kind and reliable but who later turned out to be cruel, unpredictable, even physically violent. Ms S also felt that, although she had been seen as brilliant academically, she could not find a professional outlet for her talents.

Ms S had been brought up to believe that she had had a happy childhood with devoted parents, but she was now convinced that she had absorbed a family myth. She wondered whether her pattern of choosing men who were not what they seemed might have originated in an early relationship with her mother which was presented to the world as idyllic, although it was actually deeply troubled. Perhaps, Ms S speculated, her mother might, beneath a façade of devotion, have actually felt profoundly angry with the baby who consolidated an already disappointing marriage. Ms S might have been forced to comply with her mother's insistence that hatred and resentment were unalloyed love. She now found it very hard to recognise her own negative feelings, and to distinguish people who meant her harm from those who had benign intentions towards her.

Ms S described her father as having been dominated by her mother, who quite openly had special friendships – perhaps even affairs – with other men in the neighbourhood. Ms S so dreaded humiliating men as she felt her mother had humiliated her father that she repressed her own aggression absolutely, particularly in her dealings with the male sex. The only way in which she could express this part of herself was through men who behaved towards her in destructive or violent ways. She rapidly terminated relationships with men who would treat her well because of her unconscious fear of acting out her identification with a mother she had experienced as castrating. 'When they asked to see me again, I'd say "No" and leave them wondering what was going on', she said. But this did not help her to achieve more equal partnerships. Having rejected her mother's role, she found herself constantly taking up her father's position with men who, beneath their urbane public façade, were contemptuous and cruel. Ms S therefore became the helpless victim of men whom she unconsciously experienced as her ambivalent mother. In this way she avoided the imagined dangers of rivalling or identifying with a terrifyingly powerful mother-figure.

Ms S had been active in feminist groups for many years, and felt disturbed by what she described as a 'masochistic' sexual fantasy life. Since her teens she had had sexual fantasies about a repulsive, dirty, 'macho' man who would penetrate her forcefully. Only through this image could she have an orgasm, whether on her own or with a partner. The fantasies enabled her simultaneously to express and disown a sexuality she experienced as dangerous, dirty and overwhelming. The man in her fantasy would 'overpower me, so the sex wouldn't be my responsibility . . . He would carry me right away', she said. He forced her to enjoy her own sexuality which she experienced as dirty, dangerous and debased. As Ms S talked it became clear to both of us that this man possessed the 'masculine' ruthlessness she felt she needed in order to differentiate herself from her dominating internal mother.

Because women have so little power in the external world, they often invest more of their desire – for recognition, success or other gratifications – in their children. As a working-class woman with an unhappy marriage, Ms S's mother both wished for a better life for her daughter and envied her for having this possibility. In turn, Ms S felt desperate envy of the mother who dominated the household with a 'masculine' strength, yet could so easily attract men. In discussing how she had sabotaged her chances of professional success, Ms S said that her mother:

> pushed me forward, using me as an object to compete with in the extended family. But I wasn't a son, and so, ultimately she gave me the message – 'It's OK to succeed but not too much.' The relationship was so entwined, my success would have felt dangerous to both of us. I couldn't afford to arouse her envy, and she'd have lost me if I'd moved into a different world.

Ms S's father had seemed relatively uninterested in his daughter's academic or professional life, and she may also have feared the consequences of surpassing him.

In contrast, Ms S described her son as being very well able to assert himself and to get what he wanted by direct means. She admitted that, in producing the son her mother had always longed for, she felt that she was at last superior to her mother in one significant respect. Ms S was simultaneously preoccupied with her son's future achievements and worried that she might alienate him by trying to live vicariously through him, as her mother had done with her. Ms S was using her son to express the drive and aggression which she was unable to acknowledge in herself, seeing it as a male characteristic.

Ironically, although Ms S's mother was forceful and penetrating, this served only to exacerbate her daughter's feeling of psychic enslavement. Ms S described how her mother clung to her, while simultaneously undermining her. Dreading that she might become as terrifyingly destructive as she felt her mother to be, Ms S remained stuck in a rigid identification with stereotypical 'feminine' qualities.

The parents' unconscious communications about each other are crucial in determining how the child perceives them. Ms S's father was benign and gentle in his actions but his wife scorned him as ineffectual, so his daughter could identify with him only as her mother's victim. Her father had tried to intervene between mother and daughter but 'always got pushed out again'. Ms S described how her father had seemed quite unable to acknowledge her burgeoning sexuality. When she was fifteen he still bought her sweets and comics as if she was a little girl. Ms S said:

> I imagine that, in an ideal family, the father and daughter are very close, and she means a lot to him. So when she becomes a

teenager and has boyfriends he gets jealous, and for a while there may be explosive arguments. But in my family it would be my mother who would fly into ridiculous possessive rages.

In her relationships with men Ms S constantly enacted her internal battles with an internal mother against whom she rebelled but of whom could never break free. She berated herself about her inability to settle with a man yet, since relationships with women dominated her internal world, she could be described as emotionally bisexual. She could only be active or assertive vicariously, through real and fantasised relationships with male figures, including her son.

The cruel father

Another woman, Ms T, 31, was also unable to identify consciously with her father and to differentiate herself from her mother, but for very different reasons – because she did not want to identify with paternal cruelty. Ms T sought lovers who would physically hurt her, sometimes actually injuring her during sex. Mostly her partners were men, but she had had one lesbian relationship she hoped would be more loving. To her dismay she found herself re-enacting the same sado-masochistic patterns. Finally, she rejected her female lover as men had rejected her. During both lesbian and heterosexual sex Ms T lost herself in elaborate fantasies, about a man who was violent and abusive to his pregnant wife and their children. As in Ms S's fantasies, the man was notable mainly for his dirty and unpleasant appearance. Ms T came into psychotherapy because she was feeling depressed and worried about the self-destructiveness inherent in her more dangerous sexual activities.

Ms T described her working-class parents as uninterested in her struggles to get on well at school and unsupportive, even obstructive, of her wish to go to university. Nevertheless she had persevered with her studies against great odds. When she came to psychotherapy she had recently embarked on a career involving art restoration, having through determined effort won a much-coveted job in preference to other applicants with more experience in the field.

Ms T's childhood had been bleak and frightening. As the first child of a depressed mother who had recently lost two close relatives, Ms T was often left crying desperately on her own. In toddlerhood she escaped into what she remembered as an idyllic father–daughter companionship. She felt entirely abandoned when her father suddenly transferred his interest to the first in a long line of sons whom he often hit.

Ms T insisted that her father had never sexually abused her, but his interest in her seemed quite obviously sexualised. When she was four he took baths with her and put great effort into dressing her up prettily to take her out. In her teens she remembers him flying into rages where he would hurl sexualised verbal abuse at her. Her often pregnant mother was unable to protect her children from her husband's verbal violence and bullying. Her father never hit her mother, but he allowed her to wear herself out with physical work in the home without offering much help or support.

Ms T had identified with a debased image of the sexual mother whom she saw as subjugated to her father. Now she saw all heterosexual involvement as self-abasement. Unconsciously she saw her father's violence towards her brothers as a kind of love, and this may have strengthened her childhood wish to be 'one of the boys'. Although she did not continue to get special attention, she was the only child who was never hit. Once her father became preoccupied with her brothers, Ms T sought out the company of a gang of risk-taking older boys whose leader alternately favoured and mistreated her physically, an experience which greatly influenced her sexual life.

Ms T had read some psychoanalytic literature in an attempt to understand her own pleasure in pain. Freud's paper, *A Child is Being Beaten*, resonated with her own experience (Freud 1919). Freud explains a girl's fantasies of a boy being beaten as a disguised, masochistic way of enjoying the exclusive love of the Oedipal father. Ms T could see that in imagination she was receiving a form of painful, sexualised paternal love. Benjamin disagrees with Freud's emphasis on heterosexual incestuous desire. She argues that the girl's forbidden homoerotic wish to be the father's son underlies the beating fantasy. If the father can say 'Yes, you can be like me' this will help the child to confirm her paternal identification and so enhances her sense of being a subject – rather than an object – of desire (Benjamin 1995).

Ms T also found it far more difficult to talk about her lesbian relationship than her experiences with men. At first she said that she now considered it to be wrong, and did not want to have sex again with another woman. The vehemence of her view on this surprised me slightly, since she was well aware that the sexual violence she allowed male partners to perpetrate against her would have aroused far more abhorrence among her friends and colleagues. I later wondered whether she wanted to avoid her own sadism towards women (including myself in the transference) so absolutely that she would also rule out the possibility of lesbian desire.

After two-and-a-half years of three-times-weekly psychotherapy, Ms T had given up her more dangerous sexual practices. But then a new set of problems arose. Previously she had projected her own destructiveness onto lovers who had abused her body. Now she began to turn it against herself, beginning to unravel the successful life she had so painstakingly built up for herself. Her work, in which she was utterly absorbed, seemed to have had a reparative effect on her emotional life. In fantasy she constantly damaged her internal family, but through restoring works of art she attempted to make up for her own destructiveness. Sexual fantasies are also psychic survival fantasies: in reality Ms T constantly survived the exquisite tortures enacted on the fantasised women and children and this may also have temporarily allayed her anxieties.

I was seriously worried about how depressed she was becoming, and how near she was to losing all financial security. I was also beginning to realise how determined Ms T was never to imagine herself as aggressive. This was worrying too, since if she was ever to move out of the victim role, an essential first step would be to recognise that she could hurt or abuse others, including myself. Ms T insisted that in her fantasies she identified only with the tortured mother and siblings. She could not even think about the possibility that she might be punishing her mother for infantile neglect and betrayal. Nor could she think that she might in fantasy be torturing her brothers.

At the beginning of psychotherapy Ms T had experienced me as the perfect nurturing maternal figure. But once she lost her job she began to feel intensely critical of me, so that I felt I could do nothing right. If I tried to help her to explore her imperviousness to danger she would become defensive, and accuse me of being critical and undermining like her father. But when I decided to say less she was equally angry because then she saw me as passive and neglectful like her long-suffering mother.

I began to feel tortured as she re-created in me her own victimised state of mind. I felt continually criticised and misinterpreted, as she had felt with her father. She told me that the therapeutic impasse had nothing to do with her. It was I who had changed and become a cruel father-figure. Again she could see herself only as the innocent victim. At this point she expressed a wish to see a male analyst who would speak with confident authority and also wield real power in the world of psychotherapy. Her hope now, as in childhood, was that she'd be rescued by a powerful idealised male who would magically whisk her from the quagmire of her early relationship with her mother, which was re-emerging through the transference.

Beneath the feeling of persecution was a longing to regress and be looked after by an unconditionally loving mother. She was desperately envious of the maternal riches that she felt I was withholding from her. She had heard that I worked at The Women's Therapy Centre and told me that my female colleagues must be lavishing me with the nurturing that she herself longed for. A feeling of 'being driven up to the edge of things' may emerge in the transference with patients whose internal worlds are dominated by fantasies of destructive parental intercourse, argues Betty Joseph, a Kleinian psychoanalyst. Both patient and analyst feel tortured. Joseph speculates that infantile experiences that might have led to depression became instead terrible tormenting pain. To defend themselves against this torment small children may take over the task of inflicting mental pain onto themselves and build it into a world of sado-masochistic excitement. As infants these patients withdraw into a secret world of highly sexualised, masturbatory violence where parts of the self are turned against other parts of the body and mind. This violence is often expressed physically (Joseph 1982).

This does make sense of the inner world of Ms T, who described a quality of frantic sexualised violence both in her play with older boys and in her solitary quasi-masturbatory games. Instead of moving forward into real relationships with people, Ms T seemed as a child to have retreated into herself. She then lived out sexualised relationships in fantasy and sometimes in violent bodily activity. In therapy, as elsewhere, she used her enthralment with self-inflicted pain as a defence against depending on others who might hurt or abandon her. She had come to rely on these fantasised scenarios more than on everyday relationships with others, and believed that she would never enjoy sex without them. They also represented a protection against a breakdown into suicidal despair.

Ms T's sado-masochistic sexual life had its roots in early pain and emotional abandonment by her mother and a failed identification with a cruel father who sexualised the relationship and transferred his interest to his sons.

Theorising female submissiveness

If one partner controls the other, restricting their ability to have an impact on the relationship, is it useful to describe the relationship as sado-masochistic? Obviously there are elements of submission and domination in all sexuality. When does a play with domination become real domination? In this area, where the psychotherapist's own moral and political biases can rapidly emerge, there has always been controversy.

Both of the patients I have just described dreaded losing their love-objects through their own destructiveness. Unable to assert their own will, each felt they had no option but to submit, becoming what the other wanted them to be. To ward off abandonment they recognised other people's needs without expecting reciprocation, accepting that they could make no real difference to what happened while they remained in the relationship.

I have looked at the way experiences of infantile powerlessness and exclusion are subsumed into a distorted view of sexual difference as children become aware of their position in the gender hierarchy. But class also played a part in the difficulties of Ms T and Ms S, whose cases I discussed above. Incredible pain and difficulty are associated with the transformation that success in education can bring for working-class girls. Contemporary middle-class girls may have other difficulties, such as being hothoused into an academic life for which they are unsuited, but they do not have to tackle separation of the kind experienced by Ms S or Ms T. Ms T, whose parents obstructed rather than supported her academically, is very similar to a type of working-class girl described in a recent British research study. Closing herself off from early emotional deprivation, she singlemindedly focused on succeeding against all the odds, but at an enormous emotional cost (Walkerdine *et al.* 2001).

Similarly, Cheryl L Thompson describes the self-sacrificial attitudes of some successful African American women who respond with a form of 'survivor's guilt' when the rest of their family express open or covert envy and hostility. This can lead highly competent women to sabotage their careers and choose partners, friends and colleagues who are comfortable with their tendency to deny their needs. They may also feel that they must single-handedly provide emotional and financial support for their extended families (Thompson 2000).

How are we to understand the psychic elements of female submissiveness and self-sabotage? There is no place in classical theory for a constructive version of female aggression, an active life force that might give a woman the necessary determination to succeed or the ruthlessness to assert her own needs. According to Freud, the Oedipal girl becomes submissive as she becomes heterosexual. She gives up her own active desire – initially expressed in relation to her mother – and accepts that she can only be assertive by proxy – through relationships with men and producing babies (ideally male). The girl becomes particularly self-sacrificial if her erotic desire becomes tied up with a cruel super-ego, representing a cruel internal father. The girl's sadism, allowed no other outlet, is turned back on herself (Freud 1919, 1924c, 1931).

Women's inability to cope with envy and hostility towards both parents is crucial in maintaining the vicious circle of female subordination. Social factors, including real sex discrimination and devaluation, interact with psychic difficulties in separating from the mother, which the girl may try to resolve through idealisation of men. Having identified with a mother experienced as dangerous, the girl may feel that her vagina is dangerous to others, or, if she projects her destructiveness outwards, she may fear that she herself will be damaged through sexual activities.

Jessica Benjamin describes a special variant of female masochism, 'ideal love', where the woman idealises and yearns for unattainable men – the 'heroic sadist' – who can arouse their passion and desire in a way that no one else can. This need for 'ideal love' relates to a cultural failure to provide images of powerful female desire. Fundamentally the masochist does not seek pleasure in pain, but an opportunity to submit, to surrender the will under conditions of control and safety. Through the relationship with a dominating or withholding lover the woman is searching for an experience of excitement and containment that she lacked in childhood. She longs to escape from an internal mother seen as weak, engulfing and long-suffering, as Ms T felt her mother to be. The lover is so detached that the woman assumes he won't be destroyed by the intensity of her anger or need, as she dreaded that her mother would be. Beneath the eroticisation of power and powerlessness lies a distorted wish for recognition and intimacy with an equal other (Benjamin 1988).

This is a most convincing explanation of the way psyche and society interact in creating female submissiveness. Benjamin's early work focused on male–female interactions but her analysis could equally well apply to relationships between women. The domination–

submission dynamic is often played out between partners who continually move together and then detach emotionally. In the following extract a lesbian sado-masochist parodies the emotional plays of power in relationships between women. This could as easily describe a heterosexual interaction.

> Let's start a relationship and hurt each other a lot, OK? You be needy and demanding and fearful and manipulative, and I'll be cool and tough and withdraw further from you while meanwhile becoming totally dependent on you. Then you fall in love with someone else and leave me with no warning. We'll both be broken for months by grief and guilt. Sounds like a good time?
>
> (Samois, quoted by Merck 1993a: 250)

Many women including Ms T, described above find it easier to experience themselves as suffering victims than cruel perpetrators, especially in relation to other women. Negativity towards our own sex is often extremely hard for women to acknowledge. But sadism and masochism always coexist in the personality, even though the individual may be aware of only one of these characteristics.

Another way of thinking about 'masochism' might be that we come to desire what enslaves us. There has been surprisingly little recent feminist or psychoanalytic literature on the practice of heterosexual sado-masochism. In contrast, the issue has been the focus of fierce controversy among feminist lesbians, who have developed an extensive literature on sado-masochism even though there is no evidence that sado-masochistic sexual practices are any more common among lesbians.

In *Lesbian Lives*, North American analysts Miller and Magee explore how bodies are made feminine and how sexual fantasies and patterns of arousal are formed. Returning to Freud's description of the way little girls cede their capacity to actualise their desires as they become heterosexual, they argue that adult women must make another kind of renunciation if they are to reclaim their desire as their own. They must give up a lifetime of body-based gender training in order to feel sexually assertive and expressive without imagining that such behaviour renders them 'masculine' or immoral. A 'proper girl' is still expected to keep her legs together and her skirts down. Women do not move their bodies through space with the degree of assertiveness that men are trained to exhibit. Those that do may well be seen either as sexually provocative, a 'siren', or as a 'butch' woman with a 'gender identity disorder'. It is therefore not surprising that in sexual fantasies many women see themselves as bound, enslaved, overtaken, rather than active and eager. It is also unsurprising if women project their own desire onto an imagined wanton woman, a prostitute or nymphomaniac (Magee and Miller 1997).

Female submissiveness is often rooted in a variety of early difficulties, including extreme deprivation, trauma and problems with psychic separation. Difficulties in relation to mothering are often compounded by the girl's lack of paternal identificatory figures. I believe it is vital for women to face up to their aggression, including their capacity to be sadistic towards others. Only once we acknowledge that aspect of our personalities will we be able to draw on this 'masculine' forcefulness and use it creatively to fight for personal and political equality.

In the following section I return to my earlier discussion about the interaction between psychic and cultural factors in maternal self-sacrifice, an issue which has been central to psychoanalytic discussion of female masochism. I discuss how one woman withdrew from sex after her first child was born. She herself saw this as an unconscious attempt to regain a sense of control in the face of the helplessness and vulnerability engendered by the experience of mothering.

Maternity and sexuality

Ms D came for twice-weekly psychotherapy for over five years, leaving just before the birth of her first child. When she first sought help she had been in a state of shock because her husband had suddenly left her. In that relationship she had relinquished all her own needs, using the withdrawal of sex as a form of covert revenge. Ms D told me that without her husband she realised that she had little sense of her own identity. During psychotherapy she made major changes in her life, embarking on a new, creative career and – eventually – another relationship. Ms D gained psychic strength through exploring her inner world, but there seemed to be a piece of emotional work that she still could not do. 'There's a corner I can't turn', she told me just before she left. Her internal world was still dominated by relationships where one figure was powerful and idealised, the other denigrated and submissive. In psychotherapy she had become fixed in a pattern of enviously depreciating me as a way of controlling me in fantasy.

Two years after her daughter's birth Ms D returned to see me four times. She told me then that she had become depressed after the birth. She did not feel able to afford regular sessions at that time, but we left open the possibility that she might come back for more help in the future. My discussion here is based on her reflections in those sessions about what had remained unresolved when she left psychotherapy the first time.

Ms D told me that after her child's birth she had again lost all sexual desire, even though her new relationship had initially been exciting and fulfilling. Ms D described how she had at first felt very emotionally secure with her young lover, who 'never ran away or pretended not to be interested'. She went on to say:

> In the beginning I was dominant. I paid for everything. I could then. I felt in control and could be sexually relaxed, submissive. I play-acted being a feminine soft thing. But in outdoor life I was confrontational, bold and cruel. But what I really loved was getting into the passenger-seat of his old van, and going out on a date. I was 36 then, but I felt fifteen to twenty years younger. Then a man-friend went away and lent me a sleek new Porsche. When I got behind the wheel, he looked like a poor vulnerable thing in the passenger seat. I'd have liked him to turn the tables on that when I was at my most helpless – after having the baby. I've always had to maintain a controlling role and yet because I can't solve our financial difficulties, I feel passive. I can't breathe or function. The only way I know how to be dominant is to say 'No' sexually. We'd both like there to be more give and take, but I don't seem good at equality.

While in the emotional driving seat Ms D could be sexually open, but she was afraid that she would become subservient if she let herself be emotionally vulnerable. After the birth of the baby she initially felt she'd completely lost control over her life. She described the shock of feeling absolutely on her own with her infant. She had assumed that she and her partner would share the baby's care, but this did not happen. Ms D could not find part-time work in her field and her partner did not want to give up his promising career. She felt cheated, since he had wanted a child at least as much as she did.

Ms D suddenly felt that she had lost all social value once she was out of the workplace. It is true that motherhood is simultaneously idealised and devalued. But just as significantly, the mothering role puts the parent – male or female – in touch with infantile experiences of humiliation, helplessness and envy from which activity in the external world can provide an escape.

Despite her depression, Ms D soon came to feel that the freedom she had lost appeared 'a poor empty thing' in contrast to the joys of motherhood. Since her daughter's birth Ms D had identified with her mother, recreating the kind of exclusive twosome that she imagined she might have had in infancy. But Ms D's inability to envisage equality in relationships also caused difficulties with her daughter. She thought that as an infant she might have felt entirely controlled by a dominating maternal figure. The only way that she felt able to avoid tyrannising her daughter now was to relinquish her needs entirely and to submit herself to the child's desires. 'I see myself as a robot, my daughter's life-support system', Ms D said. 'I'm a safety-net for her, not an individual apart from her. But the bad side of this is that sometimes I get lost in her. I simply react to her, rather than taking up a strong position and guiding her.'

Ms D was worried that her daughter might later have problems in creating equal relationships. Indeed, if the cycle of domination and submission is to be broken the mother must find a way of balancing her own needs with those of the child. But to set limits while allowing her child to experiment with aggression and independence the mother herself needs a sense of autonomy which Ms D was still struggling to develop.

In her own childhood her father's lack of involvement had exacerbated Ms D's problems in coming to terms with being separate and different from her mother, a dynamic she later re-enacted with me. Reviewing her psychotherapy in retrospect she pointed out that she had always resisted facing the fact that she was my patient rather than my friend. Perhaps she maintained the illusion of being in an idyllic mother–daughter couple to avoid facing early bleakness with a mother who found babies boring? Ms D thought her mother might have idealised her when she appeared to be a 'pretty sweet thing' and rejected her when she didn't.

Ms D imagined her utter shock when, during her fourth year, her mother had suddenly arrived home with a new baby sister who became her father's favourite. She could not remember having been close to her father, who tended to shut himself away from the children. Had her mother excluded him from family life? The only child to whom he had paid special attention was the new little sister. In her new family Ms D was repeating the pattern of excluding the father, so that there was never a threesome or a close parental couple. When her partner was home he looked after their daughter alone and the rest of the time she did. Ms D felt so envious of his capacity to escape from the family and pursue his career that she wrought an unconscious revenge, depriving him of sexual and emotional intimacy, even though she knew she would feel devastated if he left her.

She went on to tell me that she had begun to treat her partner in the same way as she had treated me. 'Why did I always need to criticise you and keep you at a distance?' she asked. Her answer now was that she denigrated me in order to avoid feeling envious and inadequate. 'When I admire someone I want to be them. When I realise I can't become them envy sets in and I start to tear them to bits', she said.

By projecting disliked parts of herself onto myself and others, and then controlling us in fantasy by constant contemptuous criticism, Ms D kept herself from turning the corner into depression. But she also avoided psychic change by unconsciously trying to stir up her own uncomfortable feelings in me. For instance, near the end of one session she had suddenly remarked that everyone would agree – it was a fact – that she was prettier and had more sense of style than I did. She went on to say that she hated all pot-plants and particularly the ones I had in my consulting-room. My decor was dated and the plants belonged to a previous era. I felt shocked by the suddenness of this attack, and was momentarily unable to think clearly. Indeed that day I did feel very tired and drab and I wondered whether it really was true that my pot-plants looked that way too.

During the next session Ms D talked about her own current feelings of inadequacy, telling me, 'I can never grow plants and I desperately envy anyone who can keep them alive'. She went on to talk about her lack of progress in psychotherapy. She felt lifeless and empty inside and unable to grow emotionally. In contrast she envied the fact that I seemed to have more internal resources. She also talked about her alarm at seeing the visible signs of her body ageing. She felt anxious about losing her good looks and appearing to be a relic of a bygone era, a characteristic she had attributed to my pot-plants.

Contempt for women and their sexuality can be one of the hardest aspects of the maternal transference for a female therapist and patient to tolerate. Often there is no man present in the room but the patient speaks with the internalised voice of the chauvinist men she so often criticises. It may be difficult for the therapist to help the patient explore this aspect of the transference when the patient's comments resonate too closely with her own feelings of self-devaluation as a woman.

Now that she had a child of her own Ms D felt angry that her father had not helped her find a pathway out of the claustrophobic frustrations of infancy into the external world. She told me that she had got from me the kind of 'objective' attention her father had only given to her sister, and it was this attention that had enabled her to begin her new career. Her sister had been able to develop her own needs and interests through getting from their father a more unconditional love than their mother could give. At six her sister already geared her day around hobbies, something Ms D's father greatly admired, while my patient was looking for her own reflection in other girls, and, increasingly, boys. 'I was a flibbertigibbet, a butterfly. Thank goodness I was pretty, they said.' It was assumed (quite rightly) that she'd marry young. Accordingly, as with many middle-class girls of her generation, no one bothered to talk to her about what work she'd do until she'd actually left school.

The toddler can deny helplessness through identification with the idealised father, but the girl who cannot do this will have no alternative but to confront her own helplessness, which may result in her losing much of her exploratory enthusiasm. If there is no actual father in the family, the mother's own relationship to her internal father and to the male aspects of her own psyche is crucial.

In most psychoanalytic theories there is still a tendency to assume that the movement from the mother is emancipatory: the girl is saved from an undifferentiated immersion in the infantile world into the sturdy autonomy engendered by heterosexual closeness with the father. His authority is supposed to protect us from irrationality and submission. But this theory reflects and reinforces the devaluation of women and motherhood. It also underestimates the way many real mothers devote considerable energy to fostering independence, inculcating the social and moral values that make up the super-ego. It is usually they who set limits to the child's desire for erotic closeness and wish for omnipotent control. But, paradoxically, the father's distance and mother's closeness conspire to produce a disproportionate idealisation of the symbolic father (Benjamin 1988).

The girl needs to identify with 'phallic' masculinity, with an image of active femininity as well as with receptive, containing functions. We need to recognise both the 'holding' mother and the exciting father as elements that make up desire. The child needs to be able to play in infancy with a range of cross-sex identifications, accepting difference by making it familiar. In this way the girl might be able to sustain her own curiosity about exploring the outside world, as well as her agency and desire.

The women I have discussed so far in this chapter belong to a generation who were told as adults that women now had sexual and professional equality. Yet both their unconscious fantasy lives and external realities militated against this. Although their mothers were not necessarily passive or subservient in reality, each had identified with a debased, subservient image of female sexuality. This was reinforced by their inability to identify with qualities they associated with men and masculinity, which they idealised as unattainable. Their unresolved envy and internalised contempt for their own sex emerged in quite dramatic ways within the maternal transference, evoking intense countertransference reactions in me.

It is clear then that women need simultaneously to fight for cultural and psychic change. In the following section I discuss how one woman began to break through this cycle, through becoming aware of and questioning her own sense of herself as a helpless victim. In psychotherapy she began to integrate the desire and aggression which she had previously projected outside herself through obsessive fear of male violence.

The woman who stood up for herself

Ms X, 27, came for a consultation at a publicly funded clinic because her colleagues were concerned that she had completely lost her professional air of calm competence and cried all day. This was her story: She had woken up one night to see a young man standing by her bed. He jumped on to her bed. She was terrified but stayed calm, kept the bedclothes pulled up, and asked him what he wanted. 'Sex', he replied. He then asked her whether she had any cash. She said that she had very little because she hadn't been able to get to the bank. She was used to dealing with young men like him, she said – he reminded her of those who used the project for which she worked. 'Do you believe in God?' he asked. She said she did and he left without harming her or stealing anything. But since then she'd become increasingly disturbed, wondering obsessively why the man had broken into her flat. Her lover of five years had recently gone abroad to work. She wasn't sure why she hadn't gone with him, and now thought of joining him. When she mentioned that to her parents, her mother, who had a history of depression, had taken an overdose and put herself in hospital. She was the only child of work-ing-class parents who were determined that she should have greater opportunities for fulfilment than they had.

Ms X felt unable to fully differentiate herself psychically from her mother and was constantly drawn into the middle of conflicts in a passionate yet fraught parental relationship. She felt that her father had always tended to bully her mother. I offered her the only space available – six months' brief psychotherapy – to focus on psychic separation from her mother. She said, 'I can usually do most things with a bit of help'. Professionally she was highly competent, had stable relationships and up to now had sailed through difficulties with aplomb.

It soon became clear that the police were certain what the man was looking for. They were full of admiration for Ms X since they believed that she alone had managed to protect herself from a serial rapist who had assaulted many women in her neighbourhood. But she could not accept the fact that she had managed to avoid rape, something she had always feared intensely.

Her early sessions were full of very chaotic images of sexual vio-lence and attack which had been lurking in her mind since child-hood. This alternated with the re-emergence of her cool, composed façade. For instance when she talked about her perfect relationship with her absent boyfriend I felt puzzled – it was just too good to be true. The intensities of vulnerability, passion or anger were denied, associated unconsciously with dangerous destructiveness or loss. This repression of passion was associated with two abandonments. The first was very brief. Her mother developed a fever after her birth, and her father had been unable to look after her and had left her in a different hospital for a week. The second abandonment happened when in her sixteenth year her apparently happy mother had suddenly admitted herself to a psychiatric hospital for depression.

Even at sixteen my patient had demonstrated a capacity to stand up for herself, telling her father, who had left her to do all the washing-up while her mother was in hospital, that he must do his share, and could not bully her as he did her mother – she had her homework to do. Through the encounter with the rapist she had been able to use this assertiveness. But she had also been confronted with an assertive part of herself which had previously been projected onto violent men. An incident at work illustrated her attempts to come to terms with these aspects of herself. She'd been advising a couple who'd been illegally evicted. When it emerged that they were members of a neo-Nazi organisation her colleagues pointed out that their anti-racist charter meant that their organisation could not help such people. She argued that she had good communication with the couple and felt they should be challenged into discussion about their politics rather than banned. In the same way she was wondering whether the aggressive aspects of herself could be negotiated with and integrated, rather than being completely excluded as before.

As she began to acknowledge that she had stood up for herself physically she began to think she might risk more emotional autonomy from myself as a maternal figure. After twelve weeks she decided to join her lover but returned six months later, again distraught, because the relationship had ended. We made a new six-month contract, so that in all she would have seen me for nine months.

She now began to see me as an envious clinging maternal figure, begrudging her happiness. She embarked on a new relationship where she could be more emotionally open. But at first she did not tell me because she feared I might spoil it with envious interpretations. On the other hand she was delighted to discover a book I'd edited, with a chapter by me on mother–daughter envy. She was relieved to see that I could get on with something in her absence and that I might understand about envious mothers. A different, more resourceful and independent aspect of her mother's character began to emerge within the transference. She remembered that her mother had been a pillar of the local community, always active and highly competent. Now that she was more able to acknowledge maternal strengths with which she had identified, she could also acknowledge her need to depend on others, for instance on me.

I also represented a caring paternal figure who stood by while she faced up to the reality of her relationship with her mother. Before her last session she dreamed that an old bearded man, associated with me, sat at an easel on a cliff-top painting a picture on a piece of cloud. While this therapist–father looked on, creating evanescent images of her internal world, she walked onto the beach. It was entirely covered with driftwood; she knew that for some reason she had to clear it into an orderly pile. She felt daunted by this but knew by the end of the dream (and her therapy) that she had tidied up the driftwood, even though she had no visual image of the neat pile.

She had initially disparaged her father, saying that he was thoughtless and emotionally withdrawn. But I was struck by how sensitive he had been in his behaviour to her after the break-in. He also gave her much practical help. When I mentioned this she said that her colleagues always called him 'your wonderful father'. She was interested in but only partially convinced by the idea that he might have been a better parent than she had previously thought. She observed that she had previously feared her mother's jealousy if she acknowledged closeness to her father. But she also pointed out that he had failed to look after her at crucial times – after all, why had he taken her as a baby to the hospital? And she bitterly resented his bullying of her mother and the way her parents burdened her with their marital difficulties rather than sorting the issues out between them. It also became clear that her mother might also have had 'paternal' strengths, for instance the capacity to help her daughter gain confidence in the external world. Ms X linked her own success in most spheres to the absolute certainty both parents had that she would be good at everything she undertook.

It was now clear that inside her were two separate worlds. The later, very positive and affirmative, relationship with both parents was a shallow layer on top of a fracture. The rapist's intrusion had precipitated the eruption of an earlier, more persecutory relationship, resulting from the early separation. In a follow-up visit after the ending of therapy it emerged that the family obsession with protecting her from male violence stemmed from her parents' experience of violent abandoning fathers. She also knew that her mother had suffered some childhood trauma, perhaps sexual. My patient had internalised a threatening male figure, through her father's repudiated identification with his own violent father, and her mother's experience of victimisation.

The combination of involvement and protectiveness from a father who is valued by the mother is unusual in women who seek psychotherapy. This woman was also fortunate in that she felt her parents to be devoted to each other despite their rather tortured relationship. This gave her some basis on which she could begin to build loving sexual attachments herself. Her success in the external world was due to identification with the personal efficacy of both parents. Even more significantly she did not suffer the envy or obstructiveness described by the other female patients. The two parents were united in a strong desire that she should do better than they had. A combination of vulnerability (her heightened expectation of attack) and strength (her ability to stand up for herself) had helped her to avoid attack. It was also crucial that her parents had been physically and sexually protective, even though her mother might herself have been an abuse victim.

Conclusion

How does a woman come to 'own' her powerful desires, to experience them in her mind and body in a way which allows her to assert her wants both in sexual life and in other spheres of existence? And how can psychotherapy assist her in this? In the clinical setting, feelings of internal persecution or psychic enslavement, of being the object rather than the subject of desire, can emerge as intense contempt, envy and denigration of women and 'femininity' within the maternal transference. If this resonates with the psychotherapist's own feelings of self-devaluation as a woman, countertransference difficulties may arise. Women who enter the caring professions often have an intensely critical super-ego, which demands continual perfect attention to the needs of others. Thorough analyses may help to increase women's self-esteem but they cannot alter the fact that in our society women's second-class status is continually reinforced in ways too familiar to notice consciously.

To forge a psychic link between freedom and sexual desire, girls must find a way of attaining autonomy from the mother and identifying with the father, or psychic 'masculinity', without devaluing womanhood. The parents' wishes and desires towards the daughter, and the way she situates herself in relation to these desires, are crucial determinants of the success of this process. In particular, the daughter, who may have the potential for a much more fulfilling life than her mother, can find herself the object of intense envy. Class, race, culture and sexual orientation play a significant role, as guilt and envy combine with actual external sexual discrimination to form a serious impediment to change. It is crucial that parents protect daughters from their own envy and rivalry, instilling in girls their own desire that they succeed in both conventionally 'masculine' and 'feminine' activities. This parental belief in the daughter's capacity for personal fulfilment is a vital antidote to the cultural devaluation of femininity.

We need to think more about the parameters within which we discuss female sexuality and physicality. Have 'binary' ways of thinking rendered our theories – and our sexual experience – unnecessarily predictable? How might we think about women's bodies and their erotic experience in ways that enable and empower us? Certainly the girl who internalises a range of cross-gender identifications will still have to struggle to synthesise this sense of independent selfhood with the reality of being a woman, since there are so few images of active and autonomous female sexuality. Female sexuality will not alter through psychological change alone. There also needs to be a restructuring of social attitudes and institutions – including the institution of psychoanalytic psychotherapy. Psychotherapy is no more immune to issues of gender-based power and status than any other arena of activity – indeed, the nature of the therapeutic enterprise makes it inevitable that such issues will be at the heart of the therapist–client relationship. Male social power and female subordination are among the crucial forces structuring the transference and countertransference, as the following chapter explores.

Chapter 6

Gender in the
transference relationship

In a classic psychoanalytic textbook, the North American psycho-analyst Ralph Greenson wrote in 1967 that 'all cases of eroticised transference I have heard of have been women patients analysed by men' (Greenson 1967: 339). The image of the female patient who falls passionately in love with her male analyst has also become a popular media stereotype. During the 1980s there was intense debate about why this kind of highly eroticised transference has been reported less often between female analysts and male patients.

When female analysts did write more about the erotic transference, their concerns often differed from those of male psychotherapists. While acknowledging how arousing sexuality in the consulting-room can be, female therapists did not seem to feel in nearly as much danger of actually becoming sexually involved with their patients. Their male counterparts have in recent years discussed the positive aspects of countertransference desire, and the difficulties of man-aging their own arousal. In contrast, female clinicians describe their problems in processing the anxiety, horror or aversion they sometimes feel when their clients – often the victims of childhood trauma – profess passion or desire. Female psychotherapists have also seemed to be more aware of the eroticised maternal transfer-ence, focusing on the re-enactment of sensual pleasures or eroticised pain associated with early feeding, nappy-changing, bathing, and a range of other physical ministrations (Welles and Wrye 1991). Indeed, although remarkably little has been written about same-sex eroticism, female clinicians have discussed their experiences slightly – but still only slightly – more often.

Why should male and female therapists react in different ways to erotic transferences? Are these female therapists denying their erotic arousal? Perhaps they might overemphasise the infantile elements of their patients' experience rather than confront adult sexuality? On the other hand, are male therapists too preoccupied with the erotic feelings in the room, so that they avoid the powerful hostility, contempt and infantile need that so often underlies erotic transferences ? Are they perhaps gaining gratification from wallowing in eroticised adoration, rather than helping the analysand understand herself more?

In this chapter I address these questions, examining recent literature on gender in the erotic transference in the light of my own clinical experience. In this context the psychotherapist's countertransference – his or her emotional attitude towards the patient, and the patient's transference – is again crucial. I explore how the therapist's own theoretical biases and unresolved conflicts about sexual identity may inhibit her capacity to differentiate homosexual paternal desires from heterosexual transferences and the phallic mother from the intervening father.

The impact of gender on the erotic transference

In his 1915 paper on transference love, Freud discussed how the (female) patient would inevitably fall in love with the (male) analyst. This would be due to the workings of transference rather than to the analyst's charms. The patient would be projecting aspects of her own internal world onto the analyst – re-enacting past feelings and fantasies. But, Freud went on, this transference love is just as real as any other love. All adult sexuality is at root incestuous. And all love and hate involves illusion, even delusion. The only difference is the context. Ultimately the patient has to face the narcissistic pain of rejection – transference love can never be satisfied. Again, the difference from all other desire is how it is dealt with. Ideally it is not acted upon but thought about, and used in ways that might further the work of analysis.

Freud described a certain kind of woman patient who cannot see the analyst 'as if' he is the desired parent. Instead she insists that the analyst actually becomes her lover (Freud 1915). Obviously some patients take a long time to understand that they are not actually going to become the therapist's lover or best friend. But what Freud was describing was the very extreme case of the patient who never does grasp that analysis is a meeting of minds rather than of bodies. Elizabeth Zetzel gives an amusing example – the woman who comes into her analyst's office and says, 'Before I lie down, I would like to get one thing straight. If I divorce my husband, will you divorce your wife and marry me?' (Zetzel 1970: 243). Freud said that this 'outbreak of passionate love' is largely resistance, an attempt to short-circuit the process of emotional change. He also notes the intense hostility and contempt behind such idealised love. The patient is trying to reduce the analyst, to 'bring them down to the level of a lover', he says (Freud 1915: 163).

I have experienced many erotic transferences with male and female patients, but, interestingly, I have had only one patient who actually did come to believe that I was the love of her life in a very absolute and literal way. I saw her twice weekly for two years, as one of my first counselling clients, before I went on to further training as a psychotherapist. Ms V was a lesbian, but women who think of themselves as heterosexual can also develop intensely sexualised transferences to female therapists. Her erotic transference was idealised. She described me as a perfect mother, but rejected any links between this and her sexual desire for me. She was in love, she said, and wanted me to be her partner. In fact Ms V had had very similar feelings for another female professional during her long psychiatric history. She found it very hard to tolerate intervals between sessions and would connect these with constant separations from her mother in babyhood. Her idealised love seemed to be partly a defence against the pain and rage that she felt about these abandonments. I constantly worried that her intense erotic feelings towards me might become uncontainable or that I might unwittingly be acting in a provocative way. My situation was all the more difficult because in the organisation where I worked the boundaries between client and counsellor were often blurred, and she frequently managed to see me in extra-therapeutic contexts.

When it became clear that the counselling centre for which I worked had lost its funding, her idealisation of me broke down and she began to threaten me with rape, even murder. She had identified with a childhood aggressor, an uncle who'd raped her at eight, and had originally sought help because of fears that she would injure her son. She also told me that she had raped her last lover when the woman ended the relationship. My personal reaction to her threats was one of anger. I was only slightly frightened and wondered whether I did not feel seriously threatened by her because she was a woman.

Fortunately, this enforced therapeutic ending helped her to work through some of her feelings of destructiveness towards her love-objects so that she became less terrified of acting them out. I met her by accident some years later and was delighted to discover that she had formed the kind of stable (if stormy) partnership with a woman for which she had longed. She was also getting on much better with her son. Nevertheless, she followed up this meeting with a letter telling me that I was still the love of her life, thus suggesting that she might not have entirely resolved her transference love.

Was Ms V's erotic transference to me lesbian, or was she seeing me as a male figure? It was clear that one strand of the transference revolved around the intensely painful experience of an insecure mother–infant sensuality, where the longed-for physical closeness was constantly interrupted. But another aspect of her erotic feelings towards me reflected heterosexual experience. At times Ms V re-enacted the abusive relationship with her uncle, casting each of us alternately as perpetrator and victim. The erotic transference can be a particularly compelling vehicle through which 'forgotten' early traumatic experiences can be communicated. The North American analyst Joyce Slochower suggests that when the sexual transference is rooted in trauma the clinician may feel aversion rather than desire (Slochower 1999). Despite my alarm about how to handle such an intense and complex transference, and the anxiety and rage she sometimes aroused in me, I found Ms V deeply engaging and often enjoyable in the early stages of her therapy. When do feelings like this become attraction or desire? How do we differentiate emotional and sexual seduction? These are complex questions. What I am certain about, however, is that I usually find patients of both sexes more desirable later in psychotherapy as they work through childhood traumas and bring more adult sexuality into the consulting-room. This process was curtailed by the premature ending of Ms V's therapy.

Whatever their sex, clinicians sometimes gain narcissistic gratification from a highly sexualised transference and may collude with it rather than looking at the more unpleasant feelings beneath it. It can be flattering to be idealised. Being the object of intense desire can be exciting or frightening. One of my male patients expressed his own confusion about the origins of his sexual feelings towards his mother and myself. He told me that he could not decide whether his mother really had been seductive or whether he had wished to see her in that light. He went on to say that he had found one of my interpretations, made in the last session, 'charming . . . it wasn't that you fancied me but you were behaving in the way that we all do without realising it in order to please people'. He then told me how difficult he himself had found it to tell when he was flirting. His friends had said to him, 'That girl fancies you and you were flirting'. He'd said, 'No I wasn't! I was just being nice.'

On reflection, I thought he had a point. My interpretation had been entirely accurate, but I could see that the words I'd used might have been seductive or flirtatious. Certainly that is how he saw them. At times this patient was extremely enjoyable, seductive and entertaining. He had a glamorous lifestyle, and I can remember wondering what it might be like to go with him in his fast open-top sportscar to a party full of famous people. Yet there was something very manipulative, cold and contemptuous about his attitude towards me as a mother–sister figure, which militated against the arousal of any consistent desire on my part. I was all too aware that beneath his wit and charm was a desolate psychic wasteland. He often had fantasies of killing off a family experienced as neglectful and abandoning and there was a sense that all women, including myself, were ultimately dispensable. I found his comments about some of the women he seduced quite chilling. Through my flirtatiousness I had momentarily acted out my reluctance to engage with the hatred and cynicism that accompanied his erotic feelings about me.

I was surprised in the 1980s to read papers by women psychoanalysts who argued that highly sexualised transferences from male patients to female analysts are rare. The reasons given included the stronger cultural taboo on mother–son incest and on sex between younger men and older women. In fact such transferences are much commoner than these writers assumed.

Women psychotherapists often say that the transference changes as they age. Some male analysts make the same observation, while others do not. Here, as so often in discussion of gender in the transference, it is very difficult to know whether such reports reflect the emotional reality of the patient or the therapist's own countertransference reaction. For instance, we may assume as we get older that younger patients do not have sexual feelings towards us and this might lead us to miss such feelings when they do appear in the transference. Male patients may feel more anxious about expressing sexual feelings towards a female therapist who is old enough to be their mother, but this does not mean that they do not have these feelings.

Female clinicians may have less to say about the sexualised transference of male patients because their experience of it is different. They might not have been able to identify with the agenda set by their male colleagues. Contemporary male analysts often stress the positive ways in which the erotic countertransference can be used. They argue, for instance, that patients need to be able to express their own Oedipal desire in a safe context and see that even when this is reciprocated by the therapist it will not be acted upon: an experience they may not have had with their opposite-sex parent (Samuels 1993, Mann 1997). Or, on the other hand, male analysts discuss the temptation for their own sex to collude with or to act out the sexual countertransference (Lasky 1989, Meltzer 1973b). In other words, they seem either interested in dispelling anxiety about the dangers of therapists acting out their own sexual desires towards patients, or concerned to understand the unconscious fantasies that might underlie such a misuse of the countertransference.

Is it easier for the male clinician to remain aware of his counter-transference arousal because his female patients cover any hostility or contempt with a veneer of idealised eroticism? In this way the female patient and male analyst would be following culturally pre-scribed gender patterns whereby the woman submits admiringly to the powerful male. It is difficult to know. Some male therapists obviously feel that they must guard against the dangers of seducing their female patients, but generally women analysts do not share their worries. Therefore female therapists tend to discuss the erotic transference in a different way. Instead of addressing the dangers of initiating sex with a patient, they offer explanations about why they do not respond with arousal to the sexual transference. They worry about being seen as provocative or flirtatious rather than about whether they will commit acts of sexual abuse against patients or be perceived by the public as likely to do so. Certainly this was my anxiety both with the lesbian patient Ms V and with the male patient who thought I was flirting.

Women therapists seem to have their own gender-specific anxieties about containing the aggressive or abusive aspects of their male patients' sexual transferences. In the following section I look in more detail at the way the analyst's sex may affect the heterosexual transference and countertransference.

Freud's women patients presented a veneer of idealised love and flattery, beneath which was hidden enormous hostility, even contempt. This reflects my own experience of the erotic (lesbian) transference with Ms V. In contrast some male patients do exactly the reverse. Their sexuality is extremely overt and their hostility is out on the surface. An aggressive form of sexuality operates as a defence against dependency needs and loving idealisation.

Do male patients usually fall in love with their female analysts in the way Freud describes – using idealised love as a resistance to change? In my experience male patients are just as likely to retreat from love or vulnerability into discussion of overtly sexualised feelings. If the transference of a male patient to a female therapist is sexualised, it is often aggressive rather than loving. The male patient who idealises the female analyst may well keep sex out of the transference. Chasseguet-Smirgel describes one man who did idealise her in the sexual transference, something she considers rare enough to designate a 'special case' (Chasseguet-Smirgel 1986a).

An example of this is the patient described in Chapter 4, Mr A, who sexualised the transference, like all his other relationships with women, as a defence against anxieties about childhood separation. He constantly fantasised that I would make him tea, have a chat or stop the session and make love. In this way he tried to eradicate the differences between us – represented by the therapeutic boundaries – in order to return to an illusion of symbiosis with me. The woman patient who fell in love with me, Ms V, found me perfect physically and mentally. In contrast, Mr A accompanied his requests to stop the session and make love with fantasies of 'tearing my body to bits' – a very primitive aggression which emerged initially as a criticism of bits of my body. Before each break he defended himself against overwhelming feelings of loneliness and abandonment through threats of murder and rape, an unconscious attempt to project his own fear and helplessness onto me. Sometimes I found him arousing or flatteringly seductive. At other times he was charmingly innocent and childlike. But my greatest anxieties were about the sexualised hostility and contempt with which he masked his infantile vulnerability. At one point I also looked seriously at whether I might be in real physical danger, or whether he was arousing my own partly irrational fears of male violence. It is interesting that Mr A felt convinced by the end of psychotherapy that his mother had inadvertently eroticised certain aspects of his physical care.

Men may show cruelty or sadism towards a female therapist because they become so strongly aware of a dread of losing their masculine identity through incestuous fusion with the mother's body. Perhaps the same threat of loss of feminine identity is not there for the girl in father–daughter incest since it does not involve a psychic return to the earliest relationship – usually with the mother. The girl can also draw on her sense of having a different body. This might partly explain why the sexual transference of female patients to male analysts appears to be Oedipal rather than infantile and less overtly aggressive than those described by female therapists with male patients.

Another explanation for the sadism which accompanies the sexual transference of some male patients is the different relationship women and men still have to sexuality and power in many cultures. Male authority and financial control are often seen as sexually desirable. The woman who is in an authority position may well be regarded by men with a combination of fear and attraction. Perhaps unconsciously, she is associated with an imago of the dangerously omnipotent early mother. The greater taboo on mother–son incest might also be related to the fact that it overturns the patriarchal order, putting the male in the submissive position, where he – and his male body – become the sexual property of the woman.

In contrast, male patients, unaccustomed to taking up the passive, vulnerable role in relation to a woman, may feel a strong need to give up the unacceptable position of the passive analysand for the acceptable position of the male suitor. The man I described earlier, Mr A, told me of a sexual dream, saying, 'it was an equalising experience . . . If we made love, I'd be quite powerful. I'm much bigger than you. You'd be aroused, surrender passionately.' The erotic transference enabled him in fantasy to turn the tables and restore himself to a dominant position.

Describing this dynamic between female therapist and male patient, psychologist Lisa Gornick points out that in three Hollywood films directed by men (*Spellbound, Zelig, The Man Who Loved Women*) the woman analyst restores her male patient to power through having sex with him. Once the analyst falls in love with her patient, he then takes up the dominant position in relation to her (Gornick 1986).

If the sexual transference of the male patient towards the female analyst rapidly becomes overtly aggressive rather than idealised, a defence against love and need rather than a retreat into it, the countertransference difficulties will also be different from those described by male analysts. The female psychotherapist may feel frightened, undermined or humiliated by the aggression that accompanies the sexual transference of male patients more often than she feels flattered or aroused.

Statistics seem to back up the public perception that the mental health professional who breaks sexual boundaries is far more likely to be male than female. Why is this? As a profession we do need to understand more about why this does happen, so that we can prevent its occurrence in future. In Chapter 4 I described how male patients can find it difficult to allow themselves to feel vulnerable and helpless in relation to a female therapist. They feel threatened by the unaccustomed sense of being passive with a more active and powerful woman. In a similar way, male therapists may feel unbearable anxieties about their own homosexuality or psychic 'femininity' when working with assertive female patients who are able to express powerful aggression or desire. They may be quite unused to having a woman take the initiative in discussing – or even demanding – sex. If his anxieties prove unbearable, the analyst may actually become sexually involved with the patient in an unconscious attempt to assert that he is indeed masculine and heterosexual. I have often found that therapists who act out sexually towards patients have themselves experienced some abuse from their own therapist, usually in the form of broken boundaries – although not necessarily sexual boundaries.

A few female therapists do embark on sexual relationships with their male or female patients. More often they create a tantalisingly seductive or mutually idealising atmosphere where change is impossible. And of course they are just as likely to be incompetent or neglectful in other ways. But there is far more discussion in contemporary analytic literature about how difficult women clinicians find it to acknowledge or work with sexualised transferences. Seeing themselves primarily as the mother, they may infantilise their male patients, relating all desire to childhood experience rather than seeing it as adult sexuality.

In recent years more attention has been paid to the topic of erotic transferences and countertransferences with same-sex patients – an area that was previously very much neglected by clinicians of both sexes (O'Connor and Ryan 1993). Increased awareness of homophobia within the therapeutic relationship has added layers of complexity to discussion of how 'adult' or 'infantile' homosexual transferences are. Anxieties about unresolved same-sex desire may lead the heterosexual therapist to dread being the object of homosexual transferences. Or the therapist may become inhibited through misplaced attempts to avoid being homophobic.

Female clinicians' reticence about sexuality in the consulting-room must to some extent reflect a more general cultural silence about all aspects of female desire. Women psychotherapists have lacked the support of a tradition, language and imagery to express their own erotic experience, including their ambivalence about being the object of male desire.

Female analysts who do not often find sexual transferences might be avoiding the perverse contempt and sadism of their male patients (Goldberger and Evans 1985). Spanish analyst Torras de Beà describes an analysis which ended in stalemate because the female analyst could not identify with her male patient's debased projections onto her of a fat, smelly, dirty old prostitute, and so did not engage in the erotic transference (Torras de Beà 1987).

The reality that women are at far greater risk of male sexual violence than vice versa will inevitably affect what transpires in the transference and countertransference. It certainly affects referral patterns. The potential for violent or perverse sexual transferences from male patients seems to be borne in mind both by those professionals who do consultations and by female psychotherapists in private practice, some of whom are careful to avoid such referrals. Lucia Tower mentioned this issue in 1956, describing a patient whose transference was so aggressive that she thought he might not be a suitable patient for any woman. His problems might, she said, be better worked through with a male analyst who the patient could perceive as more of an authority figure and 'better able to control him'. So the female therapist has to deal with the reality that she may be at risk from an aggressive male patient as well as her own irrational anxieties about male violence. She also has to contain the male patient's great anxiety about becoming physically violent towards a woman therapist (Tower 1956).

There is a tendency with some male patients for aggression and contempt to appear soon after the maternal erotic transference manifests itself. This often seems to be defensive against anxieties about loss of male identity through incestuous merger or against Oedipal feelings of humiliation. When confronted with the emotional power of the female analyst, some male patients may have particular difficulty in acknowledging aspects of themselves that are often projected onto women and other less powerful social groups. This can result in particularly aggressive power-battles within the transference. The female therapist may avoid the emergence of the patient's sexualised hostility and contempt by creating a seductive idealising maternal transference, or by denying the existence of the patient's sexual feelings towards her.

In the following section I explore another way that external reality may affect the transference – the impact of the therapist's sex on the transference. I focus on my own experience of the paternal transference with male patients, although equally complex issues arise in other therapeutic dyads.

The paternal transference: female analysts with male patients

In classical psychoanalytic theory it is often assumed that the sex of the psychotherapst will not affect the way the transference unfolds: the patient will re-enact real and imagined relationships with significant figures of both sexes. However, as psychotherapists we may not always be aware of how our unresolved conflicts about sexual identity affect our ability to understand cross-sex transferences. For instance, Freud suggested that women therapists might be more effective in eliciting the early maternal transference. He admitted that in that area he was impeded by his own feeling of being 'so very masculine'. On the other hand, I have also come across male psychotherapists who do not realise that their patients are experiencing them as being like their fathers, brothers or uncles because they are working with mother-centred theories and see themselves as stereotypically 'feminine' or motherly. The argument that male patients rarely experience female analysts as paternal may reflect similar theoretical or personal biases (Kulish 1986, Lester 1982). Even though there has been a recent revival of interest in the father among British psychoanalysts and ego psychologists, his role tends to be seen as complementary to, or sometimes even interchangeable with, that of the mother. This might make it difficult for the analyst to distinguish when the patient is seeing her as an aspect of the actual or symbolic father.

Psychotherapists of both sexes often find it difficult to distinguish different aspects of the transference because of the kaleidoscopic rapidity with which images merge with each other or momentarily separate. The patient may well have a multitude of identifications with different aspects of significant figures. So the analyst may at a given moment represent a part of the self, or of the super-ego, or any one of a range of internalised figures. This complexity results in swift changes even within a session between aspects of the father, mother or siblings, omnipotently kind objects and dangerous persecutors, and internal and external figures. Sometimes the mother and father are experienced as an amalgam.

Some patients choose a female psychotherapist with the unconscious hope of preserving the illusion that the father is impotent or non-existent. Perhaps it is easier for some male patients to see a psychotherapist of their own sex as female than a female therapist as male. This is especially the case with regressed male patients who may, early in psychotherapy, cling to the reality of the female therapist's gender, in order to reinforce their very tenuous masculine identity. This can reflect a dread of losing a sense of themselves as different to the therapist lest they find themselves merging with her in an indistinct sexual amalgam, where their identity as male becomes completely obliterated.

In order to work in this area as therapists we need to be able to move freely between our own cross-gender identifications with the maternal and paternal functions of each parent. Nevertheless, the process of assigning gender to aspects of the transference remains fraught with difficulty, since what the psychotherapist perceives as masculine and paternal, or feminine and maternal, may not accord with the patient's experience. In the limited literature that exists in this area it is immediately obvious that psychoanalysts themselves disagree, ostensibly because of differing theoretical perspectives.

For instance, Kleinians often assume that the provision of a consistent setting, including an unchanging location and time-boundaries, is a mothering function, which helps the patient internalise a secure containing maternal object. Similarly they believe that interpretations strengthen the patient's capacity to process and understand emotional experience, an ability that is seen as maternal.

In contrast, from a contemporary Freudian perspective the analyst's maternal capacity facilitates regression while the paternal function involves (penetrating) interpretation and boundary-setting. Within this tradition the father is associated with the acquisition of language, and with providing a way out of the illusion of early symbiosis with the mother. Janine Chasseguet-Smirgel argues that the ending of the session is like a father providing a boundary – paternal assurance that the patient can return to the everyday world of consciousness. 'In its role as boundary, the setting is law, a cut-off point, a representative of the father. There exists a dialectic relationship between the setting as the definition of a space and the regression which it induces and allows' (Chasseguet-Smirgel 1986a: 41). These different perspectives reflect varying views on the father's role in the psyche. But it is also true that the paternal role can be perceived in different ways, according to family and cultural experience.

Over-reliance on theories which stress the power of the early mother can lead to neglect of the paternal transference and the misinterpretation of authoritarian or aggressive aspects of the father as the castrating 'phallic' mother (Kulish 1986).

I have often found that a feeling of dreariness or stasis in the therapeutic relationship alerts me to the emergence of a paternal transference. In the following case-example I represented the prohibitive intervening father of a male patient, Mr H. The boredom I felt might have coincided with his own frustration that he felt, as he described it, psychically 'tethered' to me as an eroticised internal mother or elder sister.

Mr H's father had died when Mr H was in his late teens. This made it difficult for him to consolidate a paternal identification which was already tenuous because of unresolved Oedipal rivalry. Mr H told me that he wanted to become a 'better man', to break the pattern of falling out of love with women once he felt sure that he had won their affections. Men who have not fully identified with the father but have instead idealised a cruel, anal version of masculinity often treat women with indifference or contempt. They have developed a homosexual idealisation of their own sex, and reserve their love and admiration for other men, so that women are treated as sexual objects. Mr H described himself as 'roaring round the country' with a gang of male friends 'drinking and whoring', as he imagined his father had done in his youth.

Discussing an anxiety attack he had had while speaking at a conference, Mr H said, 'I'm up there on the platform, and it's like saying "I've got the biggest penis, the biggest member. It's a penis in the mind, about having power, being the centre of attention." ' He went off into an eloquent speech, as if declaiming before an audience, and I began to lose track of what he was saying. 'Are you still listening?' he asked, even though he couldn't actually see me, because he was lying on the couch. I said that he feared losing me, as he worried about losing his audience during presentations. This stopped him in his tracks, and he said in good-humoured amazement: 'Are you saying that I'm boring?' I said that here, at work, and in his childhood he felt he had to entertain but was convinced that he was inadequate and empty inside. He said he'd always felt that his mother delighted in her entertaining, loquacious son. But at a certain point his father might have become irritated and said 'Shut the fuck up', and told his mother to keep him under better control. He was experiencing me as a father who could cut him down to size, setting some limits on his grandiosity.

A few sessions later he showed his immense relief at what he'd experienced as my paternal intervention. He said that psychotherapy had felt a bit stuck and slow-moving for some weeks until the session where I'd 'said he was boring'. Now he could see some changes. He was less 'paranoid', had listened to a female colleague without trying to charm her and had talked as an equal with a new friendly boss (perhaps both representatives of myself). He felt strengthened by internalising an aspect of the father and more equal to his internal mother and other women, less in danger of being swallowed up, rejected or defeated. Furthermore, his drinking, into which he'd retreated after his father's death, had 'fallen away'. He was becoming more able to think about his own emotional experience and did not need to obliterate it through alcohol.

When male patients begin to see a female therapist as having qualities that they associate with the father and men, they often recognise with relief that they can be similarly flexible, showing desires and aspects of themselves that they might previously have seen as 'feminine' or womanly. At this point the homosexual transference towards the father may emerge more clearly. This part of the paternal transference may be hard for the psychotherapist to distinguish from the maternal erotic transference. These difficulties are exacerbated when transference projections alter rapidly, as in the session with Mr H that I describe next. I was the first to speak in the session, something I very rarely do. The consulting-room seemed cold to me, and I asked him if he was warm enough. He said, 'It's VERY warm in here. AND the hallway smells strongly of fried onions.' There was a silence and then he went on:

> When someone keeps their distance, for instance, a job interviewer, or a woman in a relationship behaves as if they can take you or leave you, you think, this person is worth something. Some people are desperate. They say, this is a wonderful job we're offering here. Or a woman you spend the night with will be all over you the next morning . . . Yes, I am talking about you, as a matter of fact. You've come over all chatty all of a sudden; you are usually very schoolmarmy, cold and distant.

I was about to interpret this within the maternal transference, but realised that this felt stale and boring. However, a bossy, impatient and contemptuous aspect of himself, associated with his mother, was definitely coming to the fore. 'You're slow today', he said as he rushed to make the interpretations he expected from me. The fact that I refrained from making transference interpretations too soon may have helped him to remember aspects of his relationship with his father which had previously been quite inaccessible to him.

Mr H was soon telling me about his teenage years when his father, a big, macho, heavy-drinking labourer, would escape to the hot steamy kitchen to cook up vats of sausage-stew, wash up and darn socks while the family watched television. Mr H, fascinated, would keep going into the kitchen for big plates of the food which was so much better than his mother's cooking. He'd asked his father whether he minded doing all the cooking. Work was hard to come by, his father said, and now that his mother was the main breadwinner it would be a poor show if he did mind. By this time it was obvious to both of us that the heat and fried onion smells were associated with his father's reign in the kitchen. The sausages in his father's stew reminded him of a dream of childhood sexual rivalry and inadequacy in relation to a greatly admired but sometimes denigrated father who could do women's work yet remain a man's man.

I said that he'd felt today a similar combination of sexual fascination and contempt as with his father in the steamy kitchen. There had been something incestuous and overpowering about the unusual closeness possible with his often unavailable father, and he had also felt that with me. 'You mean I had homosexual feelings towards my father?' he asked. 'Do you think I did?'

Then Mr H retreated into safer and more familiar territory, the guiltily desired elder sister. 'I don't fancy my sister. But we're so close she's the obvious person for me to have a relationship with.' He wondered whether acting on incestuous feelings was actually harmful for children, or if it was simply a social law that we all felt we should obey. I said that at this moment he was seeing me as a sister figure, so close I was an obvious person for a sexual partnership. He wondered whether it would be actually harmful for him to act this out in reality or if he would merely be breaking a therapeutic convention. He agreed that he did see me as being like his sister, and that they had recently joked about how they might have to marry each other if their sexual partnerships continued to break up, as in the past. Then he said, 'Well, I've talked more about myself to you than anyone else'.

A few sessions later Mr H linked me with his father, describing us both as 'sweet' when we stepped out of our conventional gender roles. His father cooked; I'd used a word he saw as masculine, vulgar.

When I pointed this out he agreed, saying that 'sweet' wasn't a word he used often. Then he said 'something came up last week about sex . . . it was something to do with my father cooking . . . what do we mean by sexual?' He then went on to describe a dream of anal inter-course with a close man friend: 'I don't feel alarmed by having feel-ings like that . . . It was cosy, warm, like you're having chatty sex with a woman you're close to, not a great passion.' In fact, he said this was exactly the way he felt about talking to me.

At this point it seemed that Mr H's homosexual fantasies were an attempt to absorb masculinity; to be like, as much as to be with, the father. In order to explore and integrate his own psychic bisexuality the patient needs to see that his therapist can draw on conventionally 'masculine' or paternal as well as maternal capacities. If a patient can move from the maternal to the paternal transference in the same session, as Mr H could, it indicates that he is firmly anchored in his sexual identity (Chasseguet-Smirgel 1986a). Grappling with ques-tions about what kind of man he was, Mr H was fascinated by how his 'macho' father could have maternal functions and I could appear masculine.

I have focused in this chapter on quite well-developed transference images of the Oedipal father, showing the impact of patients' grow-ing awareness of triangular relationships. But the paternal transfer-ence – a glimmer of the 'other', a third force – will be there from the beginning of psychotherapy, even if it is reflected in confused images of an undifferentiated parental amalgam, or represented by a silence or a gap in the discourse. The patient will always know unconsciously that the psychotherapist has a life outside the thera-peutic relationship. Over-reliance on theories that stress the power of the early mother can lead to the misinterpretation of authoritarian or aggressive aspects of the father as the castrating 'phallic' mother (Kulish 1986). If the patient has been through a long period of pre-occupation with the early mother, as in Mr H's case, a feeling of frustration or 'stuckness' may herald a new willingness to face the presence of an 'other' as well as the pain of differentiating from the mother.

Conclusion

In some areas the sex of the therapist and patient does make a differ-ence to the way the transference unfolds, and it also influences the therapist's countertransference anxieties and biases. These differences reflect both the unequal position of the sexes in our society and the asymmetrical nature of boys' and girls' early experience. The countertransference is affected by the therapist's own unconscious conflicts about sexual identity as well as by his or her theoretical stance. But it is impossible to generalise about exactly how these gender-based differences will emerge since each therapeutic dyad is so unique.

Recent increased interest in the impact of gender on the therapeutic dyad reflects changing cultural attitudes towards sexuality, and especially that of women. Male analysts have traditionally been well able to speak about their experience of the heterosexual transference and countertransference but have said very little about the homosexual transference. Women psychotherapists are showing increased interest in theorising all aspects of female erotic experience.

My brief review of classical and contemporary literature suggests that male and female clinicians continue to report different kinds of experiences of the heterosexual transference with opposite-sex patients. For instance, it seems that female patients (even with therapists of their own sex) often retreat into the love transference, using it as a resistance to change, while male patients are more likely to retreat from love and dependency into overt expression of – often defensive – erotic desire. Men in psychotherapy may feel a particular need to mobilise their sadism and cruelty in the maternal transference as a defence against losing their male identity through incestuous merger with the mother.

These differences reflect the varying relationship each sex has to authority and sexuality. The erotic transference can be a fantasised way of reasserting gender dominance. The male client's aggressive sexual fantasies of dominating the needed object can create particular countertransference anxieties in the female therapist, which reflect her position in the gender hierarchy, as well as her own unresolved conflicts in this area.

Some contemporary women – including lesbian couples – consciously choose to act as both father and mother to their children. Others find themselves in this position without having planned it. These changes create particular anxieties for contemporary men, who are concerned about the increased marginalisation of their sex within the family. It is not surprising, then, that since the 1980s there has been a renewed analytic interest in the paternal transference. Theories that revolve around the emotional power of the mother often minimise the importance of the father's role in the reproduction of patriarchy and as an object of erotic desire and identification for children of both sexes. This bias may lead to particular difficulties in distinguishing paternal from maternal authority, or the male patient's homosexual desires towards the psychotherapist as a father-figure from those towards the mother. The psychotherapist's ability to draw freely on a range of same- and cross-sex identifications will profoundly influence his or her ability to help patients integrate the maternal and paternal strengths of each parent within the transference.

My emphasis in this chapter has been mainly – though not exclusively – on my experience of erotic transferences with male patients. In the next chapter I return to the question of female sexuality, focusing largely on transference issues between women patients and therapists, including the psychotherapist's difficulties in recognising and negotiating the homosexual desires of same-sex patients. Chapter 7 explores another important, and highly controversial, intersection between fantasy and external reality within the therapeutic relationship – the question of whether psychotherapists might deny the reality of actual childhood sexual abuse, or encourage the fabrication of fantasies of such events.

Chapter 7

False memories of sexual abuse?

Since psychoanalysis began there have been dramatic swings between theories that assume that patients' accounts of sexual abuse derive from unresolved Oedipal desire, and those that assume that the patient is describing a real event. These theoretical shifts reflect changing public perceptions of the prevalence of childhood sexual abuse. In recent decades questions about the 'real event' of sexual abuse have again become controversial. During the 1980s the accusation most commonly made by feminists against psychoanalytic theory and practice was that it denied the reality of sexual abuse, sentencing patients to confused, guilty silence, while exonerating abusers. But by the 1990s a fierce public debate was raging on whether psychotherapists might be so keen to discover sexual abuse that they would encourage impressionable patients to fabricate fantasies about childhood incest.

Freud may well have fallen into both of these traps as he developed his theory. Initially he took a strong public stand in favour of tracing all neurosis to repressed memories of actual childhood sexual abuse. Whereas hysteria had once been assumed to be physiological, a wandering womb, he linked it to the wandering hands of nursemaids and parents. But in a dramatic turnabout Freud changed his mind and decided that he was often dealing with fantasies about incest rather than actual events (Freud with Breuer 1895). He later acknowledged that he might have encouraged such fantasies, either through suggestion or by the physical contact involved in hypnosis. Indeed, when reading about his earliest cases I did wonder whether ideas of abuse originated from him or the patients themselves. Freud became particularly sceptical about women who alleged paternal incest. He argued that sexual abuse was more often perpetrated by older children or less closely related adults (Freud 1916–17). Until he died he continued to acknowledge that adult neurosis often originated in real childhood experiences of abuse, cruelty and neglect. He always held to the belief that it is what the mind does with a scene, not the original experience itself, that determines symptoms. However, Freud's own focus of interest shifted away from the actuality of these real events to an investigation of the patient's unconscious fantasies. After this, several generations of psychoanalysts downplayed the significance of sexual abuse as a cause of neurosis. Despite the protests of some notable dissenters, including Sandor Ferenczi, analysts came to be seen as complicit in the patriarchal silencing of women and children. But nowadays psychotherapists are as likely to be accused of falsifying the memories of suggestible patients, planting erroneous scenarios of sexual assault by adults.

In new millennium Britain, attitudes towards sexual abuse remain contradictory. There is a heightened awareness of the dangers of paedophilia. The public interest generated in the topic of 'false memory' of sexual abuse suggests enormous societal terror, such as comes with a paradigm shift in attitudes (Sinason 1998). The general consensus is that children who allege abuse should be encouraged to speak freely and listened to carefully. Yet, despite apparent dramatic shifts in attitude over the past century, psychoanalytic historian Philip Kuhn argues from an examination of recent official reports on high-profile British cases that children's accounts of sexual abuse are still not taken seriously (Kuhn 2002).

Abuse that is acknowledged as 'real' may also later be forgotten. It is astonishing how frequently those who have been abused in childhood do not remember. For instance, out of 129 North American women whose hospital records documented sexual abuse, often vaginal penetration during early childhood, 38% had no conscious memories of this as adults (Williams 1994, quoted in Sinason 1998). Similarly, it is well known that paedophiles often prove convincing liars, but research also shows that a significant number lose conscious memory of the assaults they perpetrate (Bentovim, 1998).

Recent neuroscientific research indicates that even if patients do not have explicit memories of traumatic events, they may suffer the symptoms associated with those experiences. These 'implicit' physical or emotional memories may later need to be connected up in psychotherapy with details of the actual events. Yet, on the other hand, when memories are 'planted' they may later come to be seen as true.

One of the most fascinating texts I have come across in reading for this second edition describes the involvement of paedophiles in publicising the notion of 'false memory syndrome'. In fact the man credited with coining the phrase, the North American founder of a well-known false memory organisation, had previously published articles under his own name in paedophile journals. This organisation, which has branches all over the United States and in Britain, has been active in providing expert witnesses to promulgate their ideas at the trials of parents accused of incest with their now adult children. In reading Marjorie Orr's closely documented and utterly convincing history of those involved in 'false memory syndrome' movements, I have begun to understand how far paedophiles have succeeded in discrediting psychotherapists. It is amazing that we as a profession are not more aware of this (Orr 1998).

In this chapter I look at how these rapid shifts in attitude towards psychotherapeutic work with incest survivors have affected my own clinical practice. I begin by describing how childhood sexual abuse which has been either forgotten or kept secret might emerge in the course of psychotherapy. For many decades up until the 1980s there was profound pessimism about the possibility of helping incest survivors through analysis, which was reflected in the idea that they were not suitable cases for students (MacCarthy 1988). But the new public awareness about the prevalence of childhood sexual abuse was paralleled by increased optimism and interest in work with incest survivors.

This emphasis on the 'real event' is very facilitating for those who are relatively certain that they have been sexually abused. But the recent climate of sympathetic interest may exacerbate the confusion of those who are not sure whether they really are incest victims. In the second part of the chapter I explore the interplay between fantasy and the 'real event' in the psychotherapy of a woman who suspects that she may have been sexually abused, but has no concrete memories. It was extraordinarily difficult for both of us to tolerate an uncertainty so intense that even after a long and highly successful piece of work, neither of us knew whether a 'real event' of abuse had actually occurred in her childhood. My work with her raises fundamental questions about the nature of memory, which I discuss in relation to recent psychoanalytic and neuroscientific literature. Finally I look at some implications for therapeutic technique, raising questions about the importance of reconstructing 'real' events as opposed to working entirely in the 'here and now' transference relationship.

An encounter with a spirit

Some patients come into psychotherapy unable to talk about child-hood experiences of sexual abuse. Perhaps they have told no one at all up to now, as in the case I discuss next, where through working intensively in the transference and countertransference, secrets from the past emerged quite spontaneously. Ms Y was a 27-year-old woman whose parents came to Britain from the Caribbean before she was born. She sought help from the clinic where I worked because she was having difficulty in studying for professional exams. She told me that it was no coincidence that she had begun this train-ing as soon as her mother had left the country on a long visit to relatives abroad, since she felt that she was particularly susceptible to her mother's destructive influence and that she had always under-mined her academically. Ms Y told me about how her mother pro-voked terrible rows and talked about spirits and ghosts in a way that disturbed the entire family.

While her siblings had all done extremely well at school, Ms Y had been labelled a slow learner. She described how, as the only black girl in a secondary school in a small provincial town in Northern England, she had been victimised and unfairly picked out as a troublemaker. At first I found it difficult to believe that this solid, quiet, vulnerable woman could ever have been seen in this way. Ms Y went on to say that after a visit to her parents' home-country her schoolwork dramatically improved, but when she was fourteen her mother had visited a spirit-medium, who told her that it was danger-ous for her daughter to carry on studying for the exams she was about to take. Ms Y's academic progress again plummeted, and it was only now, in her mid-twenties, that she had begun to train for the professional life she had always wanted.

Ms Y described how, although she worked hard, accidents con-tinually happened on her course. For instance, a long essay had got lost in the post and she did not have a copy. In psychotherapy she seemed similarly highly motivated, but sometimes she would not turn up to her sessions or would arrive when I was away. She always seemed terribly distressed by these mistakes and told me that she had left phone-messages or written letters which I had not received. The situation was complicated because I knew that the office in the clinic was going through an organisational crisis and messages did some-times get lost. But when she told me that a message cancelling the session had been left on her sister's answerphone, apparently by me, I knew something very strange was happening. I tried pointing out the similarity between the mis-communications with me and at college. She agreed, but could offer no explanation, although she made it clear that she felt disturbed and unhappy about what was happening.

Eventually I summoned up the courage to suggest to Ms Y that we might be dealing with a haunted transference. Perhaps, I ventured, a spirit had materialised between us, as in her relationship with her mother, and maybe this could explain the mysterious answerphone messages and the letters that were posted but never arrived? Ms Y looked at me for a moment and then burst out laughing. When she stopped, she said that yes, it did seem that a poltergeist, or some very mischievous destructive spirit was disrupting communication between us. We had now found a way of talking about a part of herself which was identified with a 'possessed' mother, and Ms Y was clearly delighted that I was not dismissing her as a troublemaker because of it.

In *Mental Slavery*, Barbara Fletchman Smith discusses the low referral-rates of people of Caribbean origin for psychotherapy in Britain. She argues that, since we draw on such culturally-specific theories of subjectivity, it is hard for us to realise that people who think quite differently can still be judged 'sane'. For instance, a belief in 'spirits' has often been seen as a contraindication to psychological help, indicating the lack of a capacity for symbolic thought. Fletchman Smith points out that 'personal experiences of control by external forces may be regarded as the norm by some people' (Fletchman Smith 2000: 91). She asks whether such beliefs are purely a defence used to project 'craziness' outside or whether alongside high levels of projection there might be a 'capacity [to hold] the good parts of the self alongside the bad parts' (Fletchman Smith 2000: 90). These states of mind might reflect past or present experiences of being subjected to extreme outside control or domination.

After talking about the 'interference' of spirits who blocked her attempts to learn and change, Ms Y told me another secret she had never revealed to anyone. She had been sexually abused – 'interfered with' – by a family-lodger when she was eight. Around then she had started to tear things apart – she would pull all the petals off flowers and take clocks and watches to pieces. Soon after this Ms Y came into her session distraught because her mother, newly returned from her travels, had become possessed by a spirit one weekend. Her mother's belief in spirits was frowned on by their church, Ms Y explained, but the family had called a priest who was skilled at exorcism, who understood all about spirits, and was not at all condemnatory. But unfortunately, although he knew how to calm her mother down, he was available only for short periods of time and then the family were left alone with her again, knowing the spirit might well return.

In discussing this, Ms Y admitted for the first time that she too believed in the literal presence of spirits, although she thought it was only her mother who was possessed, not herself. Ms Y went on to say that she was greatly relieved to be able to talk to me and that the weekly sessions provided a haven from the disturbing family events. I said that she was finding it very difficult that the part of her which had been so powerfully disruptive of her studies had re-emerged so forcibly in her work with me. She felt that I was – like the priest – liberal, able to lessen the power of the parts of her that could sabotage all her efforts to learn and communicate. But the problem was, I went on, that, like the priest, I was only available for a limited period of time. Ms Y agreed with this and talked about how paternal the priest was. She was also experiencing me as a kind of father-figure, a third force who could help her to differentiate herself from a dangerous entanglement with an envious internal mother. For reasons of his own, her actual father had been unable to help her to struggle with the experience of being possessed, taken over by chaotic disruptive forces. Now that she was beginning to put her terrible childhood experiences into words, the process of exorcism could begin.

Ms Y was extremely responsive to psychotherapy and very rewarding to work with. However, in my sessions with her I found myself grappling again with an issue discussed in previous chapters – the complex way in which cultural issues such as racism and class difference interact with psychic inhibitions about success and achievement. Fear of maternal envy was – as so often with women – a key issue. It was also noticeable that Ms Y needed a considerable period of time to build trust in me. Fletchman Smith mentions suspicion within the Caribbean community 'of the other – that is, of white people', and an assumption that problems should be solved within the family as factors that might inhibit the psychotherapy process. She also gives a powerful description of how the legacy of fear passed on by the slave trade disrupts the capacity for basic trust. This fear, she says, must be recognised as distinct from anxiety, 'because it is likely to relate to a real rather than a phantasised past' (Fletchman Smith 2000: 9).

On the subject of sexual abuse, Fletchman Smith argues that feelings engendered by traumatic displacement might cause human beings, whatever their race or culture, to behave in an unusual way towards their young. She points out that 'plantation society – in the Caribbean and in America – was created precisely with the intention of abusing human beings' (Fletchman Smith 2000: 92).

Ms Y knew that she had been sexually abused, but had never been in a situation where she felt able to disclose her secret without being blamed for it. Other people enter psychotherapy with no conscious knowledge that they have been sexually abused. This was the case with my next patient, Ms P.

Taking a professional interest

When she first came to see me, Ms P worked with incest survivors and attributed her interest in this field to the fact that she had seen her father touch her teenage sister in a sexualised way. I asked whether he had done anything similar to her, and she was absolutely adamant that neither he nor anyone else had done so. She did tell me though, that her mother thought it possible that her father had been abused by his own mother. And seeing her father touch her sister had created intensely contradictory feelings for her, including simultaneous relief that he had not done that to her, outrage on her sister's behalf, and jealousy that her sister had so clearly been the preferred object of paternal desire. Ms P also felt some guilt that, after both sisters told their mother about the sexual abuse, her mother had told the police and then left the house with the children. Eventually her parents had been reunited and the family had lived together again. Ms P now felt that what her mother had done was in the best interests of everyone concerned, but she could also remember how much pain the entire family had suffered during that period.

After several years of twice-weekly psychotherapy, Ms P had made significant changes. The witnessing of her sister's abuse had not been the main issue in her psychotherapy by any means, but nevertheless she had talked about it at length and seemed to have resolved many of her feelings about it. I was puzzled, however, by her continuing preoccupation with the whole question of childhood incest. It was beginning to be clear that she felt compelled to continue voluntary work with abused women, even though for practical reasons it no longer suited her to do so. I again asked her whether she was sure that she had not been sexually abused, and again she said she had not. But she did begin to talk more about her confusion about the boundaries between affection and eroticised touching. Like many feminists, she was concerned that her daughter should feel proud of her female body and genitals, especially since she herself had always questioned her own sexual desirability. She told me that she was not sure how to engender an atmosphere of sexual openness in the family without over-stimulating the children or being intrusive.

While talking about this she suddenly remembered that when she visited her father's mother, as she often did on her own as a child, her grandmother would lay her down to rest and then stroke her thighs in a way that had made her feel scared and distressed. In retrospect she could see that this had been a very sexualised form of touching, but that, because she had felt lonely and neglected at home, and her grandmother had made her feel so special, she had never been able to face the fact that there had been an abusive element in the relationship.

Ms P's question about how to talk openly about childhood sexual experience without being intrusive or stirring up an atmosphere of over-eroticised fantasy is equally relevant to the therapeutic transference. When I look back on my work with her I wonder whether I would now ask such direct questions about sexual abuse, given the present climate of anxiety over psychotherapists inciting false memories. But if I had been more reticent, I think it is possible that Ms P might have left psychotherapy without acknowledging her own childhood experience of sexual abuse. Might she then have repeated the cycle by sexualising the relationship with her own children instead?

Had Ms P repressed – turned away, or kept at a distance from consciousness – her grandmother's uncomfortable stroking? Or had she never thought of it as abuse before? And what enabled her eventually to put herself in the position of the abused child rather than continually thinking of her sister, or the women she cared for at work? Some years after her psychotherapy ended I contacted Ms P to ask whether I could write about this aspect of her psychotherapy. Having read what I intended to write, Ms P agreed. On this point she wrote:

> I needed to retain the 'good' grandmother in the absence of other attention and love. When my grandmother abused me something got buried or died. I repressed the memory because I did not want to feel that someone I loved deeply was bad. Therapy

helped me make a link between childhood experience and adult feelings. For instance, discussing my father's abuse by his mother led us into talking about my experiences with my nan and that opened up the possibility of her doing that to me.

Early childhood memories of abuse may also be repressed because they are associated with intolerable feelings, including sexual arousal. In his discussion of screen memories in 1899, Freud addressed the way in which we can keep a link with a memory we have repressed by substituting another, less significant memory. Although the memory of her sister's abuse was highly significant, Ms P's preoccupation with it may have screened out her experience with her grandmother. Freud says that screen memories represent the forgotten years of childhood. 'It is simply a question of knowing how to extract it out of them by analysis' (quoted by Laplanche and Pontalis 1967: 405).

Past events will constantly be reinterpreted in the light of later thoughts, impressions and feelings. We are continually rewriting our own history. So-called 'real memories' can be of thoughts, as well as of actual observable events. And thoughts may sometimes take the form of fantasy. For many people in analysis it is the very complexity, indeed inaccessibility, of their own personal store of memories 'with its interweaving of accuracy and distortion which is at the centre of the analytic process' (Scott 1988). The complex issue of disentangling real events from fantasy was central in the psychotherapy of the woman I discuss next.

Abuse: fantasy or 'real event'?

Ms N, a 35-year-old divorcee, came to twice-weekly psychotherapy for help with depression and difficulties in relationships. After her divorce she had a series of short-lived affairs with men and then a more long-term sexual relationship with a close woman friend, which also ended. She had enjoyed sex with this woman more than with men, and now felt unsure whether she wanted to settle down with a man or a woman. To her embarrassment, many everyday experiences were sexualised. At present she was very lonely and any social overture made to her immediately became eroticised in her mind. Ms N did not think anyone could want her except for sex. She would have an orgasm having her back manipulated by the osteopath, or her hair washed at the hairdresser's.

Her father had left the family to work abroad when she was one year old, and returned when she was three. As the third of four siblings, she described her mother as being more interested in older children than little ones. She also emphasised that there had been unusually little physical contact between family members. At this point I wondered whether she had eroticised a deprivation, a lack of early parental affection and interest.

The childhood physical contact she could remember was all linked with sex or its prohibition. She described how at six she had touched her father's penis curiously while sponging his back in the bath and he had quietly moved her hand away. She also remembered being hit by her mother for playing stimulating back-tickling games with her sister in bed. At eight she knew that she had shocked girlfriends with sexual jokes. Other memories were of seeking affection from male visitors to the house who praised her prettiness and singled her out from the other children for special attention.

I asked more about these experiences, letting her know that I wondered whether her relationships with adults had actually become sexualised. She was adamant that their behaviour towards her had always been restrained and protective. I accepted this and did not raise the subject again. My reason for wondering about possible sexual abuse was her unusual difficulty in distinguishing physical affection or everyday touching from erotic stimulation.

In most situations Ms N felt great confusion about the boundaries set by others and found it difficult to distinguish between different kinds of relationships. For instance, she became infuriated with me because I wouldn't 'chat' to her at the end of sessions. She also became resentful that I would not touch her, even when she was very distressed. Her silent rage and humiliation intensified after we encountered each other in the street. I said hello and agreed that the weather was warm but did not stop to talk. Apart from my usual professional reticence I was late and in a hurry. Nevertheless, she dodged along beside me, asking questions about my flat which I found puzzling and intrusive and to which I gave noncommittal answers. For over two years she returned continually to her feelings about this event, telling me how hurt and angry she felt that I was so distant in the street when she shared so much of herself in the sessions.

Whereas at first she had idealised me as benign and giving, she now began to tell me that I was cold, distant and formal, like her mother. What surprised me was that she would often say this straight after a session where I had felt warm and empathetic towards her, moved by her pain and loneliness. She began to greet me with an unfailingly resentful stare at the beginning of every session, regardless of how understanding she had found me the last time she saw me.

Ms N had always been well able to function in certain areas of her life, and since she had been coming to psychotherapy she had made some radical changes. For instance, she had returned to college to study, overcoming her lifelong inhibitions about learning. But within the sessions she remained frozen in a rigid, persecuted stance. She continued with her angry complaints about my maintenance of the therapeutic boundaries, but would become deeply suspicious that I was trying to manipulate her if she saw any sign that I might be deviating from them. She did not see my interpretations as a point of view that could be explored while retaining her own. Either I was right or she was. Often I would feel that we had negotiated some middle ground, only for her to come back next session having obliterated any memory of this, angrily insisting that I had imposed my view on her.

Ms N often compared me to her mother, who had died ten years before. But I noticed that her view of her father accorded with what she said about me. She always described him as implacably cold and uncaring, but when he discovered that she was seeing a psychotherapist he made what seemed to be a magnificent effort to reach out emotionally to her. I was astounded when she rejected him, responding with absolute cynicism about his motivation. I asked myself whether she was so rigid that she was unable to detect warmth when it was offered.

Around this time she described a vivid image of being a toddler hanging onto the bars of a cot, enraged at the pain and excitement of being forced to watch a copulating couple. She didn't know whether this image was a memory or a fantasy. I suggested that this might have been how she had felt about her parents' sexual relationship, whether or not she had actually witnessed it. This image fitted in with the rest of her sexual fantasies, which were often of watching others having sex. As soon as she entered psychotherapy she began to have fantasies which involved her looking at a male homosexual couple, as well as lesbian and heterosexual intercourse. Her dreams frequently contained images of coercive sex. One, in which a younger, smaller person of uncertain gender was anally penetrated by a large male bully, had been set in a location reminiscent of my consulting-room. She immediately assumed that I must be the sexual bully, forcing my penetrating interpretations on her. She was astonished when I suggested tentatively that this figure might also be a part of her.

Eighteen months into her therapy she engrossed herself in a book about how to remember forgotten childhood sexual abuse. She noted that the victims had similarities with her and wondered whether she had been sexually abused. She mentioned the frequency of sexual coercion in her dreams and also said that she had never come across anyone who confused body zones as much as she did, getting orgasms so easily from casual touch, especially to her back.

I was very surprised by her idea that she might have been sexually abused, since she had at first seemed so convinced that nothing like that had happened to her. I decided to make no judgements but to listen with an open mind. During the next few months she became more convinced that she had been abused, even though she had no concrete memories. Gradually she began to think that the abuse had been by a man, and most likely her father, perhaps after his return to the family when she was three. She linked this with the number three, which kept recurring in her dreams. She was aware that learning difficulties often result from sexual abuse, and connected her frequent dream-images of children who could not speak or learn with her own childhood academic problems. She speculated that she might have tried hard to tell her mother but not been believed, and then 'gone to great lengths' not to believe in the abuse herself.

We were both well aware that she still had no actual memories of such events. At one session Ms N demanded angrily, 'How can I know whether I was sexually abused or not? There's still no concrete proof. Maybe it's all your idea . . . After all, you raised the issue.' I felt stunned into silence. Eventually I managed to think more clearly and told her that it was true that I had raised the question in her first session, but I had not mentioned it again until she did. I was by now feeling very confused indeed and rather terrorised. She seemed to be re-creating in me an experience of having her sense of reality denied. But what had really happened to her? I thought carefully about my own reactions, realising that I felt tantalised – as she once might have done – but reminding myself also that a therapist is not a detective. I determined to say as little as possible when she talked of sexual abuse. She muttered darkly that she'd become more special to her father during the abuse and now felt that she'd made herself into a more interesting patient.

Soon after this Ms N produced a quite appalling and very precise image of herself as a toddler being held aloft and abused by her father. As with the image of exclusion from parental sex, she did not know whether it was a memory or a fantasy. I was simultaneously shocked and puzzled by the image. Physiologically it did not make sense and I could not reproduce it in my own mind. Finally I said that I was having difficulty in picturing it because the two human bodies could not fit together in the way she described.

She came to the next session furious with me, but what she said appeared entirely contradictory. She felt that I had disbelieved her image of abuse. But she also said 'it's only with your support that I've uncovered what I have. . . . I've never felt you loved or cared for me. My mother was not capable of those feelings ever.' She went on to say that I had been right – if she had been abused it could not have happened in the way she described. She didn't know whether the image represented a real event. It might also be symbolic of her state of mind – an unbearable state of suspension between the certainty that she'd been abused and her lack of actual memories. At this point my experience was that everything I said was likely to be wrong – a feeling she had often had in childhood.

Gradually Ms N's certainty of having been sexually abused eroded in the face of a continuing lack of concrete evidence. She felt humiliated and furious with me for letting her explore the topic as long as she had. 'Didn't you know how susceptible I am to attention-seeking?' she demanded. Later she said:

> I was trying to please you, to make myself special. But it was more than that. I was also trying to answer questions about my history that I've wondered about for a long time. I wanted to find a concrete reason, a cause for my problems, someone to blame. I always felt terribly in the wrong as a child. If I was abused it wouldn't be my fault. I wanted drama, an actual event. Now I'm not so concerned about the reason. It doesn't matter.

It was now clear that Ms N might have felt herself to be the victim of an assault on her personal sense of reality rather than an actual sexual violation. 'My family say that nothing happened to me, but something did', she said. Again she connected this trauma with her father's return to the family during her third year. She described how she had hated and rebelled against the strict rules her father had imposed on the easy-going, mother-dominated household and her pain at his apparent lack of interest in her.

During this discussion I said that I had never before heard her imply that there might have been anything warm or positive in her early relationship with her mother. To my complete surprise she burst into tears and began to talk about how she had withheld affection from her mother in her final illness, even though she knew that her mother really depended on her children. She went on to wonder whether she had wiped out early experiences of maternal warmth around the time of her father's return to the family, creating an internal image of someone cold and remote. I compared this to the way she had in the past obliterated experiences of feeling understood by me, returning to the next session furious at my coldness. She agreed with this and also speculated that her anger at my therapeutic boundaries might have been connected with that old rage towards the paternal rules that closed off her previous easy access to her mother.

Ms N began to remember feelings of sensual or erotic pleasure in relation to her mother, and described how she had recently begun to lick her fingers and curl her own hair, as she had been told she did with her mother's hair when she was very small. She now linked this with the eroticisation of her scalp. Her confusion of bodily zones might then be connected with an intense eroticisation of the sensual pleasures and humiliations of infancy, such as feeding, holding and nappy-changing, rather than in the later Oedipal experiences she had been describing. Ms N wondered whether her mother might have also eroticised the relationship in her mind. She concluded that there was no way of knowing. It was just as likely, she thought, that she herself might have sexualised some early feelings of insecurity, avoiding pain and anger through a sense of being 'exalted', her mother's special companion.

Around this time she dreamed of saving the life of a paternal figure, whom she linked with me, and then being selected from a group of women as his sexual partner. Perhaps, she now said, she had avoided facing the pain of feeling unimportant by fantasising that she had been secretly selected for sexual favours. Ms N then described how she felt she had to 'build a wall' psychically between herself and her parents, shutting them out because of their failure to understand her pain at exclusion from their intimacy. She now linked the recurring threesomes in her dreams with a lifelong hatred of triangles.

Some patients do, like Ms N, discover that they have many similarities with sexual abuse victims, and spend time discussing the issue. Usually, during the course of psychotherapy they either find some answer to their questions or resolve to live with uncertainty about the past. I am aware that the psychotherapist can find it difficult to accept the reality of sexual abuse, to bear the patient's pain and tolerate being seen as the neglectful or molesting parent. The Hungarian analyst Sandor Ferenczi, who always believed that incest was an actual cause of much adult disturbance, said that adults were 'often dangerous fools to whom one cannot tell the truth without risk of being punished' (quoted by Stanton 1990: 113).

When she first began psychotherapy Ms N seemed relatively well able to differentiate internal and external reality. But after a while it became clear that she was liable to confuse memory and fantasy. In psychotherapy she retreated into a fantasised past at a point where the transference relationship became particularly difficult. I asked myself whether I might have colluded with this. Certainly I had become frustrated with her fixed hostile transference and worried that she might be so preoccupied with uncaring internal figures that she would not be able to change through psychotherapy. So I could have unconsciously welcomed a diversion from an exclusive focus on our 'here and now' interaction.

I might also have felt anxious about the intensity of Ms N's fantasy of becoming close to, perhaps even part of, me and of penetrating into my habitat and activities. Long after she met me in the street she told me that she had thought I looked nice that day – she liked the dress I was wearing. And her puzzling questions turned out to be an attempt to add to the astonishingly complex picture she had already built up through observation and deduction about my lifestyle and the layout of my flat.

I wondered whether, if I had been able to help her acknowledge the eroticisation of her maternal transference feelings towards me, she might have felt less need to retreat into explorations of actual abuse. At the time of our meeting in the street I had suggested that her need for me to touch her and talk to her outside the sessions might indicate that she had sexual feelings towards me, as she did towards so many others in her life. But Ms N insisted that I was different from the women she 'fancied' and she had no sexual feelings towards me 'because I was cold' towards her. Only after she had eliminated the possibility of paternal abuse could she acknowledge that she had wanted special attention – perhaps in the form of an overt, unsolicited sexual gesture – both from me and from each parent in childhood.

Homosexual transferences to the mother or the father can be particularly hard for heterosexual psychotherapists to detect and work with. The therapist's own unresolved psychic conflicts about such transferences may well result in blind spots and defensive displacement of analytic interest. These are more common amongst heterosexual therapists than conscious sexual arousal or acting out. O'Connor and Ryan argue that psychotherapists who are anxious about containing the patient's homosexual erotic transference may too easily accept professions of sexual disinterest, as I possibly did. Or they may unconsciously infantilise a patient in order to perpetuate a sense of mother–baby fusion, thereby avoiding conflict and sexual feeling (O'Connor and Ryan 1993).

Can memories be false?

The mental confusion generated by childhood sexual abuse is often re-enacted in the transference, generating the kind of uncertainty I suffered. I did not know whether we were dealing with repressed memories, or fantasies of paternal abuse. Ms N was quite right in her observation that her confusion of perception, bodily zones and roles was similar to that of many incest survivors. Ferenczi argued that 'confusion of tongues' is intrinsic to abuse. Child and adult speak different languages, the child wanting maternal solicitude, as my patient clearly did, while the adult responds with guilt-laden desire – the 'language of passion' rather than the 'language of tenderness' (Ferenczi 1932). In the first abuse experience the child is swamped by a confusion of tactile, olfactory, zonal and emotional sensations and overwhelmed by the adult's anxiety and need. Ms N's capacity to change me absolutely from an empathetic to a persecutory figure by distorting her own perception of the previous session has similarities with the abused child's confusion between good and bad, love and abuse. If the very person who abuses and is experienced as bad must be turned to for relief of the distress they have caused, then the child must out of desperate need register them as good.

Ms N also knew that learning difficulties and distortions of thinking can be associated with childhood sexual abuse, and she linked this with her own childhood inhibitions about studying. Valerie Sinason points out that the really terrible effects of sexual abuse are not so much on the sane outraged child who has been assaulted once and has been able to tell and be believed, but on children who have been perniciously, secretly and lovingly corrupted over a long period in their own homes; children who in order to keep any image of a good parent have to smile or become stupid or blind to what is happening.

Layers of stupidity and numbing are needed in order to accommodate both the abuse and the precocious sexual awakening. 'To throw out the knowledge of an abusing trusted adult means throwing out other learning; to not see terrible corruption means becoming blind' (Sinason 1988: 104).

I also wondered whether we really were dealing with dissociated memories, or with assaults that had happened at too young an age for her to integrate emotionally. Figures in fantasies represent internal rather than external objects. But fantasies can also relate to bodily experiences. This may also be true of memories, which can emerge in bodily sensations and dreams. The reality of traumatic events is so compelling that knowledge prevails, although it may not be consciously accessible or complete. There are many different ways of not knowing about massive psychic trauma. At one extreme are complete dissociation and fugue states, where events are relived only in an altered state of consciousness. Both amnesia (partial, temporary or complete forgetting of an event) and hypermnesia (the inability to escape from memories, which are relived over and over again, often in a compartmentalised, undigested way, for instance through flashbacks) are characteristic of post-traumatic stress disorder. Valerie Sinason argues that those who have suffered in well-known and publicly shared disasters are more likely to suffer from compulsive remembering, while traumas which are private, secret, unwitnessed by others may well be repressed (Sinason, private communication).

The tendency to 'forget' entirely when in one state of mind, and to 'remember' in another, becomes vastly exaggerated when trauma occurs at a very young age and is repeated over and over again. When the brain cannot process all the information it is given, memory and emotion become severed. Severe childhood trauma may permanently alter the neurobiology that integrates cognitive memory and emotional arousal. This helps to explain the existence of body memories and flashbacks. The trauma returns at these moments of very high arousal, but not as words or memories. Because it has not been integrated into the totality of emotional experience it will emerge in the form of flashbacks, nightmares or visual images (Sykes Wylie 1993).

Once Ms N became convinced that her father had not actually abused her sexually, I began to think more about the implications of my work with her for the current debate on 'false memories'. Like many of the psychotherapy patients we now read about in the media, Ms N was utterly convinced for a while that I had brought up the subject of sexual abuse a second time, or perhaps had never really dropped it. This was not true. Fundamentally she and I had a good working alliance. If anything the therapeutic relationship grew stronger through this experience. But what if this had not been so? Might I have been denounced publicly as a psychotherapist who planted false memories?

Another problem is in knowing how to define sexual abuse. Incest is obviously very common. But there are many other ways in which children can be overstimulated or intruded on sexually, and this often leads to a sense of having suffered some kind of abuse. Ms N may indeed have felt traumatised by the sight of some sexual act. She might have been touched in an eroticised way, or exposed to the disturbed sexual fantasy-life of adults round her, although she had no direct evidence that this was so. Very concrete fantasies about incest may also be an unconscious way of drawing attention to some less tangible or visible sexualising of parental care. Someone might feel that they have been sexually abused in childhood while the adult concerned might be equally convinced – at least consciously – that their conduct had been quite proper.

Patients often need to speculate about the past, and may create hypothetical scenarios which they later discard as false. Ms N said that it might have been necessary for her to explore seriously the possibility of a real external trauma in order to dispel her absolute conviction that there must be someone to blame for her problems. Sometimes both patient and analyst may be avoiding difficult aspects of the transference and countertransference. False memories of childhood sexual abuse may, for example, be the expression of the patient's desire for special love from the parents or psychotherapist, and a way of avoiding the pain of not being the object of parental desire. The psychotherapist might be defending against anxieties about an eroticised transference, or the feelings of aggression or intrusiveness associated with it.

Reconstructing the past – an escape from the present?

Clinicians have very different views about how important it is for them to help the patient piece together their own history. For Freud, a principal aim of analysis was recollection of what had been forgotten, enabling the patient to fill in the gaps in his own story. A thing that has not been understood inevitably reappears. Like an unlaid ghost, it cannot rest until the mystery has been solved and the spell broken (Freud 1909).

Many contemporary analysts still see it as crucial to link present experiences in the transference with unresolved past issues. But others disagree. For instance, Betty Joseph, a post-Kleinian, says that discussion of the patient in the past or in other settings is distant and intellectual, like talking about a 'third person'. The main analytic task is, Joseph argues, to elucidate how the patient's deeply engrained mental structures are revealing themselves in the therapeutic 'here and now'. The analyst's primary focus should be on understanding the patient's desperate attempts to draw her into collusion with avoiding the pain of psychic change. Joseph argues that once emotional experience has become real in the present, the patient will be able to make historical links that consolidate it (Joseph 1985).

This exclusive reliance on interpreting the transference gives the analyst enormous power to define what is happening in the therapeutic relationship, especially when the patient is as impressionable – as prone to taking on others' ideas – and as anxious to please as Ms N. Yet at the same time the psychotherapist may lack the necessary information to understand what is actually happening in the room. For instance, sometimes children's memories are tampered with by adults, so that distortions of fact are woven into their psyches, as in the case of a patient who said that his memories had been 'rewritten' by a parent.

During psychotherapy we discovered that he had lived all his life with a false version of events. A story had been told to him in childhood about an event he had witnessed but later could not remember. As time went on we realised that initially we had not known enough to make sense of what happened in the consulting-room. It was not so much that I had been wrong; just that with new information everything took on a subtly different meaning. But, although work in the transference alone could not help my patient make links with the past, it is highly probable that it did strengthen him enough emotionally to enable him to face the truth. My work with this patient has made me aware that when an adult risks criminal prosecution or losing custody of their children, as may happen in cases of incest or sexual abuse, there may be very strong blocks on the memory of young victims or witnesses.

The approach that suits a particular patient may depend on their history. For instance, traumatised patients usually need to go through a period in psychotherapy where they concentrate on elucidating the traumatic past events in all their manifestations. If the analyst does not listen sympathetically to this, but instead relates everything to what is happening with her here and now, the patient might feel she is being subjected to a repetition of the self-centred behaviour of parental figures, who always demanded to be the centre of attention and concern. Alternatively the patient may feel that once again someone influential is concerned to avoid discussion of – perhaps even to distort – her version of reality.

The psychotherapist must be open to exploring that mysterious interface between memory, unconscious fantasy and imagination while absolutely relinquishing any assumptions about what may be discovered. If the analyst relies too strongly on interpreting the 'here and now' transference, the patient may become fiercely resistant, fearing that once again her psychic reality is being distorted by a powerful figure on whom she is dependent. The opposite danger is that the therapist may, because of her own countertransference anxieties, collude with the patient's resistance to psychic change through prolonged escape into a fantasised past.

There is a wide spectrum of subtle and invisible ways in which the physical care of children can be eroticised. This can lead to later confusion in adults who feel they may have been abused but have no concrete memories. Alternatively a difficulty in distinguishing between memory, fantasy and desire can reflect a childhood experience of psychic abuse. Patients may feel that their sense of reality was obliterated or ignored, or that there was some more systematic attempt to distort or sabotage their memory-process.

Now that counselling is routinely offered in schools, colleges and hospitals, it is not surprising that the public are intensely concerned about the nature of the therapist's influence. Recent discoveries about the prevalence of sexual abuse can be seen as a challenge to patriarchal power since they suggest that the traditional father-dominated family is often a dangerous institution for the child.

Freud always knew that his theory of childhood sexuality would continue to arouse fierce controversy, so perhaps it was to be expected that questions about the cultural power of the psycho-therapist would focus on the erotic status of the child.

Chapter 8

Female and male perversions?

In 1905 Freud made the observation that girls from some families grow up to become neurotic while their brothers develop aberrations (perversions) of sexual behaviour. In this chapter I explore why certain psychological problems predominate in one sex rather than the other. I compare a bulimic woman with a man who felt compelled to use hardcore pornography for solitary masturbation. Although anorexia, bulimia and self-cutting are still found mainly in women, in recent years these symptoms have become increasingly common in boys and men. This change has been reflected in an increased psychoanalytic interest in the 'hysteria' of men, which is often equated with psychic 'femininity'.

Through this comparison between symptoms that prevail in one sex rather than the other I hope to shed further light on the debates that have emerged around Freud's theory of perversion, and in particular the challenges that have been mounted to his view of perversion as predominantly male. Certainly some types of perversion, such as fetishism and exhibitionism, are still found almost exclusively in men. But some psychotherapists have argued that women suffer from their own specific types of perversion. These do not focus on the genitals, as in men, but on the woman's entire body or the products of her body – her children. Predominantly female problems such as self-starvation (anorexia) and bulimia (binge-eating and vomiting), which in the past might have been seen as neurotic or hysterical, are now sometimes described as female perversions (Welldon 1988, Kaplan 1991). Is this re-categorisation helpful? How do women's psychological problems differ from men's, and why?

According to Freud, sexual perversion is a deviation from genital intercourse with an opposite-sex adult as the main focus of desire and satisfaction. The sexual object may be perverse, for instance a child or an animal, or the sexual aim may be perverse, so that activities which should lead rapidly towards intercourse become an end in themselves, as in fetishism, voyeurism or exhibitionism. In perversion the pleasures of infancy and the anal stage are idealised, and the sexual instinct goes to 'astonishing lengths in successfully overcoming the resistance to shame, disgust, horror or pain' (Freud 1905a).

Freud stressed that there is no clear dividing line between perverse (or infantile) and 'normal' sexuality. For instance, although there is always a strong element of sado-masochism and rigidity in perversion, fantasies of mastery and childlike submissiveness are universal in erotic life. Initially Freud tried to avoid pathologising homosexuality, by defining it as an inversion, but his developmental theory inevitably implied that emotional maturity is synonymous with reaching the Oedipal goal of genital heterosexuality.

Freud's theory of perversion revolves around the boy's search for the penis which he knows his mother does not have. The son 'disavows' maternal 'castration', because he cannot face his own dread that he too will have his penis cut off, a fate he imagines his mother to have suffered. The pervert, whose sexuality is rigid and compulsive, is arrested at the anal stage of the toddler who battles for control over the mother and his physical functions. He clings to the illusion that he still exists in narcissistic union with a phallic, all-powerful mother, so that he does not have to face loss, pain or humiliation by his paternal rival.

The boy who simultaneously denies and affirms the maternal penis holds two contradictory beliefs at once. His ego or conscious awareness becomes split. This twisting of reality is fundamental to perversion, Freud argued (Freud 1940). The fetish represents the sexualisation of a crisis – the boy's rude awakening from the dream of being undifferentiated from his mother. The fetish may be the last object the boy sees before the mother's genitals. It is an object or a part of the mother's body (for instance a foot or a corset) which functions as a symbolic representation of the mother's penis. So for instance the transvestite – who gains sexual arousal through cross-dressing – identifies with the mother and makes the paradoxical statement that he has no penis but he gets an erection (Stoller 1979). Fetishism is bound up with the most primitive hatred of women, the 'aversion, which is never absent in any fetishist, to the real female genitalia' (Freud 1927: 353). Women do not become fetishists, in Freud's view, because the Oedipal girl has no reason to cling to the belief that her mother has a penis. It is her own lack of a penis that the girl may be concerned to deny, since the evidence that she lacks male potency is so humiliating to her.

It is clearly vital that children recognise the differences between the sexes and the generations. But within the psychoanalytic literature on perversion it is often assumed that the recognition of Oedipal difference is synonymous with a heterosexual orientation. This assumption, with which I disagree, has led to persistent questioning by clinicians and feminists about the usefulness of the theory of perversion (Cunningham 1991, O'Connor and Ryan 1993).

Pornography and male perversion

It is notoriously difficult to define what pornography actually is, and to distinguish it from erotica, especially given that attitudes towards sexual representations shift constantly between different historical epochs and cultures. Pornographic literature, like perverse sexuality, is not a separate and distinct category. Donald Meltzer refers to the 'knife-edge balance' where the depiction of passion in art tips over into pornographic destructiveness (Meltzer 1973c). Within pornography itself, there is a range of explicitness. The male patient whose case I discuss in this chapter bought videos depicting explicit heterosexual intercourse and lesbian sexuality, material that occupies an intermediate category between softcore 'girlie' magazines and the most overtly sadistic hard-core pornography.

Contemporary psychoanalysts argue that pornography differs from erotic art in the intensity of its sadistic fantasy and the perverse way it parodies sexual love. According to Stoller, at the heart of pornography is a fantasised act of hostile revenge. 'There is always a victim, no matter how disguised' (Stoller 1975: 65). The favourite fantasy of the pornography user will encapsulate his sexual life history. Stoller argues that this usually includes a passively experienced trauma connected with sexuality or gender. The adult user of pornography, no longer a helpless child, now reverses his childhood trauma, controlling and triumphing in fantasy over those who once humiliated and attacked him. Beneath the hostility of each perverse act is a dread of emotional surrender.

The British analyst Donald Meltzer says that the pornographer attacks the viewer's inner world, especially the capacity for love, creativity and reparation of emotional damage. The attack is on the original source of life itself, the mother and her sexual relationship with the father. For this reason there is no procreation, and sex is entirely dislocated from romantic love. As a male patient pointed out, 'No one gets pregnant in pornography'. The infant's pain at exclusion from parental sex proves so intolerable that the adult still needs to debase and ridicule that relationship in a parody of idealised romantic love (Meltzer 1973c).

Pornography expresses the perverse desire within all of us to push forward the frontiers of what is possible and to subvert reality. Chasseguet-Smirgel describes the pornographic obliteration of differences and distinctions, especially those between the sexes and the generations, as an attempt to avoid the reality of human helplessness in the face of psychic pain, loss and death. Pornography, which glorifies a universe of sham and pretence, reflects the little boy's idealisation of his pre-pubertal penis, his fantasy that he does not need to grow up in order to become his mother's perfect sexual partner (Chasseguet-Smirgel 1984).

Mr B: pornography and the 'cut-over'

Mr B came to psychotherapy at 27 because of depression about the breakdown of an affair with a woman ten years older. He could have been good-looking were it not for an air of isolation, as if he were set apart from others. He was very lonely despite working in a large, sociable organisation. His recently ended affair was the third of its kind – his ongoing relationships had usually been with an older woman who selected him and then dropped him after six months exactly. Not surprisingly, after what he experienced as a six-month 'honeymoon' with me, he began to find the therapeutic relationship excruciatingly difficult. Gradually evidence emerged that he may well have experienced weaning from the breast at six months as the first in a series of humiliating, bitterly resented losses. Mr B referred to an excessively rapid 'cut-over' point, a sudden shift from breast to bottle which may have coincided with his mother being hospitalised for an operation.

Like his elder brother, Mr B had slept in the parental bedroom until he was three. After that traumatic disruption the awareness that his father retained possession of his mother's body continually reinforced his pain and jealousy. He defended himself against desperate feelings of exclusion by turning to his own penis, seeking reassurance that he could satisfy his own needs. His compulsive masturbation was probably also a defence against early infantile fears of falling apart or ceasing to exist. Masturbation also represented a rebellion against his mother, who habitually tried to stop him from touching his genitals.

Mr B initially abandoned himself to the therapeutic relationship with the passive vulnerability of a very young infant. It was a long struggle for him to begin to engage with me in a real two-way exchange. I often felt overwhelmed by his sense of despair about being genuinely close to another human being.

In psychotherapy Mr B linked his mother's use of Mills and Boon novels – mass-market romantic fiction – with his own obsessive retreat into pornography. He was aware that both were addictive, escapist ways of avoiding the pain and frustration of emotional life. Feminists have argued that popular romantic literature functions as a form of female wish fulfilment and vicarious titillation. These books suggest that 'a woman doing what women do all day, is in a constant state of potential sexuality' (Snitow, quoted in Segal 1987: 154).

Mr B described how he had been seen as his mother's child, while his brother was closer to their father. His mother was highly eroti-cised in his mind but he also identified strongly with her. She 'wore the trousers', Mr B said, dominating a father whom he initially described as chronically passive and withdrawn. Within his culture women were expected to be strong-minded, and often headed the household. However, this identification with a maternal figure who laid down the law enabled Mr B to deny the strength of all his feelings about his father – his early need, his homosexual desire and his Oedipal rivalry.

Occasionally Mr B would refer to his mother as 'he' and his father as 'she'. He expressed this confusion through a fascination with pornographic images of lesbian sex, one of the most prevalent images in male heterosexual pornography. The female couple repre-sented Mr B and his mother, he thought. Identifying with his mother, Mr B also felt a combination of lesbian and heterosexual desire for her. Through banishing his father and turning himself into a girl, Mr B simultaneously denied his traumatic 'cut-over' from his mother and his current rivalry with his father. Lesbian sexuality has an enormous fascination for many heterosexual men because they can bolster themselves against anxieties about heterosexual potency by controlling the women in fantasy and imagining that only they can truly satisfy them. Women are far less likely to be erotically pre-occupied with fantasies of male homosexuality. This may reflect the dual significance of the mother for the heterosexual boy: she is the first object of identification and of desire.

Mr B spoke of his father as weak and castrated at the beginning of therapy, but in sharp contrast he later described a childhood dream where his father was represented as a powerful, unassailable sexual rival, an evil knight who kidnapped a beautiful princess–mother. After hearing him denigrate his father for several years I was amazed when he suddenly disclosed that this weak pitiable creature was actually physically strong and handsome – 'a fine figure of a man'. He now told me for the first time that his father had been an amateur boxing champion and a teenage war-hero who had survived gruelling experiences as a prisoner of Hitler's army. Mr B could also now acknowledge that a childhood revulsion against touching or sitting near his father might have masked a powerful homosexual fascination with him.

As the omnipotent voyeur of heterosexual pornographic couplings, Mr B unconsciously engaged in a shifting kaleidoscope of painful and pleasurable identifications with each parent. Through his total power over the celluloid images Mr B reversed his helpless infantile exclusion, and revenged himself on both parents. 'My dad stole mum away . . . she chose him over me. Perhaps when I see women being dominated, I feel I'm getting my own back.' He was, he acknowledged, unsure whether the women he watched were crying out in anguish or delight. Through this confusion Mr B satisfied his conflicting desires simultaneously to protect his princess–mother from the evil knight and to punish her for her unfaithfulness.

Gradually this Oedipal battle moved from the video screen into my consulting-room. Mr B fought to maintain an illusion of being the centre of my emotional life, as he had imagined himself to be the focus of his mother's. After seeing a mechanic in the street mending a car he believed to be mine, Mr B embarked on one of a series of bitter and prolonged battles for control of my presence and the therapeutic environment. It began with him noticing a weakness in one of my chairs. 'Chairs that might break,' he pointed out later, 'are like mothers who aren't there when you need them.'

Soon, his attention shifted to the perimeters of my flat. He declared my neighbourhood dangerous and the doorlocks flimsy. Angrily projecting his own aggression outside himself, Mr B pointed out that I might be intruded upon or attacked by violent men. He then stayed away for several sessions. During one of his session times he occupied himself with a pornographic book in which a man violently attacked and seriously injured his girlfriend in a sexualised assault. He came back worried about having for the first time bought such overtly sadistic material. He did not want this to continue.

Mr B realised that he used pornographic fantasy to 'bind' or contain aggressive urges. But at the same time he dreaded that constant exposure to debased or cruel sexual imagery would corrupt him, leading him to actually attack women, including myself within the maternal transference. Unconsciously he had stayed away to protect me from an actual aggressive attack, and was mortified to realise how violently he had assaulted me in fantasy.

Interestingly, given my focus on escapist psychological activities, I responded to this alarming incident by immediately forgetting the vicious details of this fantasised attack on my body. This imaginary assault seemed temporarily to suspend my ability to think about the therapeutic material, and I only remembered it when re-reading my notes months later. Presumably Mr B was projecting onto me his intolerable anxieties about acting out his aggressive feelings, and I was reacting with an only partly conscious fear of male violence.

For his part, Mr B gradually admitted how anxious he was with me, as he had been with his mother; that the boundaries between aggressive or sexual fantasy and real events might become blurred. He experienced this with particular acuteness at the beginning and ending of sessions, 'when the barriers go down and then come up again'. If we really looked at his inner feelings and fantasies, would we, he wondered, be able to maintain the transference as an 'as if' relationship? Would I be able to ensure that the professional boundaries remained intact, or could we be talking about a real love-affair, or an actual physical attack?

Pornography had provided an addictive means of escape from unresolved infantile anxieties. I was becoming increasingly aware that Mr B might be using the therapeutic relationship in a similarly escapist way. 'I was waiting for you to do all the work . . . become my girlfriend, take me out', he said. With me, as with his mother, a façade of passive compliance belied a silent eroticised rebellion.

Mr B's use of pornography was a compulsion rather than an addiction. It was not an organised perversion, since he could enjoy genital sex without the use of pornography. He reduced his dependency on it greatly during his short-lived relationships with women. Yet Mr B's fantasies were extremely convoluted. I found some of the literature on perversion helpful in understanding how he drew me into collusion, 'twisting' my sense of what was actually happening between us. Freud observed in 1914 that people whose sexual lives are deeply committed to perversion do not come to analysis to be cured. Like all those for whom addictions or perversions have become more real than social relationships, Mr B wanted initially to moderate his use of pornography so that he could continue to use it while maintaining a veneer of stable heterosexuality. Pornography was like a treasured love-object, always there when he needed it, unlike an actual woman who might eventually leave him. It was a great struggle for him to give up such a reliable love-object. He would tell me he had incinerated it all, but later confess that he had kept one pornographic magazine, which would eventually become the basis of a new collection.

The danger for a therapist with a patient like Mr B is that he will 'make a concerted effort at certain stages . . . to dislodge the analyst from his accustomed role and to convert the entire procedure into one which has the structure of their perverse or addictive trend' (Meltzer 1973c: 136). For instance, in one session I was puzzled by jokes he was making about a bawdy passage of Shakespeare and only realised afterwards that he was trying (with some success) to draw me into collusion with a pornographic discourse.

The perverse transference is characterised by extremes of idealisation for the analyst and the psychotherapeutic process, combined with cynical contempt, argues Meltzer. Mr B's attitude did shift with extreme rapidity between scorn for me as a deluded fool committed to a useless process and idealisation of me as the source of all wisdom.

Likewise, at times I found myself idealising Mr B's progress in therapy. I was like a doting mother, seeing signs of change always around the corner, however slight the evidence. Does the female therapist more easily fall into this countertransference trap, taking up the role of the idealising mother? And are male therapists more likely to be drawn into a collusive form of infantile sexual enjoyment with such a patient, as Meltzer suggests? In one session I thought that Mr B was working hard and using all my interpretations creatively. I afterwards discovered that his main preoccupation had been with the strip-show he planned to visit as soon as he left my house, as a prelude to a weekend 'pornographic binge'. This replicated the way he had bided his time helpfully until his unsuspecting mother went shopping so that he could then raid his brother's hidden stock of pornographic magazines.

The despair at the root of this determination to keep the perverse or addictive habit must, Meltzer argues, be resolved in therapy before the struggle against the underlying problems can be initiated. Mr B was also desperate not simply to 'paper over the cracks' but to achieve radical change.

He decided to end psychotherapy after beginning a new and apparently serious sexual relationship, the first since he had begun seeing me. After four difficult years, distinct changes were visible. I suggested to him that he might stay longer to consolidate some of these psychic shifts, but he felt strongly that he was ready to leave. It had been noticeable for a while that he had developed sociable hobbies, a network of real friends and, astonishingly, a reputation as a dynamic social organiser. His air of being set apart from the world, perhaps the result of an identification with an elderly sick mother, had dissipated and his natural good looks were now visible.

His new girlfriend differed from previous lovers in being slightly younger than him and more a peer than a maternal figure. His use of pornography had diminished and then stopped a few months before he met her. He could now think about his need and destructiveness in a new way. He did not now feel so compelled to 'bind' his aggression through perverse eroticism for fear of actually acting on his impulses. His ambivalent preoccupation with a dominating internal mother had lessened now that his father had emerged as someone worth identifying with.

Bulimia: hysteria or perversion?

Ms K was a depressed, recently divorced 28-year-old. As far as she knew, her infancy was relatively contented until, when she was eighteen months old, her much-loved father died. She might have coped with that loss were it not for another death. Her little brother died during her fourth year. She held herself responsible for this accident, the mysterious circumstances of which were never discussed in her family.

Ms K remained constantly preoccupied with this second death. Through her bulimia, which began when she was 20, she attempted to vomit up a dead internal object, which her guilt had prevented her mourning. This followed a childhood habit of binge-eating, since in her family food was seen as 'the only legitimate female pleasure'. Like Mr B, Ms K felt that her mother had unwittingly aroused her sexually, by stroking her legs in a way she found tantalisingly erotic. She also, like him, experienced her mother as possessive and controlling, yet also absent or preoccupied at crucial moments. During and after her marriage Ms K rebelled absolutely against the strict religious prohibitions against female sexual pleasure which she had internalised as a child.

Ms K's mother defended herself against her own feelings about these two tragic family deaths through immersing herself in fundamentalist religion. She expected her daughter to do the same. 'God wanted little James' was all Ms K's mother would say about the accident. As a result, whatever capacities the little girl had developed to tolerate and digest emotional experience disintegrated. She would rush into her early therapy sessions, flood me with desperate, disorganised emotion, gulp greedily at my interpretations like a starving infant, and rush off again to binge sweet milky food and vomit up the whole experience in secret.

Ms K's fear of damaging me was intense, since she felt that her childhood rivalry had killed the little sandy-haired brother who was now re-emerging in the transference relationship with me. Initially, her intense need, rage and rivalry were evacuated secretly through bulimia. As her brother's mysterious death was slowly reconstructed from fragments of memory and dream, her actions communicated her overwhelmingly powerful sense of guilt. I became worried by the strength of her urge to destroy herself or allow herself to be destroyed.

The theory that women tend to somatise psychic conflicts was crucial to Freud's early writing on hysteria, and also to contemporary arguments about female perversion. Freud recognised that hysterics could be male, but he focused on women's tendency to express their more culturally repressed sexuality in a disguised way through hysteria – physical symptoms that are emotional in origin, such as anorexia, nervous 'tics' and partial paralysis (Freud with Breuer 1895). The prevalence of hysteria in women, Freud argued, was due to their peculiar difficulties in transferring their love from mother to Oedipal father. Poised between the maternal and paternal object, the hysteric 'wanders' between them, forever rejecting those who love her, always seeking the unattainable. She is unable to love when sex is present because of her inability to resolve the incestuous Oedipal conflicts at the root of all human desire.

From a Lacanian perspective, the hysteric does not know whether to identify her body as male or female. The culturally imposed sexual divide is, according to Lacan, the cause of a fundamental psychic split which sets both sexes on a path towards incompletion. If anyone is pushed beyond the limits of their knowledge and capacity to articulate emotion they can become hysteric, Lacan argues. Hysteria is seen as an expression of dissatisfaction with the limits of existing knowledge and convention. Attention to the questions underlying the hysteric symptom can advance cultural, clinical and academic knowledge (Ragland-Sullivan 1992).

In many ways Ms K did fit the category of hysteria – as indeed did Mr B – but is this way of thinking helpful? It is possible to understand bulimia in other ways, without defining it as hysteria – or indeed perversion. Contemporary analysts who have abandoned Freud's central emphasis on erotic life might relate Ms K's somatising of emotional pain to unresolved conflicts in relation to the mother. These re-emerge at crucial points of the physiological life cycle, such as puberty, pregnancy and the menopause (Pines 1986). As Luce Irigaray says:

> The girl has the mother, in some sense, in her skin, in the humidity of her mucous membranes, in the intimacy of her most intimate parts, in the mystery of her relationship to gestation, birth ... she does not want to master the mother, but to create herself.
> (Irigaray 1989: 133)

Freud's grandson Ernst threw a spool of cotton backwards and forwards in an attempt to come to terms, in a symbolic way, with his mother's coming and going from the room. Irigaray points out that the girl cannot objectify the female body as the boy does, symbolising it as something quite other, a spool. The girl is more likely to react to the mother's absence by becoming so distressed that she can neither eat nor sleep – symptoms that may be precursors of adult eating disorders.

Girls do not, Irigaray says, play with the backwards and forwards, angular, in–out movements made by Ernst with his spool, movements that are reminiscent of the penis in masturbation. In play, girls keep their entire bodies moving, their skipping games, dances and drawings often describing a series of womb-like circles, turning around and inside themselves. The girl is 'split differently in two', and the aim of all her movements is to reunite, to make whole, while keeping separate, the lips of her vagina, her breasts, her mother and herself (Irigaray 1989: 134).

Ms K's maternal preoccupation was exacerbated by the lack of a significant third force, someone 'other' than her mother, a paternal force who might arguably have been male or female. Ms K experienced herself and her mother as identical, both simultaneously beautiful and repulsively fleshy. In therapy sessions it was as if, in fantasy, she wrapped herself around me and became me. When this first happened, I had the sudden alarming feeling that, without understanding how or why, the ground had been cut from under my feet and I had lost all sense of who I was. When I expressed this feeling of intense disorientation, Ms K began to voice her fantasy of having stepped into my skin, sat in my chair and become the therapist rather than the patient. At this point, I began to regain my capacity to think and understand.

During this phase of the therapy Ms K arrived wearing clothes as similar to mine as possible. For the first time she became visibly enraged with me in a session. Her anger focused on the fact that I wore an unpredictable colour, one she disliked too much to copy. In fantasy she could control us. Imagining that she possessed all our attributes, she could avoid experiencing envy or other uncomfortable emotions.

But her bulimia also revealed a deep dilemma about her sexual orientation. Ms K wanted to come between her parents and have exclusive possession of each. She could not, she insisted, face the idea of her mother or myself being part of a sexual couple. 'It makes me feel ill', she said. After arriving an hour early for her session one morning, she acknowledged fantasies of bumping into the man in my life and luring him away. Her feelings about parental sexuality may have remained unresolved because of her father's premature death. They were exacerbated by her own guilt about her brother's death. But she also felt a desperate need to bring her parents together, accepting them as a couple inside her, so that she could relinquish her obsession with them and build her own adult emotional life.

Ms K insisted that, although she wanted a permanent love-relationship with one person, psychically she would always be bisexual. I might nowadays wonder aloud about what Ms K meant by this. For instance, would making a commitment to one person be more problematic for her as a lifelong bisexual than it would be if she were lesbian or heterosexual? Or would she simply be able to accept that she was with a person she loved, and was therefore happy to sacrifice all the other attractions she might feel?

In her therapy, as in her life, Ms K wanted a woman when she was with a man, and a man when she was with a woman. This had repercussions for her identifications as well as for her desire. Soon after a holiday break, feeling overwhelmed by a rage and devouring need, she attempted to vomit up the therapy by visiting a male psychiatrist. Yet in reality her mother had acted as both parents, and was, Ms K told me, a 'sexually ambiguous figure whose behaviour was sometimes more male than female'. She associated the psychiatrist's emphasis on adjusting surface behaviour with her mother's methods of control. But he also 'gave her licence', as she imagined her father might have done, to risk a period of depression if she gave up her bulimic symptom. Angry at the psychiatrist's confrontational style, she decided 'out of cussedness' that she could give up bingeing and vomiting while remaining in therapy with me, 'rather than doing it with strangers'. In fact, she did give up vomiting, and – more gradually – binge-eating. She had begun to internalise me as a paternal figure who could set limits and boundaries.

Seeing herself as very feminine and wanting a stronger identification with 'masculine' forceful decisiveness and personal authority, she had fantasies of having a penis temporarily attached to her. When she stood up tall and erect to give an important paper at an international conference, she had the momentary feeling that her body was like a penis.

Nowadays an epidemic of obesity threatens to affect both sexes in some societies. But still women remain more prone to anorexia and bulimia. Why is this? The girl's identification with her mother's capacity to produce food from her body before and after birth may well be crucial. Ms K's observation that within her sexually repressive culture eating was women's only legitimate pleasure is vitally important. Stereotypically, her mother's life revolved around the providing of food.

The cultural ambivalence towards women's bodies and procreative capacities – which are simultaneously idealised and denigrated – is another fundamental reason for female anxiety about weight and size. The desire to maintain a certain image of femininity may serve to exacerbate eating problems that might otherwise remain minor.

The female bulimic – or the hysteric – clings to an illusion of omnipotence through fantasised control of the maternal body while resisting full identification with its reproductive capacities. It is significant that Ms K both sought and resisted identification with what the father represents in our culture. She eventually relinquished her symptom as she took up a more influential position in the wider world.

In contrast, men often act out their dilemmas about differentiation from the mother and identification with the father through a preoccupation with the penis, and with eroticisation of early need and aggression. For men in our society there are many institutionalised ways of simultaneously denying and clinging to the repudiated 'feminine' aspects of their own psyches, most obviously through a preoccupation with denigrated – or pornographic – representations of the female body which can be controlled in fantasy.

In different ways, bulimia and the compulsive use of pornography reflect a preoccupation with objectification and sexual looking. But in our society women are usually the object of the male gaze, while men watch. Ms K described herself as feeling from infancy onward like a pretty, passive doll, to be displayed enticingly and played with by others. It had taken her a long time to realise that she could actively engage in her own sexual life. This sense of objectification was reflected in her concern with the physical functions of her body and its fluctuations of weight. It also revealed itself in her anguished fascination with attracting and repelling the advances of voyeuristic men.

Mr B's main preoccupation was in looking at others, who represented his mother or the parental couple. But the voyeur is always an exhibitionist, and he also experienced himself as a passive feminine object awaiting the advances of motherly princesses, an identification which was enacted through pornographic images of lesbian sexuality.

Each of these patients identified with a maternal figure committed to emotional escapism – romance and fundamentalist religion – through whom they could not internalise the capacity to process and learn from their own psychic life. Instead there was a demand that they maintain a veneer of total filial conformity or 'polished perfection'. No paternal figure (of either sex) helped them develop an internal regulatory capacity through which they could set limits on their physical and emotional appetites. Instead they each remained preoccupied with psychic struggles against a dominating internalised mother, who laid down the law, against which they secretly rebelled.

Sexual perversion: is it male?

Is perversion a gendered category? Freud, as we have seen, categorised perversion as male, arguing that the boy's pride in the penis induces a fear of losing access to paternal potency and privilege. In Freud's theory the perverse male disavows his knowledge of sexual difference. He avoids Oedipal rivalry and identification with his father by idealising his own infantile sexuality and becoming fixated on a perverse search for the maternal penis. Freud argued that the girl reacts to her genital lack with humiliation and envy (Freud 1910b). The female sex is therefore less ruthless, more tender and sentimental in all areas of life, including the sexual, he claimed.

Janine Chasseguet-Smirgel endorses Freud's view that boys are far more likely to short-circuit development through perversion. She argues that mothers often collude with the son's fantasy that he is already her ideal sexual partner, as Mr B's may have done. The mother of the neurotic girl does not make her feel special and desirable, but excessively devalued. The girl who has been loved too seductively by the father becomes neurotic rather than perverse, because she has usually been 'made to wait' until toddlerhood for her father to become interested in her. She is not so easily seduced into the illusion of being the centre of a parent's life (Chasseguet-Smirgel 1988).

The strongest part of this argument is Chasseguet-Smirgel's stress on how the boy is encouraged to overvalue his genitals and his sexuality. But this is not purely because of the mother's seductive attention. It relates to the general cultural fetishisation of the penis, which is regarded with awe and admiration as well as fear. Like many contemporary analysts, Chasseguet-Smirgel blames the mother for perversion, thus leaving many questions unanswered. It may well be true that, since the father is usually not the primary parent, a seductive attitude on his part may not have such a fundamental effect on the child's identity as maternal incest. But this ignores the prevalence of actual sexual abuse, which is most often perpetrated by the father against the daughter and inevitably has a fundamental and entirely destructive effect. I also disagree with Chasseguet-Smirgel's assumption that mothers will not desire their daughters unless they are perverse. Many actively heterosexual women have a strong component of bisexuality, and the mother's sensual pleasure in the daughter need not be harmful unless she is unduly seductive. In fact maternal desire is an important component of the girl's sense of herself as beautiful and lovable.

Some analysts agree with Freud that certain perverse sexual acts are a mainly male phenomenon, but they give a different explanation. They argue that each sex has a separate line of sexual development based on their different physiology, which leads to gender-specific ways of defending against psychic pain. For instance, they say, women do not need fetishes as the sole means of arousal because they can conceal their lack of sexual excitement or pleasure. For men, in contrast, interference with potency obviously and drastically affects sexual performance. Female pride is, therefore, usually less invested in erotic performance. Therefore fetishism usually occurs in women only when the idea of being male is strong enough to become a delusion (Greenacre 1979).

Similarly, Freud argued that since women experience their lack of a penis as a narcissistic injury, exhibiting the genitals outside the sexual act as a way of gaining sexual satisfaction does not reinforce female pride. In contrast, the male exhibitionist who 'flashes' his genitals protects himself from extreme castration anxiety and gains a gratifying sense of potency through the fear and shock of his female victim. Men may well be more proud of their erect penis than women of their genitals. But what is even more significant is that both sexes associate the male genitalia with rape. Behind many male perversions is an implicit threat of sexual aggression. In contrast, where the female genitals are displayed, as in pornography, the expectation is that the onlooker will be aroused. The woman who shows her genitals offers herself as an object, inviting rather than threatening the viewer.

Expectations of female sexuality have changed greatly since Freud's day in many societies. His assumptions about the differences in men's and women's erotic life now seem dated – as does his resort to physiology to back them up. Indeed, there is no evidence that women experience less sexual desire than men, although it is often mobilised in different ways. Ms K, although similar in some ways to Freud's 'hysteric' patients, was actually far more sexually active and adventurous than Mr B, whose symptom was more directly eroticised. For instance, she acted out her bisexual desire towards women, while Mr B only gradually became able to mention his attraction towards men. There is much current media interest in the idea of a new, sexually assertive and perhaps predatory female who might be interested in softcore pornography and male strip-shows. Some feminists argue that the 'conventions of gender and sexuality are . . . being actively tampered with . . . Maybe it isn't a sexuality which wholly breaks free from the oppressive codes of women as sexual commodities but neither does it straightforwardly reproduce them' (Winship, quoted in Segal 1987: 154). Yet despite these cultural changes, as Ms K pointed out, most women are still brought up to think about attracting and pleasing others rather than satisfying themselves sexually.

It is certainly true that some organised perversions are mainly found in men. This seems to be related to men's overvaluation of the penis and the cultural assumption that male sexuality is beyond conscious control, as well as to a different early relationship with the parents. In contrast women tend to remain preoccupied with somatising psychic pain and aggression through their own bodies, which they unconsciously identify with the maternal body. But perverse fantasies, where aggression is more dominant than loving concern, are just as common in women, who also engage in some of the activities Freud saw as perversions.

The case for female perversions

The idea that there is a special category of female perversion has recently become influential. Eating disorders, self-cutting, female prostitution and maternal incest have all been included in this category (Welldon 1988, Kaplan 1991). It is argued that women do not direct sexualised aggression towards an objectified other, as in male perversion, but instead form a perverse relationship with their own or their children's bodies.

One reason given for this is that the entire female body is eroticised, with pleasure zones located all over the body (Irigaray 1977, 1989). From a Kleinian standpoint it is argued that, while the boy can check that his penis is still intact, the girl's fears about damage to her reproductive and genital organs cannot be so easily allayed by reality-testing (Klein 1928). These anxieties may be reinforced by the onset of menstruation, which the girl may associate with harm to the inside of her body. Women who constantly feel very concerned about their appearance, as bulimics tend to, may unconsciously be attempting to compensate for imagined internal damage and decay.

Those who argue that there are specifically female forms of perversion often define perversion in a different way from Freud, who saw it as an exclusively sexual phenomenon. They may instead focus on questions about whether sexual fantasy life reflects a capacity for loving concern or a sado-masochistic dehumanisation of the other.

Kleinians see perverse character structures as equally pervasive in women and men. Perverse sexual activities do not necessarily exist, but the distortion and twisting of truth leads to a perverse 'borderline' relationship to reality. In analysis the perverse patient 'turns a blind eye' to insight, seeking help but failing to use it (Steiner 1987).

The problem with the contemporary literature on female perversion is that the definition has become so broad that it ceases to be meaningful, often including most typically female ways of mobilising psychic pain. It is easy to see how bulimia can be described as a perversion of the eating process, since it subverts the digestive process breaking the link between eating and nourishment. But are all eating problems perverse? Similarly, Estella Welldon argues that prostitution is a female perversion because it affords the opportunity to practise perverse activities while disowning the desire to do so (Welldon 1988). Again, how do we categorise prostitution that does not involve perverse activities? And how do we view those who are forced to sell their bodies through forms of sexual slavery?

While bulimia can be compared to perversion, it is also different in many ways. Bulimia was likened to masturbation by a female patient who described how her initial overwhelming excitement came to a climax when she vomited, to be followed by a sense of postprandial depression. For the bulimic the digestive process has become eroticised, but binge-eating and vomiting differs from perversion in that it does not provide direct sexual gratification or orgasmic release. This is very significant in clinical practice. There is less secondary gain in serious eating problems than in perverse sexuality. So, when a patient is highly motivated, as Ms K was, it is much easier to renounce the symptom and begin working on the underlying conflicts.

Pornography had been Mr B's most consistent love-object since adolescence, and when he first came for psychotherapy he wanted to moderate his habitual use rather than give it up absolutely. He was intensely dependent on me, but it had become a pretend psychotherapy, and I was sometimes temporarily deluded into idealising a sham.

In contrast, Ms K's transference relationship with me was bulimic so that she binged and vomited analytic nourishment in a self-destructive way. But, because she did not idealise her bulimia and her erotic life did not revolve so strongly around it, she did not need to involve me in such an insidiously twisted collusion.

In my view the term 'female perversion' is limited in its usefulness. The really positive aspect of this debate is that it brings women's sexuality into psychoanalytic view. But the focus is still on women's reproductive role and their identification with the mother. Yet again women are not seen as sexual subjects, with their own will and desire.

Some writers draw on the psychoanalytic literature on perversion to develop a radical understanding of how gay and lesbian eroticism transgresses the patriarchal social order. I do not think it is possible to reclaim the term 'perverse' for sexually subversive ends unless we entirely alter its meaning. Intrinsic to the psychoanalytic definition of perversion is the idea of a deep commitment to cruelty, dehumanisation and twisting of individual emotional truth. Rather than describing some activities as perverse – whether these be homosexual or heterosexual – I would define perversion in a more general way, focusing, for instance, on the degree of love and concern in unconscious sexual fantasy life.

Conclusion

Both 'perversion' and 'hysteria' are seen by many as pejorative terms. I imagine that many people we see in psychotherapy might not wish to be described in these ways. And they are not value-free, but are laden with normative and biologistic assumptions. Nevertheless, a clinical literature exists that is illuminating in working with some patients.

I cannot see the point of defining stereotypical ways of mobilising psychic pain as female perversions – or indeed as hysteria – rather than simply as forms of unhappiness. I do not see perversion as a gendered category, although there are some organised perversions that are mainly male.

Cultural – and psychoanalytic – denial of the power of female sexuality reflects envy and anxiety in relation to the early mother. In contrast, men still seem more prone to sexualising pain and rage, focusing on their genitals – which are overvalued in many cultures – and attacking an objectified female body in fantasy. In these ways men can deny their early need for their mothers, since in fantasy they possess the womanliness they master.

The boy who feels that his wish to be like his father is not accepted lovingly may become fixated, continually needing to reassure himself in very literal ways that he is virile and potent. This fixation conceals an intense repudiated homosexual desire. In contrast, the girl who has been offered no pathway out into the external world and who cannot find a way of identifying with the psychic 'masculinity' of either parent may act out her sense of being trapped through attacking her own body. Clearly there is a relationship between gender-linked symptoms, early development and male–female power relations. Much more work needs to be done on these areas, and particularly on the interconnection between physiological experience, unconscious fantasy and social forces.

In Chapter 9 I continue my focus on Freud's ambiguous theory of sexual inversion, exploring sexual orientation – another longstanding source of profound and painful controversy within the world of psychoanalytic psychotherapy. In recent years, with increased access to training, gay men and lesbians have had an increasing influence on theory and clinical practice. But this increasingly liberal attitude often conceals institutional and clinical ambivalence to those who desire their own sex – or both sexes.

Chapter 9

Differing desires

Since this book was first written there has been a dramatic shift in psychoanalytic attitudes towards lesbian and gay sexuality. Homosexuality created an irresolvable theoretical dilemma for Freud, who argued against those who wanted to 'abolish' it. Writing to an American colleague who wanted analysts to take a strong moral line with patients, Freud said, 'Sexual morality as society – and indeed American society – defines it, seems very despicable to me. I stand for a much freer sexual life' (Dollimore 1991: 172). Freud and his early followers tended to have a liberal cosmopolitan stance towards homosexuality, placing great emphasis on the cultural and artistic achievements of homosexual scholars and thinkers throughout the centuries. Sandor Ferenczi campaigned for the legalisation of homosexuality (Stanton 1990) and in 1935 Freud wrote a 'Letter to an American Mother' in which he said, 'Homosexuality is . . . no vice, no degradation; it cannot be classified as an illness; we consider it to be a variation of the sexual function . . . It is a great injustice to persecute homosexuality as a crime – and a cruelty too' (Freud 1935b).

Freud stressed the continuity between heterosexual and homosexual love, saying that he had never conducted a single psychoanalysis without 'having to take into account a very considerable current of homosexuality' (Freud 1905b: 95). Freud also emphasised that inhibitions in the capacity to love may stem as much from difficulties with the same-sex parent as with the parent of the opposite sex.

It is ironic, then, that in 1993 the writers of a book on lesbianism and psychoanalysis should conclude that homosexuality has been 'the site of some of the worst excesses of psychoanalysis – gross and inaccurate generalisations, explicitly manipulative goals of therapy and a striking failure to consider vital countertransference issues' (O'Connor and Ryan 1993).

In fact Freud never finally decided whether homosexuality was a valid sexual orientation or evidence of pathology. Initially he described homosexuality as an 'inversion', differentiating it from other deviations which he called perversions (Freud 1905a). Later he wavered, sometimes placing it more clearly among the perversions. Despite his liberal convictions, he explicitly associated homosexuality with arrested development, describing it as a narcissistic object-choice – seeking the self in the guise of another.

Campaigns within the profession have resulted in the explicit renunciation of homophobic practices by at least one mainstream organisation – the American Psychoanalytic Association. The 2001 issue of its journal focused on the theoretical and clinical implications of this decision to de-pathologise lesbian and gay sexuality (*Journal of the American Psychoanalytic Association* 2001). In Britain the situation is more mixed. I have seen during the past decade a sea-change in attitudes among psychotherapy trainees on some more liberal British psychoanalytic trainings. But a recent survey of attitudes within the most orthodox trainings reveals an uneven picture of anxiety provoked by change and the continued existence of confused countertransference feelings towards homosexual psychotherapists and patients (Ryan 2002).

In this chapter my emphasis is on the precariousness of all sexual orientation and the way heterosexual and homosexual desire coexists in all of us to varying degrees. Recent theoretical reappraisals raise important questions about how we view bisexuality as an adult sexual orientation. I explore the negative clinical impact of pathologising theories and draw on contemporary writings which might underpin a psychotherapy practice that gave equal validity to differing sexual orientations. Using clinical examples, I discuss the interaction between gender and sexual orientation and the impact of internalised homophobia on the transference and countertransference.

Different cultural attitudes towards homosexuality

The idea of a homosexual identity is a phenomenon of late-nineteenth- or early-twentieth-century western society. Freud's *Three Essays* were written at the point when medical and psychiatric theories were being elaborated that described homosexuality as a condition, a part of someone's nature, perhaps even biologically determined (Freud 1905a).

Homosexuality has often been permitted as long as it does not infringe culturally sanctioned male and female behaviour. A prohibition against deviation from whatever gender roles are culturally prevalent is almost universal (Liebert 1986). For instance, although certain male homosexual acts were permitted in Ancient Greece, sexual passivity, in the form of oral and anal receptivity, was permitted only among men of the lower social orders (non-citizens). In post-Renaissance Europe and America, 'special friendships' and sometimes even sex between women were tolerated, as long as these relationships could clearly be seen as an adjunct to heterosexuality. It was when women demanded masculine social privileges, or made open declarations of a sexual preference for their own sex, that they were condemned or punished (Faderman 1992).

For a number of social reasons, including the need for an educated, mobile workforce involving large numbers of women, it gradually became possible for the first time during the twentieth century for increasing numbers of people to live outside the nuclear family in the USA and some parts of Europe. Despite the increased visibility and toleration of homosexuality, persecution has continued to the present day. Contemporary culture has expressed simultaneously the urge to displace rejected aspects of social and emotional life onto homosexuals, and the liberal desire to integrate different sexual orientations. In its theoretical contradictions, psychoanalysis reflects both of these cultural tendencies.

Male homosexuality

Believing that sexual orientation might be determined by a combination of constitutional and environmental factors, Freud offered at least seven explanations for different forms of male homosexuality (Lewes 1989). Among these were an example of the boy who had overwhelmingly loving feelings towards his mother. He might become exclusively homosexual through an unconscious wish to remain faithful to her, choosing a man he can love as his mother loved him (Freud 1905a). On the other hand, intense hatred and fear of the mother might also lead to exclusive homosexuality. However, these childhood scenarios do not provide any kind of definitive explanation for homosexuality, since in my experience they can as often be found in the histories of heterosexual men.

Freud describes another form of homosexuality as equally common in both sexes. Instead of retaining his mother as the object of desire and identifying with his father, the boy takes both parents as erotic love-objects, while identifying with each (Freud 1918). If the resulting homosexual longings are repressed, they lead to inhibitions within heterosexual relationships. Here Freud made a distinction that became crucial to later psychoanalytic theories of homosexuality. You cannot be what you desire or want to possess, and you cannot have what you wish to be, or to identify with (Freud 1921). This dichotomising between identification and desire is consolidated at the Oedipal phase, where the child takes one parent as a love-object and identifies with the other. If the two are the same it leads to disappointment or inhibition in love, as in his example above (O'Connor and Ryan 1993).

Yet even as he elaborated this theory, Freud cautioned against oversimplification in this area. He suggested that it may not be so easy to make an absolute distinction between desire and identification (Freud 1921). Sometimes we might want to possess those who are like us. Freud had already pointed out that male homosexuals are often very 'masculine' in appearance and personality, while men who take up a conventionally 'feminine' role in love-relationships may well be heterosexual (Freud 1905a).

While Freud absolutely opposed setting homosexuals apart as a group of special character, his followers often threw caution to the winds in their search for global explanations for 'the homosexual'. For instance, it has often been argued that all gay men have an over-possessive, seductive or castrating mother, and an absent, ineffectual or rejecting father, with whom the son cannot easily identify. (See Friedman 1988 for a review of the literature.) There is no evidence at all that this very common family-pattern is experienced more by homosexual than heterosexual men. Psychoanalysts typically saw same-sex desire as resulting from an infantile identification with opposite-sex characteristics, rather than from a mature Oedipal recognition of sexual difference. For instance, the gay man might be described as enmeshed in an early identification with his mother, and seeking in his male partners a sense of masculinity which he feels himself to lack (A. Freud 1949).

It is hard to exaggerate the atmosphere of negativity and contempt that surrounds much psychoanalytic writing about homosexuality up to the mid-1990s. In written case-examples the analyst seemed immediately to ask, 'What's wrong? Why is this person homosexual?'

The answer usually hinged around bad parenting. It might be more fruitful to turn the query around and ask: How did this young man or woman find the psychic resilience to form love-relationships with their own sex in a culture where homosexuality is so intensely stigmatised? However, this question is virtually never posed, even now that more liberal views prevail. And in practice clinicians do not usually show the same curiosity about the origins of opposite-sex desire. Depending on their theoretical affiliations, an analyst might be more or less interested in the kind of heterosexual relationships a patient might have, but would not so immediately ask why his or her desire was oriented in that direction.

The assumption that homosexuality was a disease or disorder to be 'cured' resulted in an utterly confusing panoply of categories and types, reinforced by lists of personality traits and family patterns. What was the point of these attempts to classify and pigeonhole, so utterly alien in their spirit to the analytic endeavour, and so irrelevant to most clinical practice? Perhaps the vigilant maintenance of categorical distinctions between homosexuals and heterosexuals is a way of preserving the psychic equilibrium of homophobic individuals and social groups (Young-Bruehl 1996).

A comparison of the writings of two psychoanalysts illustrates the profound effect of the analyst's personal values upon contemporary theory and clinical practice with homosexuals. Adam Limentani and Richard Isay write in a very similar way about different types of homosexuality, but, whereas Limentani pathologises homosexuality, Isay does not. Each describes one kind of homosexuality as a defence against heterosexual, Oedipal anxieties including fears of the internalised mother (and therefore women) as engulfing or castrating, or of the father (and men) as brutal or abandoning. Homosexuality for this group creates guilt and personal conflict since it doesn't fit in with the ego-ideal, with fundamental personal values. Theoretically, if the patient wished to become heterosexual he or she could do so. Each analyst then describes another category of 'true' or fixed homosexuals who do not feel intense personal conflict about their sexual orientation (Limentani 1989, Isay 1986).

Although their observations about types of homosexuality are almost identical, Limentani and Isay have entirely different views about the clinical outcome of work with gay men and lesbians. Limentani argues that homosexuality is a defence against serious psychic disturbance. Isay argues, on the other hand, that psychoanalysts pathologise homosexuality because they have internalised cultural homophobia. The role of the analyst is to help resolve the neurotic conflicts that prevent the establishment of the stable, gratifying and loving relationships that are possible for homosexuals, Isay argues. He points out that research (other than that done by psychoanalysts, see Friedman 1988) does not support the view that there is significantly more psychological disturbance among the homosexual community, especially when it is borne in mind that cultural persecution may well intensify any existing personal tendencies towards depression, paranoia, and low self-esteem.

In this view of homosexuality as a defence against severe depression or paranoia, Limentani is drawing on the theories of Klein and her followers. From the Kleinian viewpoint, homosexuality, like certain perversions and psychosomatic illnesses, is a 'third position' between paranoid–schizoid chaos and the depressive position. In all perverse sexuality, Kleinians argue, parental intercourse is enviously attacked through the idealisation of the diffused, pre-genital sexual play of children. Homosexuality is equated with (infantile) foreplay (Meltzer 1973a: 121).

At the root of many classical and contemporary psychoanalytic theories is a similar assumption that all homosexuality – gay and lesbian alike – is unnatural, a transgression of biological and psychic reality. One of Freud's women patients, the poet H.D., wrote: 'When I told the Professor [Freud] that I had been infatuated with Frances Josepha and might have been happy with her, he said, "No – biologically, no" ' (H.D. 1956: 152). According to Klein, the infant is born with an unconscious awareness of its own sexual organs waiting to be complemented by those of the opposite sex, because of an innate knowledge of parental intercourse. The British object-relations pioneer Fairbairn saw homosexuality as the natural expression of a psychopathic personality (Domenici 1995). Socarides, the US psychoanalyst, wants his patients to know that homosexuality is not what culture requires, that it is meaningless and extra-territorial to the biological realities of life (Socarides 1979).

The conservatism of many contemporary psychoanalytic writings on sexuality contrasts sharply with recent developments in philosophy and in social and political theory. Rachel Cunningham (1991) pointed out that Kleinian psychoanalysts still accept on trust the theory of innate ideas and 'Ideal Forms' which philosophers have long challenged (Cunningham 1991). Klein reinforced the equation of homosexuality with pathology through her belief in inborn tendencies towards heterosexuality. But her emphasis on the underlying state of mind, rather than specific sexual acts, can be used to argue that 'perversity can be equally present or absent in hetero-sexual and homosexual relationships alike' (Waddell and Williams 1991: 206). According to Klein, rivalry for the opposite-sex parent and depressive concern for the parental couple are vital for loving sexuality. But, as Cunningham points out, homosexuality does not necessarily involve hatred towards the parental couple. It may result from real love for the same-sex parent, or admiration, love and iden-tification with the opposite-sex parent, and then would not be perverse (Cunningham 1991).

From time to time psychoanalysts have suggested that homo-sexuals may gain psychological advantages from their sexual orienta-tion and may be able to make a special contribution to society. Unusually early sublimation of rivalry towards other men, Freud argued, explained the frequency with which homosexual men devote themselves to enriching the lives of others in community, artistic and cultural activities. Joan Riviere suggested in 1929 that lesbians may have less conflict about professional achievement because they feel less anxiety about surpassing the father.

Female homosexuality

If male homosexuality is seen as a perversion, lesbianism is hardly viewed as sexuality at all. In his 1920 *Psychogenesis of a Case of Female Homosexuality*, Freud set out a number of themes that were to emerge consistently in the sparse later literature on lesbianism. His 20-year-old patient had a disappointing early maternal relation-ship and envied her more favoured brothers. She had taken her father as the primary love-object at the Oedipal phase, but partially reversed this in her teens when her beloved father gave her mother another baby. Incensed at her father's 'betrayal', Freud's patient 'changed into a man and took her mother instead of her father as love-object' (Freud 1920: 384). Freud, who argued that a predomin-ance of psychic 'masculinity' was found more often in lesbians than femininity in gay men, saw his patient as a feminist who could not accept conventional notions of female passivity. She fell in love with a prostitute and courted her 'cocotte' actively, taking up what Freud described as the conventional role of the male lover.

Yet at the same time Freud's concept of bisexuality enabled him to explore how overlapping strands of homosexual and heterosexual desire influenced her choice of love-object. He pointed out that his patient fell in love with a woman who fitted in with both her masculine and feminine ideals, since she was a mother-figure who also looked like the patient's favourite brother. Freud observes that male homosexuals also choose objects who fit masculine and feminine ideals (Freud 1920).

Freud's case history is also typical of later writings on lesbianism in that it reveals an extremely unresolved countertransference which he attributed to the patient's resistance. When we studied this text during psychotherapy training our entire seminar-group was stunned by Freud's dismissal of his patient's dream of passionate love for a man and the wish for a husband. We could see no evidence for his interpretation of this dream as a lie, a transference wish to deceive him as she had her father. Nor could we understand why, after that dream, he suddenly ended her analysis, recommending that if she started again it should be with a woman. Freud observes that it was her parents who found the young woman's sexual orientation problematic, and that her lack of personal motivation for psychoanalysis made his task difficult, if not impossible. But he added to his own difficulties by exaggerating his patient's hostility towards men, and identifying too strongly with her father, as many later analysts have done with their lesbian patients. He seems to have been unable to accept that she might have been telling the truth when she described the heterosexual desire that still coexisted with her rage towards her father.

Several themes emerged from Freud's case-history that were to dominate later psychoanalytic writings on lesbian desire. First of all, lesbian desire is seen as masculine and linked with gender disorder, or confusion about sexual difference. Or it is attributed to a highly ambivalent early mother–daughter relationship which is either re-enacted or defended against through a search for idealised female lovers. Sometimes both explanations are combined, as in the once very influential early writings of Joyce McDougall (McDougall, 1980).

Freud observed that many lesbians dressed and acted like men, splitting off their femininity (Freud 1905a). But today's feminists argue that early analysts exaggerated the masculinity of their lesbian patients (certainly to a contemporary eye these assertive early-twentieth-century women do not appear lacking in femininity), and they also note how a significant majority of lesbians in our western post-industrialised society consider themselves to be 'femme' rather than 'butch'. This may reflect the fact that it more possible now for women to live outside marriage without the financial support of men. The existence of lesbian communities also obviates the need for women to signal their orientation so clearly.

There is still a strong theoretical tendency to link lesbian desire with the early mother–daughter relationship, while female hetero-sexuality is associated with a later Oedipal phase. This ignores the crucial role that disappointing or pleasurable early infantile experi-ences play in structuring all sexual life. Similarly, when the analyst (or, by extension, the lesbian lover) is experienced as an eroticised maternal figure, we need not necessarily assume that the sexuality is infantile or 'archaic', a precursor of Oedipal genital eroticism rather than actual desire. Sexual wishes and fantasies may be directed towards an Oedipal mother, who is separate from the self, a source of pleasure as well as identification (Welles and Wrye 1991). There is also a tendency for analysts to take the actual gender of the partner too much at face value. This underestimates the way that hetero-sexual women frequently re-enact their early experiences with mothers or sisters in relationships with men, while lesbians often experience their partners as representing aspects of significant male figures, including fathers and brothers.

Bisexuality as a sexual orientation

Within psychoanalytic theory bisexuality tends to be seen only as an immature state, a transitional stage on the way to a more fixed choice. Re-analysing some well-known object-relations and Kleinian case-histories, Juliet Mitchell gives a fascinating account of the way bisexuality is ignored when sexuality is explored mainly through the mother–child relationship, sidelining fathers and siblings. Psycho-analysts have, according to Mitchell, been too ready to take the patient's current sexual orientation at face value. They might fail to see the continuing significance of a previous heterosexual marriage if the patient now sees himself as gay, or be too ready to view a bisexual woman who marries during therapy as having entirely converted to heterosexuality (Mitchell 2000).

While thinking about this revised second edition, I realised that many of the female patients I wrote about in the first edition described themselves as bisexual and had significant relationships with men and women. The same is not true of the particular group of male patients I describe, even though many of them did become more able to acknowledge some attraction towards both sexes as psychotherapy progressed. Whatever they feel their sexual orientation to be, adult women do seem more aware of and able to act on their bisexual desires than men. The greater prevalence of heterosexual experience among lesbians may reflect social and cultural pressures on young girls to have sex with men. There is also a physical reality that women can passively experience sex, whereas men find it physiologically harder to conceal a lack of desire. But I think that psychic factors are deeply significant here. Women are more prone to bisexuality because of their difficulties in obeying the cultural edict to give up their early passion for the mother. The strength of the early attachment to the mother could, paradoxically, lead to bisexuality in women and to exclusive homosexuality or heterosexuality in men. Many heterosexual male patients have had homosexual experiences in their youth and may remain unconsciously ambivalent about sexual choice, but by their mid-twenties they seem less able to think about taking a lover of their own sex than do their female peers (Bell and Weinberg 1978). Anxieties about engulfment by the mother may lead the man with an insecure sense of his male identity to cling to his adopted orientation for fear that experimentation might threaten his fragile psychic equilibrium. Women might not feel the same anxiety about losing their sense of themselves as female through same-sex erotic experiences.

The Bisexual Imaginary discusses the difficulties of asserting bisexuality as a valid form of adult sexuality in cultures where it is consistently rendered invisible or attacked. One contributor, Phoebe Davidson, discusses some of the clinical material in the first edition of this book, including Ms J, whose psychotherapy I describe later in this chapter. Davidson applauds the fact that I do recognise the existence of bisexuality and explore it more than many analytic writers, but argues that I could give it more validity if I emphasised that some people feel equally attracted to both sexes and will never be able to describe themselves as gay or heterosexual (Davidson 1997).

The sex of the object does not necessarily determine sexual identity. The bisexual man or woman will not become heterosexual by settling down with an opposite-sex partner or homosexual if they choose to live life with a same-sex partner. Indeed, Davidson is right that some people choose a life-partner of one sex while remaining aware that they will always be bisexual. But people who come into therapy thinking that they might be bisexual sometimes decide eventually that they are happier with one sex or the other. Nevertheless, I do find such recent explorations of bisexuality very useful since they validate the experience of the surprisingly large number of people who cannot fit themselves into the heterosexual/homosexual binary however hard they try.

My bisexual patients defy generalisation: each of them had an entirely different childhood history and they varied enormously in their attitudes towards their sexuality. Some had long been convinced or suspected that they were bisexual, while others made the discovery with extreme reluctance during psychotherapy. For instance, one woman took over a year to spell out that this was the main reason she had come into psychotherapy – she had never before told anyone that she desired women at least as strongly as men. She left psychotherapy convinced that she wanted to live as a lesbian. In complete contrast, another patient focused on her lack of interest in sex with men, adamantly denying any interest in women, until one day, to her astonishment, she had her first sexual dream – of a passionate encounter with a woman. Even then she remained intensely reluctant to return to this subject, ring-fencing any discussion with declarations that she was never actually going to act on her sexual feelings for women and wanted to remain with her male partner despite their sexual problems. One reason for this, she admitted, was that she needed a heterosexual lifestyle to bolster her very tenuous sense of womanliness. Eventually she began to recognise that she did need to understand more about her sexuality and that she could talk about her differing desires without necessarily acting on them.

Why are some people aware of and able to act on their desires for both sexes while others are not? There does seem to be a significant relationship between sexual orientation and the ego-ideal, the sense of personal values. In the histories of lesbians and gay men there is often a relative or other influential figure who has either approved or tolerated their sexual choice, as did the mother of Freud's patient (Freud 1920). This could offer some explanation of why some bisexual women and men act out their homosexual desires directly, while others do not. Also, since many women and men do not have approving figures, feminism and gay culture have offered enormous validation for their homosexual desires.

Psychological fragility and unresolved issues about early mothering may cause a woman to fear acting on her own lesbian wishes. Such anxieties can be reinforced by cultural factors including discriminatory attitudes. So Ms N (Chapter 7) might at the beginning of psychotherapy have felt too suggestible and lacking in psychological boundaries to find another female partner after her first left her, even though at that point she felt certain that she found lesbian sex more satisfying. Also, whereas she'd left her husband it was her female lover – for whom she felt such great passion – who had abandoned her. Maybe she could not face that again. In the closing phase of psychotherapy, after intensive discussion about her sexuality, she set her cap at the man she considered most desirable in her circle and settled with him in a loving relationship. Ms N returned to see me briefly in a post-psychotherapy crisis and told me that her desire for women remained alive but she was content with her partner and had taught him to make love to her as her female lover had done. She explained that she had chosen a heterosexual lifestyle because her family, friends, and children – and most significantly she herself – had got used to thinking of her in this way.

Other women become disillusioned when they discover that the problems they have in relationships with one sex do not alter when they act on the other side of their bisexual desire. Ms T in Chapter 5 hoped when she became involved with another woman that the relationship would be gentle and loving, but was appalled to discover that she became the sadist with her female lover, having previously been the victim of male cruelty.

In my clinical experience, then, many factors may determine sexual orientation, some of which have little to do with erotic desire. These might include lifestyle choices, such as the wish to have children within a heterosexual setting. The way we want to be seen by family, friends and colleagues, or an attachment to a particular group of friends, might also be significant factors.

How does an emotional preoccupation with one's own sex differ from desire? Some women have their major relationships with other women even though they think of themselves as heterosexual. They may, like Ms K (Chapter 8) say that they love women but mainly have sex with men. Their same-sex friendships may be richer and more enduring. Or their heterosexual activity may be underpinned by a sexual fantasy life that revolves around women. For instance, Ms S (Chapter 5) maintained a heterosexual identity through compulsive sexual activity with men even though her erotic fantasies were driven by her wish for psychic separation from her mother.

The interaction between fantasy and sexual orientation is a complex issue about which we still understand little. Psychoanalysts have often suggested that once we know about the main sexual fantasies of our patients we have vital insights into their whole psychic life, including their 'true' sexual orientation. However, if a patient fantasises about one sex while engaging erotically with the other, they may be expressing their bisexuality. Early in therapy the patient may well give us a partial picture of their fantasy life, and this can change as they come to understand more about themselves. Or the analyst who takes a patient's stated sexual orientation too much at face value may fail to create an atmosphere where sexuality can be fully discussed. It is true then that sexual fantasies are very revealing, but we should not assume that they are a 'litmus test' of sexual orientation (Magee and Miller 1997).

The differences between lesbian and gay sexuality

In psychoanalytic theory it is sometimes assumed that male and female homosexuals have shared psychological characteristics. Many gay men and lesbians do not see themselves as being set apart from their own sex in this way. Instead, they suggest that lesbians have more similarities with heterosexual women, and gay men with their own sex as a whole. Obviously this raises another set of questions, since there are as many differences within each sex as between the sexes.

It is extremely hard to generalise about the problems that each sex brings to psychotherapy. Yet it is possible to discern differences in the issues that gay men and lesbians find problematic in intimate relationships. There does not seem to be any equivalent for women – whether heterosexual or lesbian – of gay saunas and 'cottaging'. But women may have their own forms of casual sex which they may not see as promiscuity. For instance, they are more likely to view one-night stands as failed relationships and brief heterosexual 'flings' in beach resorts as holiday 'romances'.

If gay men sometimes worry in therapy about a predilection for casual sexual activity, lesbians are more likely to have the opposite anxiety – that their relationships may develop a symbiotic 'merged' quality, a lack of psychic separation and distance. The intensity and depth of bodily closeness gives lesbianism a special appeal for women, who can rapidly experience themselves as re-enacting primary experiences of intimacy with the mother. But this can also lead to subsequent difficulties, such as a premature breakdown of sexual intimacy.

Is the tendency to 'merge' emotionally more a women's issue than a gay issue? In heterosexual relationships is it easier to create a stable tension between the woman, who 'clings' through fear of abandonment, and the man, who 'distances' through unconscious fear of being trapped (Elise 1986)? It is true that there is often a partner who is more 'clingy' in an ongoing heterosexual partnership, but it is certainly not always the woman. Nevertheless, the gender differences that do exist might become exaggerated in relationships between two individuals of the same sex.

However, lesbian analysts and philosophers suggest that erotic life is defined in male terms. For this reason women's desire is that which eludes or escapes conventional descriptions. It cannot be contained or represented by a male sexuality that takes itself as straight-forward, exactly what it seems: easily categorised in terms of goals and locations. Rather than worrying about how often we 'have sex', perhaps women – whatever the orientation of their desires – should create much broader definitions of sexuality that do not privilege genital sex above other erotic pleasures, since 'sexuality and desire are part of the intensity and passion of life itself' (Grosz 1995).

Maintaining love and sexual passion in long-term marital rela-tionships is a problem for everyone, whatever their sex or orientation. The often-cited tendency towards promiscuity and anality in gay men might be gender-related. Anal obsessiveness seems to be more common in the fantasy-life and personalities of men – regardless of sexual orientation – than in women. It may well be associated with an unconscious need to control a powerful maternal figure as well as unresolved difficulties in relation to the father. Men who are beset by feelings of inadequacy can idealise a caricature of masculinity – cruel and unemotional – while feeling intense contempt for 'femi-nine' vulnerability in themselves and others. Whatever his sexual orientation, the man who is unconsciously preoccupied with psycho-logical power-battles can find it difficult to bring together love and desire. This may lead a gay man to have a long-term partner whom he loves but no longer desires, while he has transient sex with others. Or a heterosexual man may value his male friends more than women, in whom he may lose interest after brief affairs.

Some men may be more aware of a desire to withdraw from intim-acy, while some women are only in touch with their vulnerability and 'clinginess'. But in psychotherapy it is not possible to maintain such splitting, and the patient may rapidly be confronted with the aspect of himself which he so often projects onto others.

Counter-transference and sexual identity

Recently there has been some very interesting new theory that explores how all identity is structured through internalised homophobia. It is argued that heterosexuality is maintained through a cultural hatred of homosexuality which also reverberates through gay identity. Particular attention has been focused on how an unconscious heterosexist bias might impact on the therapeutic relationship through an 'obscured' countertransference (Frommer 1995).

Instead of focusing on the gay man's supposed failure to resolve his Oedipus complex by identifying with his father, the current emphasis is on the paternal rejection all boys might feel as they negotiate societal taboos against homosexual love for their fathers (Domenici 1995). Domenici describes how in Fairbairn's object-relations theory the son is not expected to be aware of his father until the toddler Oedipal phase, when he is experienced as a prohibitive Oedipal figure who curtails the boy's 'feminine' expressions of love towards him. The boy's super-ego or moral sense is then likely to be structured through an extremely melancholic identification with a rejecting father (Butler 1997). This results in a heterosexual identity which is obsessive and compulsive, maintained through a hostile renunciation of unacknowledged love for the father. Gay men often internalise some of the same hatred and contempt for their homosexual feelings.

Domenici argues that we need to look more at the often ignored early dyadic father–son relationship rather than focusing exclusively on early mothering. There would then be the possibility of thinking about transitional spaces where the child (or adult patient) could 'play' with different coexisting desires and gendered identities. If we think in terms of an identity formed through multiple coexisting identifications within which the child could mourn both homosexual and heterosexual love-objects, then a range of desires might remain metaphorical and imaginable. What is crucial, then, is not to create an 'appropriate' sexual orientation but to tolerate the ambiguity and instability of all identity and desire. We would need to emphasise the importance of recognising similarity in those who appear different as well as acknowledging what distinguishes us from others. Then, repudiating an identification with the opposite-sex parent might be seen as a failure to come to terms with difference rather than a sign of psychic maturity. If we cannot do this, then heterosexuality is the reassuring sense of not being the other, or a defence against envy of the other, rather than a full relationship with difference (Benjamin 1995).

Domenici's critique of Fairbairn's homophobia is fascinating and long overdue. But I wonder whether he is discussing the boy's actual relationship with a father-figure or his fantasies? Could this 'father' be a woman – for instance a lesbian lover, sister, grandmother – or indeed the 'paternal' aspects of the mother? It is often said that orthodox Oedipal theories place too much emphasis on the literal sex of the parents. But this confusion also exists in critiques of mainstream theory. Homosexual identificatory love serves as the boy's vehicle for establishing masculinity, both creatively and defensively, Benjamin argues. She goes on to say that the absence of a literal father may mean a more complex tension between experienced relationships and cultural ideals. This is very helpful, but sometimes it is unclear whether Benjamin herself is talking about 'real' or symbolic parental figures. For instance, she discusses the post-Kleinian thesis that the paternal function, the 'third', is a mental function or capacity rather than an actual person and so can be developed through the mother–child relationship or therapeutic dyad. She argues that the notion of a third can be disentangled from any given gender or sexual constellation, since the parental couple is not necessarily heterosexual (Benjamin 2000). But again, what does she mean exactly? Is she talking of someone who has been brought up by same-sex parents or addressing the fact that our fantasy-life may be dominated by a homosexual parental couple? The interaction of fantasy, symbolism and 'real' experiences is an area that we need to understand much more about.

The work of Judith Butler has become integral to many new studies of sexual desire and identity. She argues that heterosexual identity is fragile because it is based on the loss of a homosexual love for the same-sex parent. This cannot be spoken about or mourned because it is not seen as a loss at all in societies where only heterosexuality is seen as 'true' love, a love worth having. The man becomes a man by repudiating femininity and his heterosexuality is structured through that repudiation. Therefore 'he wants the woman he would never be. He wouldn't be caught dead being her', therefore he desires her (Butler 1997: 137). Similarly the girl becomes a girl through a prohibition against having her mother as the object of desire. She therefore installs her mother as a part of her ego, a melancholic identification. Homosexual desire is then seen as a serious threat to heterosexual identity: it 'panics gender'. Wanting 'a girl brings being a girl into question' (Butler 1997: 136).

Butler seems to suggest that the hostility towards homosexuality that pervades so many cultures is partly a result of envy of same-sex intimacy. Heterosexuality is formed through the incorporation of the love it disavows, of what is unspeakable in sexuality. The heterosexual man says 'I never loved him, I never lost him' (Butler 1997: 138). This, Butler points out, makes sense of the peculiar phenomenon whereby homosexual desire becomes a source of guilt.

Butler asks whether we need to rigorously repudiate one or other orientation. In traditional Oedipal theories separation and loss are seen as inextricably bound up with sexual differentiation. Could there instead be a sense of declining one orientation, but in a less permanent and absolute way, in a society where all identities were seen as valid? Again this raises questions about how we might view those women and men who desire both sexes equally – a topic that Butler does not address directly (Butler 2000).

In an interesting paper, Joanna Ryan draws on Butler to discuss the plight of the well-intentioned therapist who wishes to validate her patient's homosexual identity but finds that she freezes, distances or becomes dumb. At such times the therapist may be reacting to unacknowledged fears, longings and grief about homosexual intimacy with early love-objects. Ironically, the liberally minded therapist may be more vulnerable to their own conflict-ridden unconscious feelings about homosexuality than the more orthodox analyst who locates all the pathology in their gay or lesbian patient. Such anxieties may lead to a dread about being the object of homosexual erotic transferences or to worry about revealing ignorance of lesbian or gay sexuality or lifestyles. Or the therapist may fear being homophobic and therefore make strenuous efforts not to be, thus stifling creative thought and impeding the capacity to make imaginative identifications (Ryan 1998).

Until very recently, pathologising theories resulted in case-material where the homosexual patient was objectified, thus 'obscuring' the analyst's countertransference. The patient was described in such negative moral and emotional terms that any uncomfortable feelings the analyst might have could appear to be a rational response, argues Martin Stephen Frommer (1995). He also emphasises that the depth and resilience of shame and self-hatred, the hallmarks of internalised homophobia, are not fully appreciated by psychoanalytic psychotherapists. This continues to have a profound effect on the clinical encounter. Looking specifically at the heterosexual male analyst/gay patient dyad, Frommer argues that the patient may well be able to sense any mixed feelings the analyst has even if they are not expressed verbally. If the analyst is to help the patient negotiate shame and self-hatred he needs first to explore his own heterosexist bias – a bias also introjected by the patient. Otherwise he may be able to commiserate with the patient's shame and self-hatred but will not be able to help him move beyond it.

Traditional Oedipal theory allows the male analyst to polarise himself as identified with 'masculinity', in contrast to his 'feminine' patient. Negative countertransferences are then triggered when the patient's material resonates with the analyst's own unconscious feared and hated 'femininity' (Frommer 1995). The clinician then appears to respect homosexuality but does not create a climate where the patient can talk about it – a pattern that is very common indeed nowadays.

I go on now to discuss 30 sessions of brief focal psychotherapy that took place in a low-fee clinic during the 1980s, when more overtly homophobic attitudes prevailed. My main focus is on identity and the countertransference.

Ms J was a 29-year-old woman from a working-class immigrant background who sought help in a state of extreme anxiety about her financial and emotional security. She had fallen far behind on the mortgage repayments on a house she shared with her partner C and C's small son. During their two-year relationship Ms J had supported C financially so that she could go to college, an arrangement she had also made with her previous female partner of eight years. Sex had long since ceased. Now that she could no longer provide financial support, Ms J felt constantly belittled by her partner and had begun having affairs.

In childhood Ms J had felt excluded from the intimacy between her mother and elder sister and had compensated for this by closeness to her father, who seemed to favour her. She felt herself to be emotionally inarticulate like her father, and saw her mother as valuing him only as a breadwinner. I suggested that Ms J might be re-enacting with her lovers the role her father had played in the family. She agreed with a mixture of interest and reluctance, saying that he also had affairs.

In two further ways Ms J was re-enacting family patterns. She feared losing her job because of a serious conflict with a senior female colleague who resembled her sister. Furthermore, she had managed to make an enemy of her lover's younger sister, L, through a highly complex triangular relationship. Ms J had once had a brief affair with L, who left her. Then Ms J quickly become sexually involved with C, the older sister, despite continuing to feel far more attracted to L. Thus she had managed to recreate and reverse the childhood triangle. Now she was the powerful older woman over whom a pair of sisters competed, and it was the younger one (herself) for whom she felt more passion. Ms J declared herself utterly bemused by the aggression both sisters now felt both for her and for each other.

When I discussed my first session with Ms J, a supervisor made the comment that she was not a 'real lesbian', since she had made a heterosexual choice for her father at the Oedipal stage which she reversed in her late teens. The supervisor went on to say that in therapy Ms J might either become heterosexual or develop more fulfilling lesbian relationships. I wondered whether I was being told that 'real analysis' would make Ms J heterosexual and that remaining lesbian was a second-best option. I reacted to this by feeling rather protective of her same-sex desires. But then I worried that this over-protectiveness might not be helpful to her since from the beginning she had raised questions about her own sexual feelings. This kind of unhelpful self-consciousness pervades much twentieth-century clinical discussion about gay and lesbian patients, and may account for some of the analytic 'failures' described in the literature.

In retrospect I think it would be helpful to see Ms J as a potentially bisexual woman who had made a choice to be lesbian (see Davidson's discussion of Ms J – or 'Sharon' in the first edition – in *The Bisexual Imaginary* 2000). In contrast to Freud's 'beautiful and clever girl of eighteen', Ms J could act on her lesbian desires despite her mother's disapproval. This change in cultural attitudes and possibilities further undermines analytic attempts to predict which kinds of family history will produce a particular sexual orientation.

Ms J and I agreed to concentrate on resolving past issues that she was re-enacting in her current acute crisis during the 30 sessions available. However, it was clear to both of us that issues about sexuality might well emerge. Ms J did not enjoy sex, she told me in the consultation. In fact, the only time she had felt any pleasure at all was in the weeks with L, the younger sister. Ms J described how her first long-term girlfriend would complain that they weren't having sex so she would then make love to her, without enjoying it much. L's view that sex was 'about exploring' had been a revelation and a release from a burdensome feeling of responsibility. Ms J had no wish to have sex with men. At sixteen she had got engaged briefly, but there had been little physical contact because 'you know how girls dread sex'. Then, through friendship with a gay couple, she had come across the idea of being a lesbian. An older lesbian couple had questioned her about her desire for women, wondering whether it might reflect a rebellion against and a refusal to be like her mother. When her mother discovered she was going out with girls at eighteen, she had thrown her out, and for ten years they had hardly talked. Her father had gone out of his way to keep contact and to give her money, saying that 'whoever her friends were', she was always his daughter. Although her father had not condemned her, none of the adults around her had positively validated Ms J's teenage choice. So shame and self-hatred about being a lesbian might well have played a part in her difficulties with sex up to now. I said that we would not have time to discuss her sexuality in any depth, but that if she wanted I could later refer her for private psychotherapy which she might be able to afford once her present crisis was resolved.

Painfully, in those early sessions Ms J recalled how at nine her mother had 'terrified' her by beating her so violently that she broke the stick. This attack was even more unforgivable in Ms J's eyes because her mother never hit her sister. She described her father as always gentle, 'good at playing', although often out of the house. He was proud of her athletic ability and she wondered 'Did he want me to be a boy?' But she'd been called after the mother he'd lost in childhood, so maybe not.

She suffered a traumatic abandonment at thirteen when her mother became acutely ill. Left with relatives in Cyprus while her mother went into hospital in Britain, Ms J felt terrified that her mother would die and she would be to blame. Her periods then started, but her relationship with her mother had deteriorated so much that Ms J could not tell her. Hurt and defiant, she asked her parents whether she could stay in Cyprus, where she felt accepted by her aunt and cousins, 'the other boys', as she unwittingly referred to them.

As a result of her mother's violence, a part of her disappeared. Before she had happily played on her own for hours, but afterwards she became totally outer-directed. She began to rediscover this inner world of feeling and imagination in the sessions. Now she was delighted to find herself keeping a journal, reading novels, and exploring her fantasy-life. She made a new woman friend with whom she discussed her feelings in a new way.

At this point, three months into the therapy, I suddenly missed a session through illness. Ms J, devastated, took to her bed with acute asthma until the next session. On her return, she talked about her desperate teenage grief for a dog who had died after being treated for a tooth-ulcer. 'Everyone liked the dog. It was good-looking, tall, with a proud walk.' This description also fitted her handsome athletic father, and herself 'a bit'. Like a dog, she felt capable of absolute loyalty and devotion to those who looked after her. But dogs, like children, could turn on people suddenly and then I, like her mother, might reject her. She was also afraid that she'd made me ill. 'How can I stop feeling like this? Rationally I know you can't make someone get ill – can you?' She had began to re-experience the traumatic teenage months when she'd feared her mother's death. Whereas then she'd started menstruating, now she was asking fundamental questions about her sexuality. And again, she'd been abandoned. Having, like the dog, come for treatment in a crisis, she would also die – of neglect.

As Ms J extricated herself from playing her father's familial role with C, her parents temporarily separated for the first time in 30 years. Around this time she talked more about sex, which she seemed to associate with madness, danger and the emotional rift between her parents. She did not want to give up being a lesbian and still felt no attraction for men. Yet she pondered the fact that she had always had easier relationships with men than women. 'It's generally said that you should taste a drink before saying you don't like it', she ventured thoughtfully.

At this time Ms J alternated between experiencing me as the accepting Cypriot aunt and the mother with rigid ideas of how girls should be. I asked myself whether I was really pushing her towards heterosexuality or if I was leaving her free to make her own sexual choices. Ms J continued to be witty and considerate but this belied her pain and dread about the impending termination of therapy. Conflict with men was tolerable, but with women it was always 'terrifying', she explained. 'Couldn't we make it come out so I feel good about the ending?' she begged, tearfully.

By the end of therapy Ms J had worked hard, with some success, to communicate again with her mother. She was proud of being like her father in some ways, but no longer saw herself as sharing his emotionally inarticulacy quite so strongly. Now that she felt closer to her mother and could draw on previously buried identifications with her, Ms J was more able to think about what kind of women she herself might be. She resolved her difficulties at work and got promoted. She could continue to grow through nourishing the inner world of fantasy and imagination to which she had regained access. And she saw the possibility of developing more genuinely intimate and passionate relationships with women. Nevertheless, she wanted to think more about her sexuality and so I made a referral for ongoing psychotherapy.

The apparent masculinity of some lesbians does not necessarily reflect a strong identification with male figures, as many analysts have argued. In fact, although Ms J sometimes looked boyish, I would never have described her as 'masculine' in character, but might instead have used words like 'sensitive', 'shy' and even 'demure' – words that are more usually associated with femininity. Since identity is formed through layering and fusion of fragments of memory, fantasy and desire, even if we do appear to have made conventionally heterosexual identifications, our unconscious wishes may belie this. So the little girl who plays with dolls is not necessarily expressing early heterosexual femininity. She may be showing that she is too exclusively preoccupied with re-enacting her early relationship with her mother to view her father as a significant love-object (Freud 1931). And the man or woman who feels rejected by a parent may identify with them as a way of defending against loss.

It is important to separate identification and sexual orientation as far as possible theoretically, rather than assuming – as many traditional psychoanalysts have – that they are inextricably linked. If cross-sex identifications are problematic it is usually because they originate through trauma or deprivation and are highly ambivalent. For instance, the so-called 'New Man' who attracts women because of his apparent 'femininity' may prove to be intensely envious and hostile towards his female partners. This is because in early childhood he might have identified with a caricatured version of a mother who was felt to be profoundly disappointing or rejecting.

Similarly, Freud's lesbian patient showed through a major suicide attempt and the ferocity of her anger towards men that she had serious psychological conflicts, but her self-destructiveness could be linked to her very ambivalent identification with a father whom she simultaneously hated and desired. A similar argument could be made about Ms J, who changed significantly in brief psychotherapy through strengthening positive identifications and lessening the power of negative paternal internalisations, rather than by altering her sexual orientation. What is significant, then, is the nature of our identifications with aspects of early figures, rather than whether or not they share our sex.

Women are placed in a particular dilemma if they are patholo-gised for being too 'masculine', while at the same time they suffer because they have not been able to identify with those more highly valued psychological qualities associated with men. Similar ques-tions need to be asked about how men can accept and integrate identifications with qualities seen as 'feminine' rather than projecting them onto women and gay men whom they then devalue. Both sexes would benefit from the integration of a wide range of cross-sex iden-tifications, so that conventional notions of gender became more detached from biological sex and from sexual desire.

Conclusion

There might be a limit to how far we can amend traditional psycho-analytic assumptions. Instead we may need simply to listen to our patients and to lesbian and gay analysts as they describe the dis-crimination and oppression they suffer and the resulting internalised shame and self-hatred. At the same time we need to be open to their accounts of the joy and fulfilment possible within same-sex relation-ships and to deal with any possible envy this may arouse in us if we are heterosexual. Recent writing about lesbian and gay sexuality gives us new insights into all sexuality. It also helps us to highlight areas that need urgent attention. These include the complex inter-action between sexual fantasy, dreams and object-choice, as well as the interplay between heterosexual social forces and psychic life.

The demand for a new theory to 'explain' homosexuality might reflect a wish to establish another set of categories or developmental templates. This process has always been strikingly unsuccessful in the past, since lesbians and gay men seem to have as much in common with their own sex as with each other. Some psychotherapists may feel themselves cast adrift without theories to underpin more liberal attitudes. But 'How did the patient become gay or lesbian?' is no more crucial a query than 'How did he or she become heterosexual?' Rather than asking such questions it may be more important to focus on the continued existence of hidden countertransference feel-ings that undermine heterosexual psychotherapists in their analytic work with homosexual patients.

Nothing we have loved or desired is ever fully relinquished. Lost loves and attachments survive in our identities through incomplete mourning. We need to remain aware of our similarities to others, to think about what links us to them as well as the ways in which we differ. These ideas might offer more scope for the expression of psychic bisexuality within heterosexual as well as homosexual relationships as notions of sexual identity become less rigid. Hopefully, as psychotherapists continue to abandon some of our more facile assumptions about what constitutes 'normal' sexuality, we will be able to acknowledge that such changes may well offer new possibilities for sexual happiness, a more open way of being for all of us.

Conclusion: Feminism and psychotherapy – an agenda for the future

The encounter between psychoanalysis and feminism is now almost a century old. What has been gained through this intense off-and-on engagement? Ongoing questions remain. How have feminists dealt with the challenge that psychoanalysis poses to conventional notions of sexual identity? To what extent have psychoanalytic theorists and clinicians been willing to address the political issues that feminists see as central to any dynamic psychology? And finally, at a point when power relations between the sexes are beginning to shift significantly, how can future collaboration between psychoanalysis and feminism promote an agenda for sexual equality?

The two movements have always had much in common besides a central concern with sexuality and gender. Psychoanalysis highlights aspects of mental life and behaviour that are usually experienced as unacceptable or at least profoundly uncomfortable. Similarly, feminism has illuminated the disparities between what our society wants women to be and what we, as women, actually want: again, an uneasy insight. As a result, each movement arouses highly ambivalent feelings.

Today psychotherapy seems almost to be viewed as a new religion, a contemporary bastion of truth and morality. Its practitioners are subject to the same type of idealisation/denigration associated with much religious belief (and infantile emotional states). This has been reflected recently in the fierce controversies surrounding childhood sexual abuse, in which therapists are viewed either as perfect parents coming to the rescue of abused children or as evil interlopers into the family scenario. Incest is an issue that invariably blurs boundaries between fantasy and reality in this way. But today the erosion of older patterns of gender relations has made the discussion of incest even more emotive. As traditional family structures give way to new, those who point to the vulnerability of children within the family arouse very primitive anxieties. Both feminists and psychotherapists find themselves sharing this dangerous ground, as they challenge conventional attitudes towards parenting and the place of children within erotic life.

Despite this shared field of concerns, the feminist attitude towards psychoanalysis has often been very suspicious. Why is this? Psychoanalytic psychotherapy provides access to a more embodied way of thinking. This opens up the possibility of integrating political ideals with psychic experience, and exploring how cultural expectations might be imprinted on the body, as well as the mind. There is now an increasing understanding that male and female psychology cannot be considered in isolation from each other. But some of those aspects of femininity that psychoanalysis highlights are difficult to confront, particularly female envy and aggression. Women who still place a premium on being 'nice' would often rather foist these less nice aspects of the psyche onto men. Yet in so doing we forfeit the possibility of mobilising our aggression in creative ways, diminishing our capacity to demand, insist and take what we need personally and in the external world. We also restrict our understanding of the forces that lie behind women's apparent collusion in certain forms of personal and cultural subordination. We need to know more about why women tolerate cruelty, frustration or even violence within personal relationships and what makes it so difficult to claim an equal share of cultural power. What is it about femininity that continues to constrain us, and how can psychoanalysis help us to understand or even change this?

The degree to which psychoanalytic perspectives have proved useful to the feminist political project has undoubtedly been limited by the hesitancy and prejudice with which the analytic world has approached gender issues. There is still a clear male bias in all mainstream psychoanalytic theories, a tendency to view female sexuality as structured through a 'lack' or as inextricably linked to reproductive and mothering functions. Women are not seen as agents of their own destinies, with their own pleasure-oriented sexuality, but are viewed through the eyes of men or children. Men, on the other hand, have often been idealised in most mainstream analytic writings (unless they are homosexual) and as fathers they tend to be viewed in a more positive light.

These biases are strengthened by the tendency of psychoanalytic theorists to present their views as universal and timeless.

Contemporary feminist literature has placed an increasing stress on the historical and cultural factors behind the formation of sexual identity and the multiplicity of forms sexual subjectivity and orientation can take. In contrast, psychoanalytic theorists have been disappointingly slow to acknowledge the cultural specificity of their theories. Only very recently have there been the first signs of a sustained attempt to understand how different cultural values and belief-systems might be reflected in personality development.

Ideas of normal/abnormal development are still offered as universal psychoanalytic truths, despite all evidence that such norms are culturally weighted. Until the 1990s this was particularly true of theories of sexual orientation. In this second edition I have shown how theories that pathologise homosexuality are being tentatively reappraised. Theoretical attention has now shifted to an exploration of the fragility of a heterosexual identity – and culture – based on unmourned homosexual losses. It is now clear that countertransference biases were previously hidden by homophobic theories (Butler 1997, Frommer 1995).

Oedipal theory sees separation and loss as intrinsic to the process of sexual differentiation, becoming psychologically male or female. Recently the idea that everyone must make an absolute choice for one sexual orientation has been fundamentally challenged. Theoretically there is a new awareness of the need to recognise a range of desires and acknowledge the triangular echoes in all relationships, ideas that I have explored through discussion of clinical work with women who feel themselves capable of sexual love for women and men.

These questions about the usefulness of the homosexual/ heterosexual 'binary' resonate with a new feminist scepticism about the complementary polarities that have for so long dominated psychoanalytic thinking about identity. Conventional stereotypes about 'masculinity' and 'femininity' reinforce gender power-imbalances, but they undermine both sexes, restricting our emotional and erotic possibilities. In other areas too there has been a move towards recognising the complexity and diversity of human subjectivity. For instance, theories which assume that the mind – and the therapist's verbal interpretations – can easily influence the body have given way to more subtle and intricate neuro-psychoanalytic understandings of how from the beginning of life brain and body are inextricably interconnected (Solms and Turnbull 2002). In a similar way, feminist philosophers now tend to reject the idea of 'outside' cultural forces that are internalised by the psyche, describing instead how we are structured within and through power. Paradoxically, since our very identities are the material through which power operates, this also gives us the possibility of standing outside and resisting existing cultural power dynamics (Butler 1997, Grosz 1995).

How do these ways of thinking relate to 'race', class and caste? In discussion of such topics there has been a parallel move away from global generalisations. Despite the current emphasis on the fluid, multi-layered nature of identity and desire, psychotherapists still often talk about male and female 'identity' as if they were single clearly definable entities. In contrast, recent writing by radical clinicians delineates quite distinct 'masculinities' and 'femininities' constructed through a range of factors including 'race', ethnicity, social class and sexuality.

The issue of trauma, so fundamental to feminists and psychoanalysts, has re-emerged as a cornerstone of new thinking about how cultural forces structure the analytic encounter. Racial traumas resonate across generations, marking individuals and entire cultures psychically and physically. In a similar way, class has layers of conscious and unconscious meaning, which live on as 'encrypted or secret identifications long after the material conditions that shaped them have altered' (Harris 2003: 111). All therapists inevitably respond to material according to their position in relation to the prevailing power hierarchy, a fact that has profound implications for our understanding of countertransference phenomena.

The impact of class and caste on the therapeutic relationship is surprisingly rarely discussed, given that the pain and dislocation intrinsic to cultural and class transition are so often central to psychotherapy. Issues of psychic separation tend to be played out within the arena of class or race as well as gender. This may mean that fear of envy from other family members may be particularly intense for a successful black or working-class woman. Oedipal guilt and rivalry with the father might be differentially determined according to boys' position in the dominant cultural power hierarchies.

Can we expect a transformation in psychoanalytic attitudes towards 'race', racism and culture now that they are under the theoretical spotlight? In this context it is significant that many in the analytic world still, despite a century-long encounter with feminism, refuse to recognise the role of power in male–female relations. I wonder whether the same will be true when it comes to acknowledging other cultural power-differentials in the clinical context. Although there is considerable interest in gender and sexual identity in psycho-analytic circles, I am often astonished to hear these topics discussed with barely any mention of the power difference between the sexes. From listening to clinical discussions one might think that the sexes were equal, or even that women really did have the overwhelming power with which the infant invests the mother in fantasy.

Why this refusal to acknowledge the psychic consequences of male power? In this book I have shown how, since its inception, psycho-analytic theory has tended to emphasise one side of the parental couple as more powerful than the other. The first psychoanalytic debate on female sexuality in the 1920s highlighted the issue of which parent appeared more powerful and enviable in the mind of the child. After Freud was accused of male bias, there was a reaction against his father-dominated theory, in which the role of the mother was marginal and women were viewed as envious and deficient. Klein and Winnicott then focused almost exclusively on the power and significance of the mother, barely mentioning the father. And, although mother-centred psychoanalysts are beginning again to explore the psychic significance of the father, and of Oedipal issues, theoretically the father remains a shadowy figure. But if we are to understand how maternal and paternal power interact in the psyche, we must first integrate the parental couple in the theoretical mind. We still do not have a mainstream psychoanalytic theory that brings the two sexes together, while giving due weight to the different kinds of power and control with which each is invested through culture or nature. Perhaps this is because holding in mind different notions of envy and power would necessitate the recognition that the sexual equality our society purports to offer does not exist in reality.

This theoretical limitation in turn limits the way psychotherapy has grappled with gender-mediated problems. For example, object relations theories explain women's propensity to eating disorders in terms of unresolved psychic separation from the mother, resulting in unconscious conflicts which are acted out in fantasy through the daughter's own body. Bulimia and anorexia are sometimes seen as forms of female perversion – indirectly eroticised abuse of the wom-an's own body, or that of her children. But these mother-centred theories often neglect the more Oedipal aspects of sexuality and the crucial role of the female body as a site for both the reproduction of and resistance to patriarchal power relations. In contrast, Freud's theory of hysteria emphasises how women use their bodies to express in a very concrete way their discontent with their devalued status and restricted opportunities. Drawing on both of these perspectives we can more fully understand the dilemmas of the bulimic or anorexic woman who cannot assert herself as a potent desiring subject in personal life or the world at large.

Turning to the male side of the gender equation, we need to see how maternal and paternal power interact in the male psyche if we are to understand why men so often sexualise psychic conflict and are more prone to acts of sexual violence. The man who focuses in a perverse way on his own genitals or fantasises about rape is expressing his dread of losing what the penis symbolises – male cultural dominance over women and their bodies, potency and privilege. Simultaneously he is expressing his own conflicts about the lost world of early 'feminine' intimacy, through reassuring himself that he has not succumbed to the lure of an imagined symbiosis with the maternal body. But is it solely the mother he has lost? Recent theory has focused on the child's need for an active, nurturing father who is not threatened by rivalry and can accept the boy's need for identification, a father who might also set boundaries. There is a new acknowledgement of how difficult fathering has become in societies where masculinities are structured around a homophobic avoidance of 'feminine' closeness between men while at the same time a retreat into old patriarchal modes is no longer possible (Frosh 2002). However, such theorising raises complex questions about what we mean by the term 'father', and whether we are talking of the biological progenitor, the symbolic image of a father within any given culture, or the person – perhaps a woman – who plays the paternal role.

It is also essential that psychoanalysis integrates its insights into maternal psychological influence and paternal power so that we may understand how the transference is formed. Gender power differentials, as I have stressed throughout this book, are reflected in the transference and countertransference. For instance, a theoretical bias towards maternal power may combine with unconscious conflicts about psychic 'masculinity', causing a female psychotherapist to mistake a male patient's homosexual desires towards the father for a maternal (heterosexual) transference. Or the woman therapist might use a theoretical focus on maternal nurturing to avoid the contempt and hostility that often emerge rapidly in the heterosexual transferences of male patients.

Male psychotherapists who remain unconsciously profoundly ambivalent towards the early mother may collude with a female patient's idealised love-transference towards the father rather than exploring the hostility towards both parents that might lie beneath it. In similar fashion, unconscious conflicts about his own disowned psychic femininity may prevent a male clinician from recognising his homosexual countertransference feelings towards a patient who shares his sex.

Many of the issues raised in the 1920s about the limits and possibilities of change in male and female sexuality remain just as topical and unresolved today, despite vast changes in the daily lives and expectations of both sexes in our society. Although we have significant new understandings about how cultural and familial experience is structured into the brain and body, we still have no definitive theory of how culture, physiology and unconscious processes interact. I have argued that sexual identity is formed mainly through culture although the experience of erotic life and the physiological life-cycle will inevitably be different for women and men. Language patterns, symbols and values systems determine how bodily sensation is interpreted in each culture, so if we want to eradicate sexual inequality we must understand and radically alter the way we symbolise and interpret the embodied experience of women and men.

There is a tendency in psychoanalytic theory to pathologise those who have intense opposite-sex identifications: so-called 'masculine' women and 'feminine' men. But these normative notions of gender identity obscure the way both sexes are impoverished through the inability to integrate cross-gender identifications.

A resurgence of psychoanalytic interest in male hysteria reflects the increased cultural visibility of male envy and fear of women now that there are fewer institutionalised ways of inducing feelings of envy and exclusion in women. Many contemporary men feel anxious about their ability to adapt to a less masterful role. In the consulting room they often wonder whether they can explore new embodied modes of emotionality and find different ways of parenting without losing access to rationality or becoming devalued as women and 'effeminate' men have always been. In a similar way female patients question whether they really can be successful in traditional male as well as female spheres of activity, especially given that men have traditionally relied on the support of a wife in order to do so. Can women find different ways of winning and using power?

The most crucial and difficult task for all of us is to face the fact that the sexes are equal in potential yet reproductively and anatomically different. To accomplish this, the envy, fear and inadequacy engendered by sexual difference must be resolved through identification with the psychological qualities associated with both sexes. For women this means finding a way of differentiating from the mother and identifying psychological masculinity without devaluing their own sex. The man who recognises his psychological similarity with women will feel more able to accept his physiological difference and less driven to denigrate them enviously.

If men must come to terms with the loss of some of their traditional patriarchal privileges, the question for women is how to build on what we have gained. We need to explore our own passion, excitement and destructiveness within safe limits, if we are to see that strong emotion will not damage ourselves or our love-objects. We might then feel more free to exert our own wishes and desires and make a real impact on the world around us.

In some areas, such as education, female disadvantage is fast diminishing. However, men often respond to this increase in sexual equality with an institutional backlash or personal forms of retaliation, as has happened in the past. There is an urgent need for psychotherapists to give up their preoccupation with maternal omnipotence and to focus equal attention on helping men understand their current dilemmas so that they can develop the psychic resilience to act as equal partners in sexual and family life.

A belief in the primacy of individual responsibility – an idea fundamental to most psychotherapy – may exacerbate clinicians' difficulties in understanding the ways we might re-enact cultural power inequalities in the consulting-room. Nevertheless, there is now a growing interest in the clinical impact of race and culture. A similar reappraisal of class issues is long overdue. New thinking in these areas both draws on and enriches feminist, lesbian and gay understandings of sexual identity.

Since desire is structured through our earliest childhood experiences, it is inevitable that the image of a helpless being acted upon by a powerful other will at times feature within the erotic imagination. But if we are to break the cycle whereby gender inequalities are structured into psychic and sexual life, men and women need to be able to find different ways of expressing and resolving the narcissistic wish to deny pain, helplessness and psychic separateness, other than denigrating the mother and subordinating the female sex.

Change at the psychological level will be limited unless it is accompanied by a transformation of attitudes, cultural imagery and social institutions. Men need to find a place for themselves in the realm of 'feminine' emotionality and childcare if women are to move out of their conventional roles. But it is women themselves who must find new ways of speaking for and about their sex, a new language and imagery to express the previously hidden aspects of their experience, and different ways of symbolising power other than through the phallus.

All of us, women and men alike, need to feel that we can take risks, while having our emotional vulnerability accepted, if we are to embrace the challenges life offers. We must be able to look to each other for support and love without feeling that such dependency overthrows our sense of independent selfhood, or deprives us of inner worth. Inextricably entwined with all our 'others', as we inevitably are, we need nevertheless to feel in possession of ourselves – travellers on our own paths, the subjects of our own destinies.

Bibliography

Abraham, K. (1920), 'Manifestations of the female castration complex', in *Selected Papers of Karl Abraham*, London: The Hogarth Press and Institute of Psycho-Analysis 1927.

Balint, E. (1973), 'Technical problems found in the analysis of women by a woman analyst: a contribution to the question: "What does a woman want?" ', in G. Kohon (ed.), *The British School of Psychoanalysis*, London: Free Association Books 1986.

Bell, A.P. and Weinberg, M.S. (1978), *Homosexualities: A Study of Diversity Among Men and Women*, New York: Simon and Schuster.

Benjamin, J. (1988), *The Bonds of Love: Psychoanalysis, Feminism and the Problem of Domination*, New York: Random House.

—— (1995), *Like Subjects, Love Objects*, New Haven, CT: Yale University Press.

—— (1998), *Shadow of the Other*, London: Routledge.

—— (2000), Response to commentaries by Mitchell and Butler, *Studies in Gender and Sexuality* **1** (3), 291–308.

Bennett, P. (1993), 'Critical clitoridectomy: Female sexual imagery and feminist psychoanalytic theory', *Signs* **18** (2), 235–259.

Bentovim, A. (1998), 'Children are liars aren't they?', in V. Sinason (ed.), *Memory in Dispute*, London: Karnac.

Benvenuto, B. and Kennedy, R. (1986), *The Works of Jacques Lacan: An Introduction*, London, Free Association Books.

Blackwell, D. (1998), 'Class, status and conflict in mind and society: Comment on paper by Lauren E. Storck', *Group Analysis* **31**, 116–120.

Britton, R. (1989), *The Oedipus Complex Today*, London: Karnac.

Brunswick, R.M. (1940), 'The pre-Oedipal phase of the libido development', in C. Zanardi (ed.), *Essential Papers on the Psychology of Women*, New York: New York University Press 1990.

Butler, J. (1990), *Gender Troubles*, London: Routledge.

—— (1993), *Bodies that Matter*, London: Routledge.

—— (1997), *The Psychic Life of Power*, Stanford, CA: Stanford University Press.

—— (2000), 'Longing for recognition: commentary on the work of Jessica Benjamin', *Studies in Gender and Sexuality* **1** (3), 291–308.

Campbell, D. (1999), 'The role of the father in a pre-suicide state', in R.J. Perelberg (ed.), *Psychoanalytic Understanding of Violence and Suicide*, London, Routledge.

Cavell, M. (1985), 'Since 1924: toward a new psychology of women', in J. Strouse (ed.), *Women and Analysis*, Boston: G.K. Hall and Sons.

Chasseguet-Smirgel, J. (1964a), *Female Sexuality*, London: Maresfield 1985.

—— (1964b), 'Feminine guilt and the Oedipus complex', in *Female Sexuality*, London: Maresfield 1985.

—— (1984), *Creativity and Perversion*, London: Free Association Books.

—— (1985), *The Ego Ideal*, London: Free Association Books.

—— (1986a), *Sexuality and Mind*, New York: New York University Press.

—— (1986b), 'The femininity of the analyst in professional practice', in *Sexuality and Mind*, New York: New York University Press.

—— (1988), 'A woman's attempt at a perverse solution and its failure', *International Journal of Psycho-Analysis* **69** (2), 149–162.

Chodorow, N. (1978), *The Reproduction of Mothering: Psychoanalysis and the Sociology of Gender*, Berkeley: University of California Press.

—— (1989), *Feminism and Psychoanalytic Theory*, London: Polity Press.

—— (1994), *Femininities, Masculinities, Sexualities*, London: Free Association Books.

Cixous, H. (1976), 'The laugh of the Medusa', in E. Marks and I. de Courtivon (eds), *New French Feminisms*, Brighton: Harvester Press.

Coates, S. (1990), 'Ontogenesis of boyhood gender identity disorder', *Journal of the American Academy of Psychoanalysis* **18**, 414–438.

Cunningham, R. (1991), 'When is a pervert not a pervert?', *British Journal of Psychotherapy* **8**, 48–70.

Dalal, F. (2002), *Race, Colour and the Processes of Racialization*, Hove: Brunner-Routledge.

Davidson, P. (1997; 2nd edn 2000), ' "Her libido had flowed in two currents": Representations of bisexuality in psychoanalytic case studies', in *The Bisexual Imaginary*, Bi Academic Intervention (ed.), London Cassell.

Deutsch, H. (1924), 'The psychology of women in relation to the function of reproduction', in J. Strouse (ed.), *Women and Analysis*, Boston: G.K. Hall and Sons 1985.

—— (1930), 'The significance of masochism in the mental life of women', *International Journal of Psycho-Analysis* **11**, 48–61.

—— (1933), 'Homosexuality in women', *International Journal of Psycho-Analysis* **14**, 34–56.

—— (1946), *The Psychology of Women*, London: Research Press.

Dimen, M. (2003), 'Keep on keepin' on – Alienation and trauma: Commentary on Ruth Fallenbaum's paper', *Studies in Gender and Sexuality* **4** (1).

Dinnerstein, D. (1978), *The Rocking of the Cradle and the Ruling of the World*, London: Souvenir Press.

Dollimore, J. (1991), *Sexual Dissidence*, Oxford: Oxford University Press.

Domenici, T. (1995), 'Exploding the myth of sexual psychopathology: A deconstruction of Fairbairn's anti-homosexual theory', in T. Domenici and R.C. Lesser (eds), *Disorientating Sexuality*, London: Routledge.

Eichenbaum, L. and Orbach, S. (1982), *Understanding Women: a Feminist Psychoanalytic Approach*, New York: Basic Books.

—— (1987), 'Separation and intimacy: Crucial practice issues in working with women in therapy', in S. Ernst and M. Maguire (eds), *Living With the Sphinx*, London: The Women's Press.

Elise, D. (1986), 'Lesbian couples: The implications of sex-differences in separation–individuation', *Psychotherapy* **23**, 303–310.

Ernst, S. (1987), 'Can a daughter be a woman?', in S. Ernst and M. Maguire (eds), *Living With the Sphinx*, London: The Women's Press.

Faderman, L. (1992), *Odd Girls and Twilight Lovers: A History of Lesbian Life in Twentieth Century America*, London: Penguin.

Fanon, F. (1967), *Black Skin, White Masks*, trans. C. Lam Markmann, New York: Grove Weidenfeld.

Ferenczi, S. (1932), 'Confusion of tongues between adults and the child', *Zeitschrift* **18**, 239.

Fletchman Smith, B. (2000), *Mental Slavery: Psychoanalytic Studies of Caribbean People*, London: Rebus Press.

Fogel, G. (1986), 'Introduction: Being a man', in G. Fogel, F. Lane and R. Liebert (eds), *The Psychology of Men*, New York: Basic Books.

Freud, A. (1949), 'Certain types and stages of social maladjustments', *Indications for Child Analysis and Other Papers*, London: Hogarth Press 1969.

Freud, S. with Breuer, J. (1895), *Studies on Hysteria*, Pelican Freud Library (PFL) **3**, Harmondsworth: Penguin 1974.

Freud, S. (1899), 'Screen memories', *The Standard Edition of the Complete Psychological Works of Sigmund Freud (SE)*, London: Hogarth.

—— (1905a), *Three Essays on the Theory of Sexuality*, PFL 7, Harmondsworth: Penguin 1977.

—— (1905b), *Fragment of an Analysis of a Case of Hysteria ('Dora')*, PFL 8, Harmondsworth: Penguin 1977.

—— (1909), *Analysis of a Phobia in a Five-Year-Old Boy ('Little Hans')*, PFL 8, Harmondsworth: Penguin 1977.

—— (1910a), 'Leonardo da Vinci and a memory of his childhood', *SE* 11, London: Hogarth 1953–74.

—— (1910b), *A Special Choice of Object Made by Men*, PFL 7, Harmondsworth: Penguin 1977.

—— (1914a), *On Narcissism: An Introduction*, PFL 11, Harmondsworth: Penguin 1984.

—— (1914b), 'Remembering, repeating and working-through', *SE* 12, London: Hogarth.

—— (1915), 'Observations on transference-love', *SE* 12, London: Hogarth Press 1953–74.

—— (1916–17), *Introductory Lectures on Psychoanalysis*. PFL 1, Harmondsworth: Penguin 1962.

—— (1918), *From the History of an Infantile Neurosis ('The Wolfman')*, PFL 9, Harmondsworth: Penguin 1979.

—— (1919), *A Child is Being Beaten*, PFL 10, Harmondsworth: Penguin 1979.

—— (1920), *Psychogenesis of a Case of Female Homosexuality*, PFL 9, Harmondsworth: Penguin 1979.

—— (1921), *Group Psychology and the Analysis of the Ego*, PFL 10, Harmondsworth: Penguin 1979.

—— (1922), *Some Neurotic Mechanisms in Jealousy, Paranoia and Homosexuality*, PFL 10, Harmondsworth: Penguin 1979.

—— (1924a), *The Dissolution of the Oedipus Complex*, PFL 7, Harmondsworth: Penguin 1977.

—— (1924b), 'The loss of reality in neurosis and psychosis', *SE* 19, London: Hogarth 1954–74.

—— (1924c), *The Economic Problem of Masochism*, PFL 11, Harmondsworth: Penguin 1984.

—— (1925), *Some Psychical Consequences of the Anatomical Distinction Between the Sexes*, PFL 7, Harmondsworth: Penguin 1977.

—— (1927), *Fetishism*, PFL 7, Harmondsworth: Penguin 1977.

—— (1928), Letter from Freud to Ernest Jones, 22 February 1928, quoted in P. Gay, *Freud: A Life for Our Times*, London: Papermac 1988.

—— (1931), *Female Sexuality*, PFL 7, Harmondsworth: Penguin 1977.

—— (1933), 'Femininity', in *New Introductory Lectures*, PFL 2, Harmondsworth: Penguin 1973.

—— (1935a), Letter from Freud to Carl Muller-Braunschweig, published as 'Freud and female sexuality: a previously unpublished letter', *Psychiatry*, 1971.

—— (1935b), Letter from Freud, in *American Journal of Psychiatry*, 1951, **107**, 786.

—— (1937), 'Analysis terminable and interminable', *SE* 23, London: Hogarth.

—— (1940), *Splitting of the Ego in the Process of Defence*, PFL 11, Harmondsworth: Penguin 1984.

Friedman, R.C. (1988), *Male Homosexuality: A Contemporary Psychoanalytic Perspective*, New Haven, CT: Yale University Press.

Frommer, M.S. (1995), 'Countertransference obscurity in the psychoanalytic treatment of homosexual patients', in T. Domenici and R.C. Lesser (eds), *Disorientating Sexuality*, London: Routledge.

Frosh, S. (1989), *Psychoanalysis and Psychology*, London: Macmillan.

—— (1991), *Identity Crisis, Modernity, Psychoanalysis and the Self*, London: Macmillan.

—— (1994), *Sexual Difference: Masculinity & Psychoanalysis*, London: Routledge.

—— (2002), *After Words: The Personal in Gender, Culture and Psychotherapy*, Basingstoke: Palgrave.

Frosh, S., Phoenix, A. and Pattman, R. (2002), *Young Masculinities*, Basingstoke: Palgrave.

Gallop, J. (1982), *Feminism and Psychoanalysis: The Daughter's Seduction*, London: Macmillan.

Glasser, M. (1984), ' "The weak spot": some observations on male sexuality', in D. Breen (ed.), *The Gender Conundrum*, London: Routledge 1993.

Goldberger, H. and Evans, D. (1985), 'On transference manifestations in male patients with female analysts', *International Journal of Psycho-Analysis* **66**, 295–309.

Goldner, V. (2003), 'Ironic gender/authentic sex', *Studies in Gender & Sexuality* **4** (2), 113–139.

Goodison, L. (1990), *Moving Heaven and Earth*, London: The Women's Press.

Gornick, L. (1986), 'Developing a new narrative: The woman therapist and the male patient', in J. Alpert (ed.), *Psychoanalysis and Women: Contemporary Reappraisals*, Hillsdale, NJ: The Analytic Press.

Greenacre, P. (1979), 'Fetishism', in I. Rosen (ed.), *Sexual Deviation*, Oxford: Oxford University Press.

Greenson, R. (1967), *The Technique and Practice of Psycho-Analysis*, London: Hogarth Press.

Grossman, W. and Stewart, W. (1976), 'Penis envy: From childhood wish to developmental metaphor', in C. Zanardi (ed.), *Essential Papers on the Psychology of Women*, New York: New York University Press 1990.

Grosz, E. (1990), *Jacques Lacan: A Feminist Introduction*, London: Routledge.

—— (1994), *Volatile Bodies: Towards a Corporeal Feminism*, Bloomington: Indiana University Press.

—— (1995), *Space, Time and Perversion*, London: Routledge.

Grunberger, B. (1989), *New Essays on Narcissism*, London: Free Association Books.

H.D. (1956), *Tribute to Freud*, Manchester: Carcanet Press 1985.

Harris, A. (1999), 'Unfinished business', in R.C. Lesser and E. Schoenberg (eds), *That Obscure Object of Desire*, London: Routledge.

—— (2000), 'Gender as soft assembly: Tomboys' stories', *Studies in Gender and Sexuality* **1** (3), 291–308.

—— (2003), 'Working in the trenches: Commentary on Ruth Fallenbaum's paper', *Studies in Gender and Sexuality* **4** (1).

Horney, K. (1924), 'On the genesis of the castration complex in women', *International Journal of Psycho-Analysis* **5**, 50–65.

—— (1926), 'The flight from womanhood: The masculinity complex in women as viewed by men and by women', in J. Baker Miller (ed.), *Psychoanalysis and Women*, London: Penguin 1984.

Hughes, A. (ed.) (1991), *The Inner World and Joan Riviere*, London: Karnac.

Hyatt-Williams, A. (1998), *Cruelty, Violence and Murder: Understanding the Criminal Mind*, London: Karnac.

Irigaray, L. (1977), 'This sex which is not one', in C. Zanardi (ed.), *Essential Papers on the Psychology of Women*, New York: New York University Press 1990.

—— (1984), *Ethique de la différence sexuelle*, Paris: Minuit.

—— (1989), 'The gesture in psychoanalysis', in T. Brennan (ed.), *Between Feminism and Psychoanalysis*, London: Routledge.

Isay, R. (1986), 'Homosexuality in homosexual and heterosexual men: some distinctions and implications for treatment', in G. Fogel, F. Lane and R. Liebert (eds), *The Psychology of Men*, New York: Basic Books.

Janeway, E. (1982), *Cross Sections: From a Decade of Change*, New York: William Morrow and Co.

Jones, E. (1928), Review of *Sex and Repression in Savage Societies* by B. Malinowski, *International Journal of Psycho-Analysis*, July, 365.

Joseph, B. (1982), 'Addiction to near-death', in E. Bott Spillius and M. Feldman (eds), *Psychic Equilibrium and Psychic Change. Selected Papers of Betty Joseph*, London: Routledge 1989.

—— (1985), 'Transference: the total situation', in E. Bott Spillius (ed.), *Melanie Klein Today*, vol. 2, London: Routledge 1988.

Journal of the American Psychoanalytic Association **49** (4), 2001.

Jukes, A. (1993), *Why Men Hate Women*, London: Free Association Books.

Kakar, S. (1989), 'The maternal–feminine in Indian psychoanalysis', *International Review of Psycho-Analysis* **16** (3), 355–362.

Kaplan, L.J. (1991), *Female Perversions*, London: Pandora Press.

Khan, M. (1989), *Alienation in Perversions*, London: Maresfield Library.

Klein, M. (1928), 'Early stages of the Oedipus complex', in *Love, Guilt and Reparation and Other Works 1921–45*, London: Hogarth Press 1975.

—— (1952), 'The origins of transference', in *Envy and Gratitude and Other Works 1946–1963*, New York: Delta 1977.

—— (1957), 'Envy and gratitude', in *Envy and Gratitude and Other Works 1946–1963*, New York: Delta 1977.

Kohon, G. (1986), 'Reflections on Dora: the case of hysteria', in G. Kohon (ed.), *The British School of Psychoanalysis*, London: Free Association Books.

—— (1987), 'Fetishism revisited', *International Journal of Psycho-Analysis* **68**, 213–229.

Kuhn, P. (2002), ' "Romancing with a wealth of detail", Narratives of Ernest Jones's 1906 trial for indecent assault', *Studies in Gender and Sexuality* **3** (4), 344–378.

Kulish, N.M. (1986), 'Gender and transference: the screen of the phallic mother', *International Review of Psycho-Analysis* **13**, 393–404.

Lacan, J. (1953), 'Some reflections on the ego', *International Journal of Psycho-Analysis* **34**, 11–17.

—— (1964), *The Four Fundamental Concepts of Psycho-Analysis*, translated by A. Sheridan, Harmondsworth: Penguin 1977.

—— (1977), *Ecrits. A Selection*, London: Tavistock.

—— (1985), 'Intervention on transference', in C. Bernheimer and C. Kahane (eds), *In Dora's Case*, London: Virago.

Laplanche, J. and Pontalis, J.B. (1967), *The Language of Psychoanalysis*, London: Karnac 1988.

Lasch, C. (1979), *The Culture of Narcissism*, London: Abacus Books.

Lasky, R. (1989), 'Some determinants of the male analyst's capacity to identify with female patients', *International Journal of Psycho-Analysis* **70** (3), 405–418.

Laub, D. and Auerhahn, N.C. (1993), 'Knowing and not knowing massive psychic trauma: Forms of traumatic memory', *International Journal of Psycho-Analysis* **74**, 287–302.

Leary, K. (2000), Racial enactments in dynamic treatment, *Psychoanalytic Dialogues* **10** (4), 639–653.

Lester, E. (1982), 'The female analyst and the eroticized transference', *International Journal of Psycho-Analysis* **66**, 283–294.

Lewes, K. (1989), *The Psychoanalytic Theory of Male Homosexuality*, London: Quartet.

Liebert, R.S. (1986), 'The history of male homosexuality from ancient Greece through the Renaissance: Implications for psychoanalytic theory', in G. Fogel, F. Lane and R. Liebert (eds), *The Psychology of Men*, New York: Basic Books.

Limentani, A. (1979), 'The significance of trans-sexualism in relation to some basic psychoanalytic concepts', in *Between Freud and Klein*, London: Free Association Books 1989.

—— (1984), 'To the limits of male heterosexuality: The Vagina-Man', in *Between Freud and Klein*, London: Free Association Books 1989.

—— (1989), 'Clinical types of homosexuality', in *Between Freud and Klein*, London: Free Association Books.

—— (1991), 'Neglected fathers in the aetiology and treatment of sexual deviations', *International Journal of Psycho-Analysis* **72** (4), 573–584.

Littlewood, R. (1992), 'Towards an intercultural therapy', in J. Kareem and R. Littlewood (eds), *Intercultural Therapy*, London: Blackwell.

MacCarthy, B. (1988), 'Are incest victims hated?', *Psychoanalytic Psychotherapy* **3** (2), 113–120.

McDougall, J. (1980), *Plea for a Measure of Abnormality*, New York: International Universities Press.

Magee, M. and Miller, D.C. (1997), *Lesbian Lives*, Hillsdale, NJ: The Analytic Press.

Maguire, M. (1997), 'Envy between women', in M. Maguire and M. Lawrence (eds), *Psychotherapy with Women: Feminist Perspectives*, London: Macmillan.

Malcolm, J. (1982), *Psychoanalysis: The Impossible Profession*, London: Pan Books.

Mann, D. (1997), *Psychotherapy: An Erotic Relationship*, London: Routledge.

—— (ed.) (1999), *Erotic Transference and Countertransference*, London: Routledge.

Mannoni, O. (1968), *Freud: The Theory of the Unconscious*, London: Pantheon Books 1971.

Meltzer, D. (1973a), *Sexual States of Mind*, Scotland: Clunie Press.

—— (1973b), 'Perversion of the transference', in *Sexual States of Mind*, Strath Tay, Perthshire: Clunie Press.

—— (1973c), 'The architectonics of pornography', in *Sexual States of Mind*, Strath Tay, Perthshire: Clunie Press.

—— (1978), *The Kleinian Development*, Strath Tay, Perthshire: Clunie Press.

Merck, M. (1993a), *Perversions, Deviant Readings*, London: Virago Press.

—— (1993b), 'The feminist ethics of lesbian s/m', in *Perversions, Deviant Readings*, London: Virago Press.

—— (1993c), 'The train of thought in Freud's "Case of Homosexuality in a Woman" ', in *Perversions, Deviant Readings*, London: Virago Press.

Mitchell, J. (1974), *Psychoanalysis and Feminism*, London: Allen Lane.

—— (1984), *Women: The Longest Revolution*, London: Virago Press.

—— (2000), *Madmen and Medusas*, London: Allen Lane Penguin.

Mitscherlich, A. and Mitscherlich, M. (1967), *The Inability to Mourn: Principles of Collective Behaviour*, trans. B. Placzek, New York: Grove Press 1975.

Mohamed, C. (2000), *The Construction of a Lie: Racism: An Arena for Psychic Conflicts*, MA dissertation, Sheffield University.

Munder Ross, J. (1986), 'Beyond the phallic illusion: notes on men's heterosexuality', in G. Fogel, F. Lane and R. Liebert (eds), *The Psychology of Men*, New York: Basic Books.

Norwood, R. (1986), *Women Who Love Too Much*, London: Arrow Books.

O'Connor, N. and Ryan, J. (1993), *Wild Desires and Mistaken Identities*, London: Virago Press.

Odes Fliegel, Z. (1986), 'Women's development in analytic theory: six decades of controversy', in J. Alpert (ed.), *Psychoanalysis and Women, Contemporary Reappraisals*, Hillsdale, NJ: The Analytic Press.

Orbach, S. (1999), *The Impossibility of Sex*, Harmondsworth: Penguin Books.

Orr, M. (1998), 'False memory syndrome movements: The origins and the promoters', in V Sinason (ed.), *Memory in Dispute*, London: Karnac.

Ovesey, L. and Spector Person, E. (1973), 'Gender identity and sexual psychotherapy in men: A psychodynamic analysis of homosexual trans-sexuality, transvestism', *Journal of the American Academy of Psychoanalysis* **1**, 53–72.

Pines, D. (1986), 'A woman's unconscious use of her body: a psychoanalytic perspective', Carl Dilling Memorial Lecture, New York.

Potts, A. (2002), *The Science/Fiction of Sex*, London: Routledge.

Ragland-Sullivan, E. (1992), 'Hysteria', in E. Wright (ed.), *Feminism and Psychoanalysis: A Critical Dictionary*, Oxford: Blackwell.

Rayner, E. (1991), *The Independent Mind in British Psychoanalysis*, London: Free Association Books.

Richards, B. (1989), *Images of Freud: Cultural Responses to Psychoanalysis*, London: J.M. Dent and Sons.

Riley, D. (1983), *War in the Nursery*, London: Virago Press.

Riviere, J. (1929), 'Womanliness as a masquerade', in A. Hughes (ed.), *The Inner World and Joan Riviere*, London: Karnac 1991.

Rosen, I. (ed.) (1979a), *Sexual Deviation*, Oxford: Oxford University Press.

—— (1979b), 'The general psychoanalytical theory of perversion: a critical and clinical study', in *Sexual Deviation*, Oxford: Oxford University Press.

Rosenfeld, H. (1949), 'Remarks on the relation of male homosexuality to paranoia, paranoid anxiety and narcissism', *Psychotic States*, London: Maresfield.

Ryan, J. (1998), 'Lesbianism and the therapist's subjectivity', in C. Shelley (ed.), *Contemporary Perspectives on Psychotherapy and Homosexualities*, London: Free Association Books.

—— (2002), 'Where now? Recent thinking on psychoanalysis & homosexuality', paper for WTC & Freud Museum Conference: Women Today.

Samuels, A. (1985), *The Father, Contemporary Jungian Perspectives*, London: Free Association Books.

—— (1993), *Politics and the Psyche*, London: Routledge.

Sayers, J. (1991), *Mothering Psychoanalysis*, London: Penguin.

—— (1998), *Boy Crazy: Remembering Adolescence, Therapies and Dreams*, London: Routledge.

Schore, A. (1994), *Affect Regulation and the Origin of the Self: The Neurobiology of Emotional Development*, Hillsdale NJ: Lawrence Erlbaum Associates.

Scott, A. (1988), 'Feminism and the seductiveness of the "real event"', *Feminist Review* **28**.

Segal, L. (1987), *Is the Future Female?: Troubled Thoughts on Contemporary Feminism*, London: Virago Press.

—— (1990), *Slow Motion, Changing Masculinities, Changing Men*, London: Virago Press.

—— (2000), 'Psychoanalysis and politics: Juliet Mitchell then and now', *Radical Philosophy* **103**, Sept./Oct., 12–18.

Shengold, L. (1979), 'Child abuse and deprivation: soul murder', *Journal of the American Psychoanalytic Association* **27**, 533–599.

Sinason, V. (1988), 'Smiling, swallowing, sickening and stupefying: the effect of sexual abuse on the child', *Psychoanalytic Psychotherapy* **3** (2), 97–111.

Sinason, V. (1998), *Memory in Dispute*, London: Karnac.

Slochower, J. (1999), *Erotic complications, International Journal of Psychoanalysis* **80**, 1119.

Socarides, C.W. (1979), 'The psychoanalytic theory of homosexuality: with special reference to therapy', in I. Rosen (ed.), *Sexual Deviation*, Oxford: Oxford University Press.

Solms, M. and Turnbull, O. (2002), *The Brain and the Inner World*, New York: Other Press.

Spector Person, E. (1986), 'The omni-available woman and lesbian sex: two fantasy themes and their relationship to the male developmental experience', in G. Fogel, F. Lane and R. Liebert (eds), *The Psychology of Men*, New York: Basic Books.

Stanton, M. (1990), *Sandor Ferenczi: Reconsidering Active Intervention*, London: Free Association Books.

Steiner, J. (1981), 'Interplay between pathological organizations and the paranoid–schizoid and depressive positions', in E. Bott Spillius (ed.), *Melanie Klein Today*, vol. 1, London: Routledge 1988.

—— (1985), 'Turning a blind eye; the cover-up for Oedipus', *International Review of Psychoanalysis* **12**, 161–172.

—— (1987), 'The interplay between pathological organizations and the paranoid–schizoid and depressive positions', *International Journal of Psycho-Analysis* **68**, 69–80.

Stoller, R. (1968), *Sex and Gender*, London: Hogarth Press.

—— (1975), *Perversion: The Erotic Form of Hatred*, London: Maresfield.

—— (1979), 'The gender disorders', in I. Rosen (ed.), *Sexual Deviation*, Oxford: Oxford University Press.

Strouse, J. (ed.) (1985), *Women and Analysis*, Boston: G.K. Hall and Sons.

Sykes Wylie, M. (1993), 'Trauma and memory', *Family Networker*, Sept/Oct., 42–43.

Symington, N. (1986), *The Analytic Experience*, London: Free Association Books.

Thomas, L. (1992), 'Racism and psychotherapy: Working with racism in the consulting-room – An analytical view, in J. Kareem and R. Littlewood (eds), *Intercultural Therapy*, London: Blackwell.

Thompson, C.L. (2000), 'African American women and moral masochism: When there is too much of a good thing', in L.C. Jackson and B. Greene (eds), *Psychotherapy with African American Women*, New York: Guilford Press.

Torras de Beà, E. (1987), 'A contribution to the papers on transference by Eva Lester, Marianne Goldberger and Dorothy Evans', *International Journal of Psycho-Analysis* **68** (1), 63–69.

Tower, L. (1956), 'Countertransference', *Journal of the American Psychoanalytic Association* **4**, 224–255.

Verhaeghe, P. (1999), *Does the Woman Exist?* London: Rebus Press.

Waddell, M. (1989), 'Gender identity – Fifty years on from Freud', *British Journal of Psychotherapy* **5** (3), 381–390.

—— (1993), 'From resemblance to identity: A psychoanalytic perspective on gender identity', unpublished paper.

Waddell, M. and Williams, G. (1991), 'Reflections on perverse states of mind', *Free Associations* **2**, Part 2 (22).

Walkerdine, V., Lucey, H. and Melody, J. (2001), *Growing Up Girl: Psychosocial Explorations of Gender and Class*, Basingstoke: Palgrave.

Walton, J. (1995), 'Re-placing race in (white) psychoanalytic discourse: Founding narratives of feminism', *Critical Enquiry* **21** (4).

Welldon, E. (1988), *Mother, Madonna, Whore*, London: Free Association Books.

Welles, J.K. and Wrye, H.K. (1991), 'The maternal erotic countertransference', *International Journal of Psycho-Analysis* **72**, 93–106.

White, J. (1989), 'Racism and psychosis: Whose madness is it anyway?', unpublished paper.

Whitford, M. (1989), 'Rereading Irigiray', in T. Brennan (ed.), *Between Feminism and Psychoanalysis*, London: Routledge.

Winnicott, D.W. (1957), 'The mother's contribution to society', in *The Child and the Family: First Relationships*, London: Tavistock.

—— (1964), 'This feminism', in *Home is Where We Start From, Essays by a Psychoanalyst*, London: Penguin 1986.

—— (1971), 'Creativity and its origins', in *Playing and Reality*, Harmondsworth: Pelican.

Young-Bruehl, E. (1996), *The Anatomy of Prejudices*, Cambridge, MA: Harvard University Press.

Zetzel, E. (1970), *The Capacity for Emotional Growth*, London: Maresfield Library 1987.

Index